Front Cover Photograph: Ecstatic Charter Class students carry the Chancellor, celebrating the news that they had scored the second highest in the US Boards of all international medical schools in the world. This was the moment they knew they had reached—and exceeded—the dream. Left to right: Phil Lahrmann, unidentified, Dave Mucci, Warren Stanton with Chancellor Modica on his shoulders, and Steve Leskowitz.

Photo taken by Danny Ricciardi, a crucial and vocal member of the Charter Class, and a lifelong champion of St. George's University where he is currently Executive Vice President for Clinical Development. He is also Director of Undergraduate Medical Education of Brooklyn Hospital. Without him this book may have not come to fruition.

Advance Praise for

Docs on the Bay

"*Docs on the Bay* is a remarkable celebration of perseverance and hope that is both unbelievable and true. It is a gripping read and contains important lessons about how rare individuals with passion and determination can overcome the odds to change the world for the better."

—**Jeffery S. Flier**, M.D., Former Dean of Harvard Medical School

"The true story about a young medical visionary who did not give up and made the world better."

—**Nicholas Pileggi**, American Author, Screenwriter, and Journalist

"The gripping tale of a young man's impossible dream—inspiring students who believed, and ultimately shattering the complacent world of US medicine by giving the US much needed doctors."

—**John Wren**, Chairman and CEO of Omnicom Group

"Charlie Modica's *Docs on the Bay* is one of the most enjoyable, entertaining, and inspirational books I have ever read. The sheer determination to create a new medical school in the face of endless impossible challenges replete with circumstances that would defeat any ordinary person, but not Charlie Modica."

—**Joe Willie Namath**, Former American Professional Football Player

DOCS ON THE BAY

The Dream that Became America's Most Unlikely Medical School

Chancellor Charles R. Modica
with **David Fisher**

A POST HILL PRESS BOOK

Docs on the Bay:
The Dream that Became America's Most Unlikely Medical School
© 2026 by Medream Entertainment, LLC, a Florida limited liability company
All Rights Reserved

ISBN: 979-8-88845-761-0
ISBN (eBook): 979-8-88845-762-7

Cover design by Jim Villaflores
Interior design and composition by Greg Johnson, Textbook Perfect

This book, as well as any other Post Hill Press publications, may be purchased in bulk quantities at a special discounted rate. Contact orders@posthillpress.com for more information.

This is a work of nonfiction. All people, locations, events, and situations are portrayed to the best of the author's memory.

No part of this book may be reproduced, stored in a retrieval system, or transmitted by any means without the written permission of the author and publisher.

Post Hill Press
New York • Nashville
posthillpress.com

Published in the United States of America
1 2 3 4 5 6 7 8 9 10

This book is dedicated to the over thirty thousand successful graduates of St. George's University who believed in a wild dream to find theirs, and who are now helping people across the globe.

This University and, hence, this book would not have been possible without the trust, energy, and hard work of many people. At the center is my wife, Lisa Modica, whose understanding, empathy, encouragement, and endless patience were key to the success of the school. St. George's would have never survived the early years without the passion and vision of Andy Belford, Peggy Lambert, Dave Brown, Vish Rao, Geoffrey Bourne, Morrie Alpert, Keith Taylor, Pat Adams, Charles Adams, Jane Sutter, Al Pensick, Steve Weitzman, Bob Jordan, Danny Ricciardi, Jack Cush, Bob Ryan, Anthia Parke, Dawne Buckmire, Jay Wilbur, Leslie Marino, and many more dedicated people who believed in the dream we were building and worked hard to get there.

Contents

INTRODUCTION

A Life Saved

In August 2025, as this book was about to go to go to the printer, I happen to call a student from one of our first classes with whom I had remained close. He is a well-respected cardiologist, he has been cited many times as one of Connecticut's top doctors, and was preparing to implant a pacemaker. It was a procedure he'd done literally thousands of times. But rather than speaking with me, he promised to call back. His patient came first. Then he went to work.

Seconds later, as he stepped into the operating room, the patient's heart stopped. There was no warning, it just stopped. She literally had minutes to live. There was no time to perform the full procedure. Instead, the doctor took the pacemaker's wires and calmly but quickly inserted them into the patient's heart. He jump-started it. Within seconds, the heart started beating again. Her life was saved.

Later, he called me back and in a very matter-of-fact manner told me the story. Obviously, I was astonished. I asked, "What would have happened if you had spent a few minutes talking to me?"

He paused, then said, "Well, the outcome might have been different."

I wondered how it felt to know that he had saved a life only minutes earlier. Wonderful, incredible, he told me, but added it was not the first time. Then he asked me how many lives I think our graduates had saved since he was part of the original classes on Grenada. I had never considered that. This episode made me pause to consider how significant just one day in the life of a doctor can be in the lives of so many others. How many lives can twenty-four thousand doctors save over almost five decades?

"Likely millions," he said.

That's twenty-four thousand men and women who probably would not have become doctors if St. George's Medical School did not exist. It's impossible to calculate how many patients have been served or saved by those physicians. Likely millions? What a wonderful thought. St. George's University, School of Medicine on the small, beautiful island of Grenada started as my unlikely dream. A lot of people still have never heard of it. But today we are the largest provider of doctors to the United States—which unfortunately is still not providing enough of its own graduates to fulfill America's medical needs.

This is the story of what those young people from the early classes sacrificed to help build the school. What they gave up, the hardships they endured, the creative and brilliant ways we found together to deal with potential disasters. I am so proud of them, every single one of them. Today our campus is among the most modern and beautiful medical schools in the world that has made our partner, the great nation of Grenada, so proud during this half century in operation and our students are still coming from dozens and dozens of countries to study there, to earn their white coat.

There are answers to the growing shortage of doctors, just as there was when we first settled in our sparse surroundings. What we've learned, what we know, what we have proven and produced, and how to approach the growing problem is in these pages.

But mostly it is a wonderful tale of some extraordinarily brave and trusting people who more than anything in the world wanted to be doctors. It is about dreams coming true.

—Chancellor Charles Modica

PROLOGUE

A World-Class Institution

I am always amazed by how many memories a soft breeze can carry. Sometimes, late in the evening, I enjoy walking through the quiet streets of the magnificent campus of St. George's University on the island of Grenada. All around me are big, beautiful mission-style buildings, each one of them crisp and clean, full of promise for the future. It is brightly lit, proudly displaying one of the most beautiful and modern university campuses in the world, equipped with all the modern tools and technology necessary to educate the next generation of doctors and nurses, veterinarians and management.

And then a gentle Caribbean breeze washes over me, the same warm whisper I felt almost fifty years ago when I came here for the first time, and I can feel the past. I can see it. It was thousands of yesterdays, long before we had graduated more than twenty thousand medical doctors and caused significant changes to the world of medicine.

I can see that past clearly…a small number of incredibly optimistic young men, and a few intrepid women—eager to become physicians, who answered a small newspaper ad announcing a new English-language medical school—had arrived on an island few of them had known existed only months earlier, never imagining the obstacles they would face.

Those first classes came from so many different places in their lives. They were recent college graduates as well as established business people, they were health-care professionals and researchers, but all of them, every one of them, shared a single dream: They wanted to become doctors.

And somewhere, at some time, for some reason, that dream had been deferred.

I had my own dream too. I was a twenty-nine-year-old law school student determined to create a world-class medical school. Those students and I had fought through so many obstacles, hurdles no one possibly could have imagined—or believed we could resolve. There were shortages of everything we needed, everything imaginable from electricity to professors, and we survived by bucking the establishment, an intervention by the United States Marines, a revolution, a coup, a massive hurricane, and a volcanic eruption.

In the beginning I'd kept my dream in a shoebox on my desk. Somehow, we had managed to transform a few decrepit, transitory, and mostly abandoned buildings, located on two campuses several miles apart on a newly independent Caribbean nation, into sixty-five Georgian buildings on forty-two acres overlooking the Caribbean Sea. From that shoebox we became America's largest source of doctors—as well as the nation's leading provider of primary-care physicians.

That dream, that desire, that determination made all the difference. It is what held the school together initially, it was the foundation on which we built, it got us through the most difficult days, and it made our students the equal of students at almost any domestic medical school. In the decades that followed, we placed more medical school graduates into first-year residency programs in the United States than any other institution, and our graduates currently are working in virtually every specialty and subspecialty in the US and around the world. We created a university that welcomes students from more than 140 countries and has expanded to include schools of arts and science, veterinary medicine, and graduate studies—including a master of public health program. St. George's graduates have practiced everywhere from the renowned heart transplant operating rooms at Houston's Baylor College of Medicine to a town in rural Georgia where payment literally was made in fish.

I remember very early, when our visiting faculty program was just getting started, a professor from Harvard Medical School came down to Grenada to lecture for two weeks. This guy was a big deal, and we were thrilled to have him. This was even before two-time Nobel Prize recipient Linus Pauling became a visiting lecturer. But as this Harvard professor finished his two weeks, he told me how surprised and pleased he had been. He wasn't used to students being so enthusiastic, so excited to learn.

And he added that he liked the beaches too!

From that shoebox we grew into a world-class institution. Our graduates are practicing in most American hospitals and in more than fifty countries. They run massive, cutting-edge programs; they head departments; they prevent, they heal, they research, they cure. Nothing has held them back from fulfilling their dreams. This all became reality because of lessons learned early in my life that implausibility and obstacles really are only challenges to be overcome by creativity and perseverance.

CHAPTER 1

Roots of an Entrepreneur

"I have an idea."

—Charles Modica, i.e., Me

For me, it began almost a half century ago when I applied to almost twenty American medical schools—and was rejected by every one of them. Maybe I didn't necessarily have a great passion for medicine, but I did have an Italian mother.

I was a good student, my grades were fine, but there just weren't enough places in American medical schools for all the qualified people who wanted to become doctors. In fact, there still aren't. That really bothered me, because I could walk into the emergency room of any hospital in the country and see a foreign-born, foreign-educated doctor who had taken my place because the American medical school establishment was not creating enough doctors for the United States. Eventually, I spent a year studying medicine at the University of Oviedo in Spain. I did well enough academically my first year to be invited back to continue my studies, but during that year I learned one very important thing that would have hindered my medical career: I hated the sight of blood.

Being in Spain, though, with so many other Americans struggling to learn medicine in a foreign language, made it clear to me that there was a desperate need that was not being met. I was astonished to discover that many of my classmates had paid placement agencies as much as a $1,000—a significant amount of money in the early 1970s (over $7,000 today)—to help them secure a spot in foreign medical schools that had direct entry. I later discovered every year almost forty thousand top college graduates competed for only sixteen thousand spaces in American medical schools.

The need was there. And as I saw in Spain the desire was there, so I decided to open my own English-language medical school, training students to practice in the States. In the ensuing years I would be asked many times what drove me to do that. What made me believe a first-year foreign medical school dropout could found his own medical school? The answer has always been the same: I wasn't smart enough not to do it.

I was twenty-seven years old. I didn't do it for money. I did it to prove it could be done—and should be done.

I was always an entrepreneur; my wife, Lisa, claims the first thing I ever said to her was "I have an idea." Before opening a medical school, I had created a number of other businesses. Maybe my greatest skill has been recognizing an opportunity and having the guts—or perhaps lacking the common sense—to try to create something entirely new to fulfill the need. For example, as a teenager I was teaching waterskiing to people on Fire Island, a twenty-nine-mile-long sandbar protecting Long Island's South Shore, dotted with numerous totally separate communities, when my customers began asking me for rides down the island. As a result, I turned my ski boat into that resort island's first water taxi service and changed the nature of life on Fire Island.

I grew up on Long Island. My grandparents were immigrants. My paternal grandfather had come to the United States from Sicily when he was a teenager. How brave he was. I would say he risked everything to come here, but in fact he had nothing to lose.

He embodied the great American success story: He arrived in this country with a few dollars hidden in his sock, a skill, and a work ethic. He was a bricklayer who worked hard, saved his money, and eventually started constructing buildings in Brooklyn. My grandfather was not a formally educated man. We always said that he didn't read books because he was too busy building libraries.

My father, Lou Modica, was the first person in his family to go to college. He attended Long Island Agricultural and Technical Institute, a two-year community college, for one year. At that time, eastern Long Island was mostly farmland, a lot of potato and duck farms, and dairies. My grandfather bought land in Hauppauge, a place nobody had ever heard of way out on Long Island. My father built chicken coops on it and raised chickens, which he trucked into the city to sell to restaurants. Just before I was born in April 1947, a virus killed all his chickens, leaving him with several acres of vacant land.

Rather than being dragged down by his loss, he embraced the opportunity. The suburbs were being created just at that time; tens of thousands of World War II veterans were coming home from the war with cash in the bank and access to GI mortgages. New parkways, an expressway, and expanded Long Island Railroad service made it possible to commute to work in New York City and live in a house in the suburbs. A man named William Levitt was building a town of affordable houses on western Long Island. Levittown was the American Dream being transformed into reality house by house by house. It was what we had fought for: truth, liberty, and a front lawn.

My father built the first residential development in Hauppauge, in eastern Long Island. It was a beautiful hilly area surrounding a lake where Native Americans had lived. Hauppauge is a Nissequogue word meaning "land of sweet water." As a young kid I would go to the site with him and sometimes dig up arrowheads and bowls. He built fifty identical two-bedroom boxes that sold astonishingly quickly. So, he started building fifty more homes. He named the company after himself and my mother—Loumar Homes, for Lou and Marian Modica. Eventually he expanded to Brentwood and Central Islip and became one of the most successful builders in Suffolk County.

My father had learned from his father that pennies eventually became dollars. Once, I remember, we were on Fire Island and he needed to make a phone call. At that time there were only public pay phones on the island.

That created a dilemma—a call cost a dime but he only had a quarter. Rather than spending a whole quarter to make a ten-cent call, like most people would, we stood there several minutes until someone came along with change for a quarter. Then he made his call.

That was the way he built his houses. He knew precisely how many nails it took to construct a room—literally. If a frame required fifty nails the workman got fifty nails. He was the most generous frugal man I've ever known; he just didn't believe in waste. A paperclip left on the floor would drive him crazy. Later in life Post-its drove him nuts! He never understood why people would buy Post-its when they could easily tape a piece of (already used scrap) paper to the wall. Yet if someone needed assistance, he would be the first person there to offer it, no matter how long it took or what it cost.

He put me to work on weekends. By the time I was twelve I was painting houses or up on the roof hammering shingles into place. I laid my first linoleum floor when I was in high school in an office building he owned in Bay Shore. He made me give him an estimate for the job. I figured how much time it would take and what my time was worth and drew up a rudimentary contract. That was the first contract I ever signed. It was a major lesson I learned from him: When you're working for yourself you work a lot faster, and when you encounter a problem, don't waste time stressing about it—solve it.

The key, of course, is figuring out which problems can be quickly solved and which ones have to be stored away for another day when conditions are different and a solution can be found. Recognizing this, accepting it, and finding a different path, a possible solution, is essential. Years later, when I faced seemingly impossible problems, I didn't let them stop progress. I put them aside and kept moving forward, and with perseverance, dedication, and ingenuity we managed to solve the problems.

My paternal grandfather was a hard-nosed, bottom-line business guy. When I got a toy for Christmas he would ask me, literally, "How can you make money with that?" In contrast, my mother's father, John Schiro, would get down on the floor and play with me and that toy. Believe me, he was tough too. He was a union organizer for the Amalgamated Clothing Workers of America, so you knew he was a scrapper. He also had come to the US from Italy as a teenager. When he got off the boat, he liked to tell people, he saw a HELP WANTED sign. A laundry was looking for a presser, someone to iron new shirts. "You know how to do this?" he was asked.

"I can learn," he said. What a great answer: I can learn. And he did learn. After the historic Triangle Shirtwaist Factory fire in Greenwich Village in which 145 mostly female garment workers died locked in a burning sweatshop, he became active in the union movement. It was a tough time, it was ugly—and he was part of the ugliness. He was a survivor, my grandfather, and he fought for other working people as strongly as he did for himself. He helped build that union and changed countless lives.

He also was a smooth talker, a charmer who had the ability to make every person in his life feel special.

He could make you believe anything was possible, that with work and dedication you could transform your dreams into your life. Whenever I left his house, every time, his last words to me were always, "Study. Study. Study."

Everybody liked John Schiro. The rank-and-file workers, shop stewards, and management all respected him because he was fair and honest. Without doubt, he was the person in my family I most identified with growing up.

It was a good two-grandfather combination. A friend of mine once suggested that the reason I did a lot of crazy things was because I was never afraid of failure. I've thought about that. It makes a lot of sense. Why would any sane person with the barest medical background decide to found his own medical school in a country he had never heard of? It makes no sense. There's no logical way of explaining it. But that spirit, that belief that I can do something I believe in, that's what I got from those two men.

That's what they brought with them to America.

I learned from their examples not to follow the safe route, the beaten path. I learned how to iron a shirt, lay a linoleum floor, to treat everyone fairly and honestly. And I learned that if I can't solve a problem, I don't obsess over it—I solve the problems that I can solve. That last trait may have proved to be the most valuable.

Like my father, I never made a back-up plan. If I didn't have a back-up plan I had to keep moving forward.

The early years of my life we lived in a small house on a shady street in the town of Brentwood. It was a very middle-class community, a wonderful place to grow up. I remember being six or seven years old and collecting and returning bottles with my friends so we could get the two-cent deposit and spend it on candy. I remember watching Cadillacs drive by and thinking, *Look at that rich guy*. Then as my father became successful, we moved to a larger house on a beautiful lake in Brightwaters—and my father bought a Cadillac.

None of the kids in Brightwaters collected bottles; they were the kids who threw them away. I learned another lesson that made it possible for me to take risks: I was equally happy in both environments. Money didn't make that much difference in my life. In fact, at times I felt guilty about living in a wealthy community because I hadn't earned it.

My father had a thirty-six-foot Chris-Craft we would take across the Great South Bay to Fire Island. Basically, the only way to get to Fire Island is by regularly scheduled ferries or private boat. My aunt and her husband had bought twenty-eight lots in a community then being developed named The Pines. Even then Fire Island was a magical place—a place with beautiful beaches and no cars, a place where deer ran free, where monarch butterflies paused on their migration, a narrow strip where the ocean and the bay were separated by only a few hundred yards. Every house on the island was no more than a five-minute walk from some of the most beautiful beaches in the world.

It was the kind of special place where I could stand on the dock in a town called Kismet at 3:00 a.m. and play a jazzed-up version of "When the Saints Go Marching In" on my slide bugle—and instead of people screaming at me to stop, they would applaud. In other words, the perfect place to be a teenager.

My friends and I spent as much time as possible there. Eventually I bought a small powerboat, a fourteen-foot Boston Whaler with an outboard, and began teaching waterskiing. I used the profits to buy a couple of old Sunfish sailboats and rented them by the hour. I had a nice business going.

Traditionally, people had traveled up and down the island by sand taxi, buggies that drove on the beach. In the early 1960s, master builder Robert Moses wanted to build a highway down the center of the island. To prevent that, Fire Islanders successfully lobbied for the island to become part of the federally administered National Seashore. But as a consequence, beach taxis were prohibited. That meant there was no easy way for people to get to distant towns.

Enter opportunity.

I didn't know any of this. I'd never heard of Robert Moses. But at the beginning of the summer season one of my waterskiing clients asked me to take her and her husband in my boat from a town called Fair Harbor to a restaurant several miles down the beach in The Pines.

Sure. I was thrilled. I charged them $1.25 and had dinner with my cousins. Then I drove them back. A few days later this same couple asked me to take them down the beach again, this time with a few of their friends. I ended up making several trips. I think I charged $2.50 a couple wherever they wanted to go. The word spread: There's a guy who will take you anywhere on the island for a few bucks.

This was the first water taxi company on Fire Island. My investment consisted of several handmade signs. When my father heard about it he told me I needed a license to carry passengers, so I took the Coast Guard exam and got a license.

I didn't stop to think about how to start a business. It was too late for that. I was already in business. By the middle of the summer I was running three boats. I hired my high school classmates. My best friend and next-door neighbor Andy Belford drove one of the boats. His friend Peggy Lambert became our dispatcher.

I had no business plan. My plan was to do what needed to be done when it needed to be done. I came from the Lou Modica See a Problem, Solve a Problem School of Management. When we had a problem keeping the boats fueled, for example, I anchored a flatbed clam boat in the middle of the bay and stored as many fuel cans as possible on it.

When I had a problem I did the most logical thing: I had no cash reserve, so I paid my captains 25 percent of their gross. That kept them hustling.

Within weeks I had competition. The biggest problem I faced was maintaining dock space. My competitors tried to buy exclusive docking rights from restaurant owners; I couldn't afford that. But I learned the extraordinary value of relationships. The restaurant owners liked me and trusted me. Instead of accepting other offers, most of the restaurant owners begged me to continue delivering patrons to their front door. I never had a written contract with any of them. But if a restaurant owner needed a boat at 2:00 a.m., my boat was there for him. If he needed supplies brought across the bay at any time, he got them.

I began distributing the only newspaper on the island, the *Fire Island News*. I worked with the owner, Bea Garfield, and was always up front and honest with her, so when she published an article about the water taxis, we always got prominent and positive mention.

Be nice to people, I learned. This is the foundation of a successful business.

I owned South Bay Water Taxi for almost a decade. When I sold it to my younger brother John, we were operating fourteen boats, and Fire Island itself had changed. The island does not allow cars in the summer, and the communities were all quite different. Some are quiet with maybe a general store for coffee, milk, and bread; some wild with many restaurants and bars; some are gay communities. Water taxis allowed people to move easily and inexpensively from sedate towns to the bright spots. The business filled a need and was a huge success.

CHAPTER 2

A Strange New World: Foreign Medical Schools

"I think I want to be a doctor."

—Me again

I didn't grow up knowing what I wanted to do with my life. Founding a medical school certainly was not on my list. We had Career Days in high school where people would come in and tell us about their professions. Once an airline pilot came in, so I decided I wanted to be an airline pilot. Then a doctor came to Career Day and told us about medicine. I liked the way that sounded, so I told my mother, "You know, I've been thinking about it. I think I want to be a doctor."

My mother was a homemaker, the daughter of Italian immigrants. It was as if I'd told her I had decided to become pope. She looked at me with astonishment. "You do?!" Her greatest dreams for her son had come true: I was going to be a doctor. From that moment on, it was cemented, etched in stone: Charlie is going to be a doctor.

I knew nothing about being a doctor, nothing about medicine. I knew if you tapped someone on their kneecap with a small metal hammer their leg moved reflexively. I think I learned that from Groucho Marx's Dr. Hackenbush. The son of my mother's close friend attended Bethany

College, a small liberal arts school in the West Virginia panhandle, and had become a neurosurgeon. I wanted to go to Villanova in Philadelphia, a fine Catholic university.

"You're going to Bethany," my mother insisted. "If you're going to be a doctor, you have to go there."

The very small town of Bethany, West Virginia, was an adjustment for me. I was a New York kid, a Long Island kid. Isolated would have been a step up. My mother knew me very well—there was nothing to do there but go to class and study, then study some more. No one played the slide bugle at 3:00 a.m. in Bethany, West Virginia.

I was a premed student. Rather than a neurosurgeon, I was going to be an allergist. One summer I'd taught sailing to an allergist, and he'd hired me to do pollen counts at Southside Hospital. That was one of the stranger jobs I'd had. Early every morning and late every night I would dab Vaseline on a slide, go up to the roof of the hospital, and collect air samples. Then I would place it under a microscope and literally count the pollen seeds.

So naturally I was going to be an allergist.

I was a good student, not a great student. I also was personable, diligent, and a successful entrepreneur. I applied to numerous medical schools. I assumed I would be accepted by several of them. Anytime in my life when I really wanted to do something I'd always figured out how to do it.

I got one interview, from the Chicago Medical School.

One. I was not accepted by a single medical school. That stunned me. I wasn't used to failure. I was Charlie; I'd always been able to figure out a path to reach my goal. But what really made me furious was that my premed classmates, many of them far more qualified than me, also were rejected. Few of them even got that one interview. That stunned me too. These were smart, dedicated, enthusiastic young people who would have made terrific doctors, and they were being denied that opportunity. I read later that in my year there had been between thirty-five thousand and forty thousand applicants for about sixteen thousand slots. The competition was made even tougher by the fact that this was during the

Vietnam War, and medical school students got a military deferment. But at the same time we were being rejected I was already reading articles warning of the coming shortage of physicians.

It was obvious there was something very wrong with the system. More than anything else, that's what gave me the attitude that carried me through this venture. I didn't know it at the time, but the entire American medical system was undergoing a fundamental change. The friendly neighborhood doctor depicted by Norman Rockwell, the man who made house calls carrying a black bag, was disappearing, gradually being replaced by corporate groups. The invention and availability of new expensive technology, including ultrasound, CAT scans, MRIs, and microsurgery, was changing the daily practice of medicine.

The Nixon administration was advocating for the new health management organizations (HMOs), which encouraged medical group practices. The American Medical Association, which had been fighting against the proposed Medicare legislation, was becoming more of a politically active organization. Within the practice of medicine, the traditional general practitioner who came to your house carrying his black bag was being replaced by doctors going into higher-paying specialties.

The American medical schools didn't respond to the projected future shortage of doctors. From 1982 to 2002 the population of the US grew by 28 percent, and the number of first-year medical school seats went down—less than 1 percent, but down.

There was an alternative path. Students rejected by American medical schools could attend a school in a foreign country and eventually try to pass examinations to practice here. It wasn't easy. While there were medical schools around the world, about 90 percent of Americans studied in Europe or Mexico. There was a stigma attached to attending one of these schools, though; the underlying implication was that you weren't as good as other students—the medical establishment considered you second rate. Not a "real" doctor. Students graduating from these schools had a far more difficult time getting a residency at a good hospital or being accepted into a specialty training. That included American graduates of the top medical schools in England, France, Germany, Italy, and India.

It was ridiculous. So many medical advances and so many procedures, techniques, and medications had come from these countries; their standards were similar to ours, yet the AMA considered their medical school graduates less qualified than American students.

The most popular foreign school for American students was in Guadalajara, Mexico. I finally decided to enroll in medical school in Spain. The admissions process for Spanish medical schools was simple: If you had a college degree and a police certificate of good conduct, stamped and restamped and translated and submitted in triplicate, admission to any medical school in the country was automatic. I submitted my application to the Spanish consulate general in New York and was accepted. I literally could attend any medical school in Spain.

I had done all the application work by myself. I didn't even know that agencies were charging desperate young Americans as much as $1,000—and guaranteeing them admission—to these schools.

Getting in was easy; staying in was tough. Most American students face an additional problem when attending foreign medical schools: They are in foreign countries. We don't speak the language—whatever language it is. Studying medicine is difficult enough in English; having to do it in a foreign language made it considerably harder. I had spent the previous summer studying Spanish at Berlitz. One on one, every day. But that first year still was extremely tough; students had to do well to be *selectivo*, promoted to the second year.

Selectivo was a weeding-out process; just a fraction of students made it into the second year.

I visited several Spanish medical schools to see where I might want to study. Generalissimo Franco, a dictator, was still in power then, and I remembered seeing combat-ready Guardia in the Madrid airport carrying automatic weapons. Guns and medicine. At that moment I began wondering what I'd gotten myself into.

I ended up enrolling in a school in the small northern Spanish city of Oviedo. Hundreds of miles from the guns and politics of Madrid. Medical school was a five-year commitment. Including me, there were twenty-eight Americans in my class. I will never forget: On our first day we were sitting together in the rear of a classroom when the professor pointed at us and said something about "*los Americanos*." None of us spoke Spanish well enough to understand exactly what he was saying, but it clearly wasn't positive. The Spanish students turned around, looked at us like we were hostile invaders—and some of them started laughing.

It was humiliating. I never forgot it.

I once heard a wonderful description of the legendary Academy Award–winning actress and dancer Ginger Rogers, who made classic musicals as Fred Astaire's partner. Ginger Rogers, it was said, did everything Fred Astaire did—but she did it in high heels and backwards. That's what going to medical school in a foreign language is like. We had to learn and memorize the sometimes very complicated terminology in a foreign language. We had to learn how to fill in the gaps between what we were able to translate and what we needed to know. It made medical school far more difficult than learning in English. Being successful required extraordinary desire and dedication.

Every day brought some kind of new and difficult experience. In anatomy class, for example, we were told we had to go to a local cemetery to buy our bones. At least that's what it sounded like. I figured my translation must be wrong. The school couldn't possibly want us to buy bones. To my surprise it turned out my translation was accurate: We studied the skeletal system before working on a cadaver, and we were expected to bring our own bones to the classroom. This was the way it was done at that time—local cemeteries sold skeletons of unclaimed bodies to medical students.

I had entered a strange new world, the world of foreign medical schools. Maybe as surprising to me as having to buy bones was learning that people were willing to pay a $1,000 fee to an agency that guaranteed them admission to schools that automatically accepted applicants. That was an enormous amount of money at that time. (Again, over $7,000 in 2022 dollars.) My classmates had responded to a small ad in the *New York Times* promising "Guaranteed admission to certain European Medical Schools." The ad had been placed by Dr. Pressman (I'll never forget his name), and he could make that guarantee because Spain,

Italy, and probably France admitted every person who applied. I believe my application cost $20. If Pressman had charged $50 or $100, okay, that would have been fine, but $1,000? That was outrageous. Even more surprising to me was the fact that my classmates were not upset when they found out they could have done the same thing for $20. They were so desperate to attend medical school they felt the fee was worth it.

In midwinter Dr. Pressman came to Oviedo, supposedly to learn more about the school from his clients, but I suspected he was gathering information to improve his recruiting pitch. I attended the meeting with my close friend, the only other American in the class who had not paid Pressman, David Byrnes. We were astonished, both of us realizing that Pressman had been paid $26,000 by the people in that small hotel room. But then he ended the meeting by explaining he had to attend a similar gathering in Barcelona, "Because I have three hundred students in class there."

The math was simple: $1,000 x 326. I didn't need a calculator to figure out how much money he was making: a lot. In just those two cities. It was impossible to know how many American clients he had placed in European schools, but in David's words it added up to "Oh, my God!"

This whole situation intrigued me. Dr. Pressman wasn't doing anything illegal. He certainly was providing a service to people who believed they needed it. It wasn't a scam; he did exactly what he claimed he could do. But to me it still seemed like a rip-off because these schools had an open admissions policy. Students just needed access to that information and instructions how to proceed with the application. Basically, I summed it up as a passport and everything in triplicate.

I decided to write a book explaining the process to interested students. I knew that had it existed I would have bought a copy. The fact that I had never written a book or that I knew absolutely nothing about publishing a book did not deter me. The demand was there, even if I was one of the few people who recognized it. I wanted to make some money out of this situation, and I wanted to help those people who couldn't afford Pressman's $1,000. Initially I intended to focus on medical schools in Spain because I had visited many of them before picking Oviedo. But my concept quickly expanded to include all European medical schools, and eventually all foreign medical schools.

I knew that the publishing company Barron's, which was well known for its college guides and testing prep books, had its headquarters in Hauppauge. This seemed to be a perfect fit for them. "I have an idea for a new book," I wrote to them. "I'm currently a medical student studying in Spain. Most of the people in my class have paid a $1,000 fee for a $20 application. This book will help them find and apply to foreign medical schools. Are you interested?" A month later I got a terse answer: "We appreciate your interest in Barron's. At this time we do not believe there is a market for this type of guidebook. Thank you for your suggestion…."

Another opportunity had found me. I could see the need for this book sitting next to me in the classrooms every day. Not to even mention those thousands of other Americans who couldn't afford the fee and didn't apply because they thought these schools were too expensive. After the school year ended I toured Europe in my Fiat 300, a small car I'd bought for $300. But rather than visiting the great museums or churches, I went to medical schools. I visited just about every medical school in Europe, gathering information about the application process and a description of the program. I interviewed American students and took photographs. There were fourteen schools in Spain, twenty-three in France, and twenty-one in Italy. Switzerland had five schools, but they admitted very few Americans. In Milan my Fiat was stolen. All my luggage was in it. I just bought more clothes and kept going.

At this same time my friend Andy Belford was crewing his way around the world on sailboats. I convinced him to research medical schools in the countries he visited. There were five medical schools in South Africa, for example. Four in Finland. Eventually I got the name and address of every accredited medical school in the world from the World Health Organization. I wrote to those schools we couldn't physically visit. By the time I was done I had compiled the requirements and at least some basic information about every medical school in the world that accepted American students.

My guidebook was going to be published by the Foreign Medical School Information Center—which consisted of me. It was a made-up name, but it sounded official and prestigious. The price of the book was $8.95, which admittedly was expensive for the time. My father agreed to loan me the seed money, but before doing that he wanted to be convinced the market existed. So before writing it, or collating the information, I needed to prove that to him. I decided to send a poster describing my not-yet-existing book and eight order forms to every college in America.

I worked out of my father's real estate office. My cover letter explained that students were paying up to $1,000 for the same information they could get for $8.95. I sent it to the premed advisors at 1,100 colleges. I know that number is accurate because I personally typed and addressed each envelope, folded and inserted the letters, and licked and affixed the necessary two postage stamps.

Within a few days the first checks began trickling in. In exchange for using his office and his secretary, Mrs. Walden, my father insisted that I not cash a single check until the book was printed. All the checks went into a locked drawer in Mrs. Walden's desk until I put the first books in the mail. The trickle quickly became a flow.

In less than a month I had received several hundred orders. Most colleges bought one copy for their library, which I didn't like, but there was nothing I could do about it. And it was a sale. After selling the book, I went to work producing it. It opened with "A Word from the Director." Me. It was my hope, I wrote, that interested students would be able to apply to the medical school of their choice without using a placement agency. "These agencies have continued to take advantage of applicants by charging enormous fees, from $500 to $3,000 for their services which, contrary to their claims, do not increase an applicant's chance for admission."

My book also included tidbits that would be helpful to applicants. Only five foreign students a year were accepted in Costa Rica; Irish medical schools had accepted only two foreign students the previous year; in addition to a college degree, Norway required applicants to pass a science exam. I offered a matching service, connecting students who would be attending the same foreign school to enable them to "practice a foreign language and find living quarters together in order to save on rent."

Premed advisors at colleges welcomed the book. It made their job considerably easier. Even they didn't know most of this stuff. Nobody did, except me. I had the pages printed by the company that produced my father's real estate listings. The book had a plastic binding, and two young women who had worked for my water taxi service, Lisa Sanders (my bride to be even though I didn't know it then) and her best friend, Helen Kappus, hand-collated it. My cost was $2 per book, including postage, so I was making about $7 on each sale.

It sold—in fact it sold significantly better than I anticipated. And believe me, I anticipated. I have always been an optimist. The sales proved that there were a large number of desperate young people ready to do whatever it took to fulfill their dreams.

CHAPTER 3

The Idea Takes Shape

"Do you know the word for colon in Spanish?"
—Frustrated me

I learned so much during that first year of studying medicine in Spain—do you know the word for colon in Spanish?—mostly that I did not want to be a doctor. In any language. It became obvious to me that I just didn't share the passion of my classmates. Telling my mother I was not going back to Spain—that I was not going to be a doctor—was one of the most difficult things I'd ever had to do. She couldn't understand it. "How could you do this to your family? You passed the test. What's wrong with you?" She cried for weeks. And when nothing else worked to change my mind she brought in the big guns: She called my grandfather.

This was a really big deal. For years every Sunday we would drive to Brooklyn to have a big Italian dinner with my grandfather. Then we would go to Coney Island. But he came to Long Island only for the major holidays. It was unheard of for him to come all the way out to Brightwaters during the week. But that's how much of a family crisis this was. "Grandson," he said, in his still-heavy Italian accent, "let's take a ride together."

He drove silently, holding the wheel with both hands and looking straight ahead. He did not turn on the radio, emphasizing the importance of this trip. He didn't tell me where we were going. Not a word. But things began looking familiar. We drove across the railroad tracks into Brentwood and made a right turn on Suffolk Avenue. He stopped directly in front of our old house. He looked at me. This was very dramatic. "Grandson, do you remember this house?"

I did.

"Grandson, I come offa the boat with ten dollars in my sock. I started from right here. And I worked. Then your mother and your father, they met at the Lincoln High School. They went from here." He always punctuated his conversation with his hands, and as he reminded me where our family had come from he waved his arms in great swings. It was a memorable performance and really affected me.

I started crying. I was twenty-four years old, and I had already started two successful businesses. But I was being reduced to an ungrateful child. "Grandpa," I pleaded, "I just don't want to go back. I can't."

"All right," he finally agreed. "I understand, this medicine, it's not for you. So it's okay, you don't have to go back." I let his words sink in…he was on my side. He was on my side! And then he added, "So, you'll be a lawyer."

A lawyer? I actually hadn't considered what else I might want to do. I'd thought I might follow my father into real estate. "A lawyer?" I responded.

The more he thought about it the more sense it made to him. "Grandson, I can accept your decision now. I can see how unhappy this makes you. But if you don't wanna be a doctor, then you have to be a lawyer."

As we drove home I began thinking about it. There is no blood in lawyering. Yeah, I could be a lawyer. I knew several lawyers who worked with my father in real estate. I could do that.

When we got back to Brightwaters, he made the announcement. "Dolly [he always called my mother Dolly], I got some bad news, but I got some good news. Your son, my grandson, he's not gonna be a doctor." He waved his index finger back and forth, as if erasing that possibility—no doctor. "But the good news is, he's going to be a lawyer."

Doctor. Lawyer. My mother agreed instantly. "Okay," she said, then said it again more firmly, "Okay."

While taking the LSAT, the tests I needed to take to apply to law schools, I continued updating and selling my book—while teaching eighth-grade math in Amityville. I had taken a job as a substitute teacher before law school started, and the principal asked me to work full time. He was desperate. "We've had subs here for a month, and you're the only one who has lasted more than a day."

I had no training. But I figured out that I didn't have to be a mathematical genius, I just had to be one lesson ahead of my students. They never knew what I didn't know. The lesson I learned from that experience was to prove very important within a few years.

It seemed like my life had no single direction. I was all over the place. Medical school, publishing a guidebook, law school, teaching, running a water taxi company. Every day consisted of an endless series of small decisions, but every one of them mattered. What I could not know was that everything counted, every experience made a difference. These experiences were like the ingredients in the Italian soup my grandmother made every Sunday—eventually they would all be tossed into a large pot, and the result would be wonderful.

I was accepted to the recently opened Delaware Law School. My uncle, a state supreme court judge in Brooklyn, had given me some guidance. I went to school there with my friend Dunewood Truglia, another one of my water taxi drivers. Dunewood wasn't his real name; he got it after his boat disappeared one night and we found it the next morning tied to a dock in the town of Dunewood, where he had spent the night. The name stuck.

After studying medicine in Spanish, law school in English came easily for me. Each case was a short story. That made it easy to remember them. There were three hundred students in the first-year class, and I finished number one. My mother was thrilled: My son the lawyer!

Unfortunately, having been founded only a year earlier, the school had not yet been accredited. A lot of students were unhappy about that, as well as the way it was being run. There was no one to answer our questions or allay our concerns. So Dunewood and I and a third friend decided we should start our own law school. If the concept of three first-year law students opening their own law school seems absurd, that's because it was. But we never let logic get in the way of our dreams.

It actually did seem like a good idea at the time. We believed enough of our classmates would transfer to our law school to make it financially viable. We did this while we were attending classes. We decided the school would be based in Rhode Island, while our admissions office would be in New York. But Rhode Island's attorney general turned down our application, informing us that the business office must be in the same state as the business.

We adapted, instead founding the Commonwealth School of Law in Washington, DC. We went through all the necessary legal steps. This time we made it work. We got our charter and opened an admissions office on K Street in the District. Our business plan was to use the tuition we collected to fund the school.

We were in operation for three months. We just didn't attract a sufficient number of applicants to make it viable. We failed, but I learned a great deal about the process. This experience turned out to be another important ingredient in the soup of my future.

Meanwhile, my book continued to sell steadily. I spent most spring weekends visiting colleges in the Northeast, meeting with premed advisors and students to sell books and answer questions. During almost every meeting a student would complain, "This is great stuff about Italy and Spain. But I want to study in English." In response I would explain the reality: Every medical school in an English-speaking country was overwhelmed with applications from their own citizens. Chances of American students being admitted to a medical school in England, for example, were significantly less than at any American school. I was blunt: "You have to get past that. The odds are really against you."

As I drove home from these weekend trips, I would think about the absurdity of the existing system. Almost a quarter of all the doctors practicing in America came from other countries. Physicians who were born and trained overseas were taking jobs that easily could have been filled by the students I was meeting every weekend—if only there were enough places in our medical schools to train them. But this system had been created and was preferred by the American medical establishment. I understood their bottom line: They had an obligation to maintain high standards. Since the days of traveling medicine shows selling snake oil out of the back of a wagon, conmen had been taking advantage of people. The AMA was established to protect the American public. I got that. I respected them for it. Its contribution had made the American medical system among the best in the world. But as a consequence of those policies there were a limited number of available seats in our medical schools.

Limiting the number of US-trained physicians led to the existing shortage. In addition, they were able to manage the number of internationally trained physicians with the residency training program. Being a licensed physician in another country was a ticket to the United States. You're a doctor? Want to become an American citizen? We'll give you a residency, we'll pay you, we'll let you bring your family with you.

As a result we were robbing countries around the world of their best young doctors while preventing smart, qualified American kids from filling that need. In fact, a Yale instructor named Rosemary Stevens—I'll never forget her name—had written a paper for the United Nations describing this as a perpetual brain drain. The medical establishment loved them because they met all of our standards and helped fill the need for primary-care physicians.

The system made no sense for anyone but the medical community. The limited number of medical-school slots created that shortage of physicians.

As I was reminded by every book I sold, there was a significant pool of frustrated students desperate to study medicine with no place to go.

I knew there was an opportunity: The "demand" for acceptance to an American medical school was far greater than the "supply" of available seats. Several years earlier an attorney named Pat Adams had rented an office in a Bay Shore building owned by my father. They had become friends. Pat was a terrific lawyer and an even better person. Our families had become close. In fact, Pat's son started working for the water taxi company when he was a teenager and eventually became a captain. Purely coincidently (it is amazing how these things happen), at that time Pat was representing a medical school in the Dominican Republic that was trying to set up an American placement service. This was one of the very few medical schools in the Caribbean. Pat knew about my book and asked me to establish a pipeline. Although classes there were taught in Spanish, even then the Dominican Republic was bilingual, making it easier for an American to study there than in Europe.

I worked as both a recruiter and admissions officer for the school for three semesters. I was paid $300 for every student who enrolled. This was another side business for me while still in law school. My book gave me access to prospective students. I knew I could recruit more students than the school could accept. I thought we had agreed to limit the class size to 150 students, but I discovered they were accepting an unmanageable number of applicants.

I had created a monster. They were even admitting students I had marked for rejection. And apparently some of their professors were running a side business manipulating test results. Pat and I were furious. We quit.

But the basic problem still existed. Once again, opportunity had found me. Seeing up front and personally a rapacious group take advantage of a bad supply/demand problem while not fixing the core problem started pulling all the soup ingredients together. I decided I was going to fill the need that was not being met. I was going to create an honest path for American medical students to study abroad. I was going to provide qualified students to reputable foreign medical schools. As the executive director of the Foreign Medical School Information Center, I wrote to just about every foreign medical school in which classes were taught in English asking if they might be interested in creating a special track for a certain number of seats per year to be set aside for qualified American students.

I had the credentials. I had written and published the best-selling book in America on the subject, I explained, which gave me access to numerous students who wanted to study abroad. As I had done for the Dominican school, my company would process the applications, conduct the interviews, and guarantee the students we recommended were qualified.

Only a few schools even bothered to respond, and those that did politely and firmly turned me down.

Big demand, limited supply. What could I do about it?

There was no ah-ha moment. No eureka instant when I suddenly realized I would start my own medical school. It had simply and inexorably evolved to this point. The idea was the sum total of my frustration, beginning with my own rejections. I was angry at an unfair system. *This is crazy*, I thought. And it wasn't just about me—I had met people in Spain who were far more qualified than me, who had excellent grades as undergraduates but maybe hadn't done well on the medical school entrance exam, the MCAT (one bad day that changed their lives), or who lived in the wrong state and due to the insane number of applicants did not get admission to a medical school in another state.

I saw what they were willing to go through in a foreign country to achieve those dreams. It wasn't just one or two people—there were thousands of them, thousands of smart, well-qualified, dedicated, energetic, enthusiastic young people who would make wonderful doctors. The soup ingredients had come together. I decided: I'm going to find a country willing to let me open an English-language medical school. It had to be in English and be structured like a US medical school, because these students eventually were going to be working in American hospitals.

That was more than twenty thousand doctors ago.

CHAPTER 4

Grenada?

"You're crazy!"

—Pretty much all my friends and family

I began my research by getting the annual reports from several medical schools, which included their operating budgets. The numbers were daunting: It cost a school like New York Medical College three to four times the annual tuition to educate a student. The tuition then might have been about $20,000 a year, while the real cost for each student was closer to $80,000. That meant if I was able to recruit one hundred students the first year, if I was very smart and cut corners, I would lose only $6 million.

Never was that old warning more accurate: Don't try this at home.

As I continued investigating, I discovered there was a reason for those losses. It wasn't that high-salaried deans were riding around in limousines. Schools were legitimately spending it on research. The LCME, the Liaison Committee on Medical Education that accredits American medical schools, mandated that schools must conduct laboratory and clinical research. The student-to-faculty ratio was 1.4 to 1, but most of those 1s were working in laboratories, publishing articles and books, rarely interacting with students. These schools boasted that they had some of the most impressive scientists in the world on their faculty, but those people were not lecturing first-year medical students. God bless them for their research, but it was not an essential aspect of educating doctors.

This was the way things were done because it was the way they always had been done. In my mind there was no logical justification for it. Conducting research certainly plays a role in educating medical students. But when the result is limiting the number of available seats, then it is out of balance. And, in my opinion, this was what was happening. It was a model that couldn't possibly work for me. So, as I began planning this new medical school, which would be created to meet modern needs rather than being restricted by standards that hadn't changed much in decades, my first decision was that it was going to be dedicated to teaching and supported by tuition. We would not focus on research. We would educate medical students, not use them as laboratory assistants.

I told only a few friends about my plan. But pretty much without exception they all reacted the same way: "You're crazy! You completed one year of medical school and now you're going to start your own medical school?"

That was the logical response, but it didn't affect me. I knew the demand was there. I knew there was tremendous waste in the operating budgets of existing medical schools. I was determined: If nobody else is crazy enough to do this, I am!

The key for me was not to get overwhelmed by reality.

The first challenge was to find a country willing to let me open a medical school. It had to be an English-speaking country other than the United States. Founding a medical school became my part-time job. I was still attending law school, living in a small apartment in Wilmington, Delaware. I spent several hours in the library compiling a list of every English-speaking country in the world. Then, on my official Foreign Medical School Information Center stationary, I wrote to the president, the prime minister, the minister of education, the minister of health, to any official whose name and address I could find, congratulating them on the fact that their country had been selected as a finalist in our extensive feasibility study about where to build our planned medical school. I sent at least two hundred letters. Maybe more.

I put every response in a shoebox I kept on my desk. There was plenty of room in that shoebox. I received about twenty polite rejections; most officials did not bother to respond. My search continued for several months. I didn't give up, because I knew it was a good idea. But in addition to being frustrated, I actually felt a little sorry for these people, because they lacked the vision to see the possibilities. Then one night I found myself reading the local newspaper, the *Evening Journal.* I was not a regular reader of that paper—I didn't subscribe, and most days I was too busy to look at it. But that night in early February 1974 I picked it up—and if I hadn't I probably would have spent my life working as a real estate attorney on Long Island.

At the bottom of the front page there was a summation of news stories called "In the World Today." These were teasers, a couple of factual sentences. One item caught my attention; it said essentially, "The nation of Grenada received its independence amid some turmoil, and British royalty did not attend. New Prime Minister Eric Gairy said..."

Grenada? British royalty? I'd never heard of Grenada, but as a former British possession, obviously its people spoke English. I had no idea where this newly independent country was, so it took me a little while to find the little black dot representing it on the globe in my apartment. (I still have that globe.) Finally, there it was, Grenada. It was an island in the British West Indies, near Trinidad and Tobago. About a quarter of a fingernail from Venezuela. It was a Caribbean nation. Perfect.

Rather than a letter, I sent a telegram. Telegrams were still a big deal at that time, and even though it cost me $15—because you paid by the word—I knew it would attract more attention than a letter. "The Foreign Medical School Information Center wishes to congratulate the nation of Grenada on its recent independence from the United Kingdom. I am pleased to inform you that as a newly independent nation you are eligible for inclusion in our ongoing feasibility study for a new American-type medical school. Since this study has been ongoing"—that was true, the shoebox had been on my desk for almost six months—"you must respond within the next 30 days to be considered...."

About a week later, when I returned from class, I found a yellow Western Union envelope under my door. It was a telegram from Prime Minister Gairy's secretary, a woman named Gloria Payne. My hands were trembling as I opened it; no one sent telegrams to turn down an offer. It read simply, "The nation of Grenada wishes to be included in this study. Please let us know what are the next steps we must take." And that is how the nation of Grenada came to be selected as the site of my medical school.

The next thing I had to do was raise seed money to get started. I needed someone to invest in my dreams. I called my father, who knew nothing about this idea. I was hoping I could talk him into going down there to see if this was feasible. "Hey Dad," I said in my most professional law student voice, "I've got some great news."

There were several seconds of silence on the other end of the phone. My father had learned to expect the unexpected from me. "What's that, son?" he asked. "Things are still good in school, right?"

"Oh yeah, yeah, school's going great. But I got an answer to the telegram I sent to Grenada."

Telegram? Grenada? "What's Grenada?"

"You know, remember, it's that English-speaking island in the Caribbean that just got its independence." Once again he paused, clearly unable to make any connection between me going to law school in Delaware and a newly independent island in the Caribbean. "I don't understand," he admitted. "Why would they be sending you a telegram?"

As matter-of-factly as possible I explained, "Well, see, I congratulated them on their independence, and they said they wanted to be included in this study I have going on for the best place to build a new English-speaking medical school."

I could almost hear his mind working as he absorbed all of this. Finally he asked, "What study is that?"

Admittedly, I had never mentioned my concept to him. "Well, I have this great idea. I want to start a new medical school, and I've been writing letters, but until now nobody had responded. But they're interested in doing it."

He answered in Italian, which he did only when he had something very serious to say. "I got two words for you, kid: *Sei pazzo!*" You're crazy!

Okay, that was a start. He didn't say no. I knew how to get through to him. I employed the traditional Italian strategy: I called my mother. "Mom, Dad really disappointed me last night. I have this great idea, and he won't even listen to me."

She responded with the magic words: "I'll talk to him."

Apparently, she was very persuasive, telling him, "If your son says he can do it, he can do it." My father called me later that day. "Okay, go ahead, tell me, what's this great idea?"

I would drive back to Long Island most weekends to fulfill orders for my guidebook. The following Saturday we sat in his office, and I explained the concept to him. This was a man who had turned chicken coops into a large and successful real estate business. He also knew how hard I worked, so he took it very seriously. But he was doubtful, which is the nicest way I can describe his response. "How can you do this?" he asked. "You don't just start a medical school."

The fact that he had never heard of anything like this was not surprising. As far as I knew, no one had ever done anything like this.

We sat at the kitchen table. Ironically, the kitchen walls were covered with colorful illustrations depicting several different types of spices: nutmeg, cinnamon, cloves. I didn't know it at the time, but these were crops grown on Grenada and the reason it is known as the Spice Island.

I knew my father was doing this to satisfy my mother. The idea seemed preposterous, but as we sat there I could see his interest growing. He asked a lot of questions to which I had no answers—yet—but what he did see was my own conviction. "Dad," I told him, relating my experience in Spain, "you have no idea what these kids have to go through. I've been there; I've seen it. They're desperate to become doctors. They'll do whatever it takes. If we can give them a way to learn in English…"

He stopped me. "I get it. I get that. But you have no idea how complicated this is. There are all kinds of rules and regulations. They don't just let anyone with a degree practice medicine.…"

I had done enough research even before going to Spain to know what was possible. I knew which tests foreign-trained medical students had to pass before being allowed to practice in America. The World Health Organization had established standards: Any student who graduated from a medical school accredited by the country in which it was located was permitted to take these tests. The path to certification was there, I told him, there was no question about that. The demand was there. "You see how well the book is doing, Dad," I reminded him. "I'm selling hundreds of copies."

We sat there for more than an hour. I made the argument every possible way. He kept trying to punch holes in it, and I found ways to plug them. He started jotting down some notes. Finally he paused, looked at those notes, and asked, "Where is this Grenada again?"

Truthfully, all I knew about Grenada was what I'd read in the *Encyclopedia Britannica*. As I was to learn, it is an absolutely beautiful island that had been struggling economically under British rule. Unemployment and poverty were widespread on the island, but it was a very different type of poverty than existed in the States. Because it was a tropical country, there was an abundance of food, including various types of fruits and vegetables. Meals literally could be picked off a tree. It also had an established educational system in which most young people had access to primary schools and, after passing proficiency exams, high schools. But access to college was limited by finances and opportunity.

My father brought in Pat Adams, who understood the economics of a medical school, and Ed McGowan, another real estate investor and the former county Republican Party leader. These were my father's friends and business associates. They were serious men who had watched me grow up. They knew me as Lou's kid. When I was twelve years old, I had delivered *Newsday* to Ed McGowan's house—he was the best tipper on my route—so it took some time for them to take me seriously.

My father moved slowly, pitching it to them as more of a real estate opportunity rather than founding a medical school. That made sense. They understood real estate. They also were aware that the Caribbean was rapidly becoming a popular vacation destination. The islands were aggressively building a tourism industry. It made investing there an intriguing idea. Even if the school failed, they would own potentially very valuable land on an English-speaking Caribbean island. Adams and McGowan were interested, but they wanted to see my business plan.

Right, my business plan. I had never done a business plan. For the water taxi service, my business plan had been to get a boat there when people wanted to travel up or down the island. The guidebook had been printed on demand. But they needed a business plan, so for the first time I had to put a dream on paper.

My business plan consisted of one page on lined ledger paper. I started with the belief that tuition would cover all the school's expenses. I predicted how many students would enroll, what the tuition would be, how many would graduate, and how large a faculty we would need. I based my estimates on what I had seen in Spain and what I had learned compiling my book. I knew the tuition medical schools in the States charged. I knew the average faculty salaries. From that I calculated how high our tuition had to be. I had been through a year of medical school, so I knew the range of courses we would offer. I also started talking to several local doctors, just trying to gather as much information as possible.

I wasn't making up the numbers. I tried to be realistic. The one thing I always believed was that we would be able to attract students. I'd seen that; I'd lived it. But admittedly a lot of it was guesswork. There was nothing in existence in any way similar to what I was proposing.

It was all sort of vague, but on paper it looked very good. My business plan proposed enrolling two hundred students who would pay $2,250 per semester, $4,500 a year. That's what I needed to make the school work. In that plan I accounted for attrition; inevitably some students would drop out, and, I firmly believed, other students would do well enough on the national boards to transfer to American schools. That had been everybody's dream in Spain. I predicted one hundred students in my first class would eventually graduate. That was a guess and a hope. It was wildly optimistic, but that's what I needed.

Within two months my father, Pat, and Ed went to Grenada to conduct their own feasibility study. I remained in the background—way in the background. They didn't want Prime Minister Gairy to know that the so-called brains behind all of this was a twenty-seven-year-old kid.

That was the first of many trips. They almost always went together. It took considerable time, but gradually they began to believe this was possible. They often met with Prime Minister Gairy, who as a former union organizer knew how to negotiate. Each time they came back from the island, we would meet to discuss the problems they'd discovered. They had pages of notes on their yellow pads. How are we going to do this? What about that? I remember Pat telling me a story about a conversation he'd had with a local taxi driver. The man had asked him what he was doing in Grenada, and he said, "We're going to open a medical school."

The driver turned around and replied, "What? Here?" He laughed.

I spent hours with the three men responding to their questions. There were endless problems. More than endless! I answered as best I could, although sometimes I really didn't know if I was correct. When I had no answer, I would respond as earnestly as possible that there had to be a way to solve that problem.

It wasn't simple and it wasn't quick. Months passed. A year. Eighteen months. The three of them continued going down there. Meanwhile, I was speaking to anyone who would answer my questions, learning about medical education. I began to understand why the existing system had developed, what worked, and what made little sense. I already knew it wasn't working for the majority of applicants. Almost twenty-five thousand applicants were being rejected each year. And most if not all of them were qualified or they would not have been applying in the first place. That's why I was doing this. Need plus quality, meet solution!

I wasn't locked into the existing system. I knew I couldn't re-create it, so to be successful we had to modify it. I began devising possible solutions to what once seemed like insurmountable problems. Instead of accepting only one class a year, which is what medical schools did, I decided we would take in a new class each semester. That instantly doubled the number of students we could accept. As for the faculty, I believed we could make it work with six instructors for the first term. Each of them would serve as both the department head and the professor. Every member of our staff would teach. We would add instructors as we needed them in the second term.

I created the curriculum from the bulletins of America's most prestigious medical schools, among them Harvard, Yale, Stanford, the Jefferson Medical College of Philadelphia, even Oxford. I practically memorized their catalogs. With some minor variations they all offered essentially the same basic courses to first-year students. That was my road map. I proposed a first-year curriculum of five courses. Anatomy (which consisted of both the classroom and lab work) was essential—that was a requirement at every school—plus biochemistry, histology, endocrinology, and medical writing techniques.

The entire course of study would be four and a half years, nine semesters including two years of clinical training. This mirrored the curriculums of the best American schools, so I knew the AMA would have to accept it.

It made sense to me. Of course, I was a second-year law student. But I believed in this concept and these numbers. I knew this would work. I had the ingredients: an independent English-speaking country able to give me a charter and an absolute right for my students to take every exam required to practice medicine in the United States. In my mind there was no question this would succeed.

I also had one more advantage: Unlike my father or Pat Adams and Ed McGowan, I had seen the passion of students up close. Incredibly, there wasn't a moment I doubted this was going to happen and that the school was going to be successful. That just wasn't part of my character. I was fully aware that the concept of a medical school dropout starting his own medical school was...strange, challenging—and really hard to accept. But rather than allowing potential problems to stop me before I even began, I kept moving forward with confidence that I could solve each of them as that became necessary. I also began to learn more about Grenada. It was, I discovered, reputed to be one of the most beautiful places in the world. The newly independent nation had been under British rule for more than two centuries. The French and Spanish had tried to colonize the island beginning in 1650 but were repelled by the indigenous Caribs.

Like England, Grenada was a parliamentary democracy, then ruled by its first elected prime minister, Eric Gairy. The population of the island was slightly more than 120,000 people. The largest city on the island was the capital, St. George's. Grenada was the world's largest nutmeg producer. There were no direct flights from the United States to the island. Grenadians said there were three seasons: the wet season, the dry season, and the tourist season. The economy of the island was largely dependent on tourism, but it didn't have the infrastructure to compete with the better-known and more-developed Caribbean islands.

That was potentially beneficial for us; it meant that land there was less expensive, labor was available, and the school would create jobs for the Grenadian people.

To my surprise, not everyone welcomed the school. I had expected that the Grenadian people would be enthusiastic about the prospect of a school that would bring investments, jobs, and positive publicity to the island. Many were. But Gairy's political opponents in the New Jewel (Joint Endeavor for Welfare, Education, and Liberation) Movement were concerned that if it was successful, he would get all the credit. So the opposition newspaper, the *Torchlight*, tried to discredit us with false information and wild accusations, vehemently opposing any success that might be attributed to Gairy for our endeavor.

Admittedly I had not anticipated these objections. It was ridiculous. I couldn't imagine who they were trying to scare. No one in Grenada believed the allegations. The opposition looked foolish even raising issues, but they had no legitimate reasons to object to the school.

The seven-member Grenada Medical Association also was against the government issuing the charter. As part of our approach to Grenada, in addition to a $50,000 government fee, we planned to offer five scholarships annually to qualified island residents. The government would select these recipients. In return for a free medical school education, these students would have to sign a contract committing them to practice medicine in Grenada for several years. I felt very strongly about that. I wanted the school to play an active role in improving the lives of the people living there, not just be located on the island.

But the seven doctors practicing on the island did not want any additional competition. These were all smart, educated men. We knew that if those local physicians didn't accept it, the government would not allow us to move forward. As far as they were concerned, five scholarships a year would eventually create an oversupply of doctors. It might, we agreed, if available medical services on the island did not expand. But our medical school required a hospital in which our students could train. The present hospital would have to be substantially upgraded. Improving it was part of our plan. We worked with those seven doctors. Those doctors ended up teaching at the school—and some of their children studied there.

When we first started I had figured, naively, we could deal with all the problems and get our charter issued in a couple of months. With a little luck we could open the school in a year. Instead, it took two years and four months. But we had used that time productively. The three founders had purchased about five acres of land, both on the beach and about two miles inland, and the basic facilities we would need. Basically, we needed dorms, classrooms, a lecture hall, a library, and, at least before the second semester, a cold room in which to store the cadavers.

Lou Modica, Pat Adams, and Ed McGowan found two suitable locations we could use. They took an option to buy the Grand Anse Beach Hotel, right on a beautiful beach, that had gone out of business. It was exactly what you would expect to find on a lush Caribbean island. That would be our faculty and married-student housing. What had been an open-air bar became our central meeting place. Smaller buildings previously used as the laundry and for storage became our administrative office, anatomy lab, and faculty offices. We made arrangements to rent space in several local schools, including the Grenada Boys' Secondary School, which was then not being used. A year earlier the Grenadian government had built a geodesic dome for the 1977 conference of the Organization of American States. It was a modern, air-conditioned building with its own audio-visual equipment. It certainly was one of the best facilities on the island. The government rented it to us to be used when it was not being used for official functions.

And then there was True Blue. The founders purchased a site about two miles away on which there were several large, mostly abandoned buildings. Both locations were in the parish of Saint George, one of six parishes. To host Expo '69, a convention of the Caribbean Free Trade Association, the Grenadian government had erected five prefab exhibition halls in the inland area known as True Blue. We intended to convert the exhibit booths in these buildings, which resembled military barracks, into dorm rooms. These five long, rectangular exhibition halls were arranged in a semicircle around a large structure. We called it "a large open-air wooden building" rather than the more accurate "big roof and floor with no walls." Half of this central space would become our lecture hall, while the other half would be used as the cafeteria, library, bathrooms, and a few offices. Several other buildings would become the histology lab and classrooms.

The lecture hall was a typically repurposed structure. It leaked badly and had uncovered louvered windows. The main improvement we made was installing a roll of plastic at the top of each window. One person in each class was responsible for pulling it down and tying it in place when it rained.

When I look at photographs of those facilities, especially when I'm standing on what is now recognized as one of the most beautiful college campuses in the world, I marvel at how far we have come. At that time it would have been impossible to envision this. Impossible.

The key to opening the school was getting a government charter. Gairy knew how vital that was to us and used it to get concessions. Pat Adams proved invaluable figuring it out. The charter permitting us to open the appropriately named St. George's University School of Medicine was finally issued in August 1976. That was much too late for us to open in September, but I didn't want to wait until the following September. I was far too impatient to wait another year. As we planned to enroll two classes every year anyway, I decided we would open in January 1977.

"You're crazy," my father pointed out. Again.

"Leave him alone," my mother told him.

By that point my father, Pat, and Lou were deeply committed to the project. And somewhat satisfied that even if the school didn't work, the real estate had great value. They told me to go ahead. That gave me five and half months to hire a faculty and convince two hundred students to enroll in a medical school that didn't yet exist.

Somehow, I never doubted I could do it. Where that optimism came from I did know: It came from the guy who turned a dead chicken farm into a large housing development.

I did have to make one concession. Having finished my classes in law school, I had intended to take the bar exam that fall. But it proved pretty much impossible to found a medical school while studying for the bar. So I decided to postpone taking the exam. As it turned out, it was a permanent postponement.

CHAPTER 5

Charter Class

"Where's Grenada?"

—Aspiring doctor Rudy Antoncic

"If this is going to be successful you have to be flexible."

—Me

I began recruiting students by running a small ad in the education section of the Sunday *New York Times*. Basically, it read, "New Caribbean medical school teaching exclusively in English. Write for brochure." I knew the key word: English. Then I wrote the brochure. I took a sheet of 8.5" x 11" paper and printed vertically on one side so it could be folded in thirds. As we had nothing on our "campus" impressive enough to use for a cover photograph, I used a photograph of the existing St. George's General Hospital.

I believed that facility would play an important role in the school. The second part of a medical education is clinical work in a hospital. That is where education meets patients. Students spend two years in a hospital exploring the various medical specialties to try to find a good fit for themselves. Most American medical schools had arrangements with hospitals to accept their students. I knew that finding spots for our students was going to be a problem. I didn't know how I was going to solve it—yet. I couldn't anchor a clam boat with young doctors in the middle of a hospital. I wasn't ignoring the problem; I was postponing it.

Part of our deal with the Grenadian government allowed some of our students to do their clinical work at this hospital. It was essentially a last resort. The 250-bed St. George's General Hospital was a converted British army barracks; sections of it were more than a century old. But it was impressive looking. And we had agreed to do at least some upgrading.

Putting a photograph of this hospital on the cover of my brochure conveyed that an established institution would be part of the educational experience. The brochure stated accurately, but admittedly optimistically, "The University is fully recognized and approved so that it may confer the degree of Doctor of Medicine upon its students."

Within two days I began receiving responses to the *Times* ad. That confirmed my belief that there was a large reservoir of desperate people willing to explore even the slightest chance of becoming a doctor. Qualified people who had a dream. I sent each person a brochure and an application. I also had kept a list of everyone who'd ordered a guidebook and mailed each of them a brochure. In fact, one of the first applications we received came from a man named Philip Lahrman. He had bought my guidebook and purely coincidently had contacted me a week earlier about applying to the Dominican school I had worked for.

Instead, I suggested he take a look at the *Times* Education section the following Sunday. "You'll find an ad for a new English-language medical school on an island called Grenada." He became one of our first students. The ad attracted a lot of attention. Eventually I mailed out several hundred applications.

A lot of potential applicants wondered if this was legitimate. Orazio Giliberti—"Raz," his friends called him—was sure of it. He was living in New Jersey, waiting to begin medical school at the University of the Sacred Heart in Italy, when his father showed him the ad. "Dad," Raz told him, shaking his head, "look at the size of the ad. This is fake." But he went to his school's library and found my book. He ordered two copies of it. A friend of his father coincidently knew my father, and the word came back to him that Lou Modica was a stand-up guy. "Maybe this guy's real," he decided and submitted an application. "I was all set to be driving an Italian sports car, having an Italian girlfriend, and skiing in the Italian Alps," he recalled, "but my father kept asking, 'Are you going to be a bum or are you going to school?'" Reluctantly, he put away his skis.

He wasn't convinced, but his curiosity was too strong. If this was true...

At least two people hired private investigators to determine if this venture was for real. At that time it was considerably harder for a woman to gain admittance to a medical school than a man. Schools didn't want to waste a coveted spot on a woman who, it was assumed, would practice for a while, then might leave to raise a family. This was a different time, and women's opportunities were limited. With few exceptions men were doctors, women were nurses. That's the way world worked. I was fully aware of that; I intended to take advantage of a vast reservoir of qualified women who had been denied an opportunity to become doctors.

Joan Mack, who had already earned her master's in biochemistry, became ill from a norovirus during her second year at University of Pennsylvania Dental School and had been forced to drop out. She was working part time as an electron microscopy technician at New York's Memorial Sloan Kettering hospital when her father saw the ad. Joan became one of five women in our charter class.

The applications continued arriving. In fact, they came in faster than even I had expected. Most applicants had already been rejected by numerous medical schools, and for them this represented a last chance. "It's hard to throw away a dream you've had for so long," wrote Carrie Zwerdling.

Initially we set up interviews for applicants at the Grenadian consulate general's office at the United Nations, which added a hint of prestige, but as we received more applications, we began meeting students wherever it was convenient.

For that first class we didn't have many written qualifications other than a degree from an established university. But we knew the future of the school was totally dependent on the success of the first and maybe the second class. If a significant number of our students did not become doctors, the school would quickly close down. And we would deserve it. It was vitally important to prove this whole concept was credible, that we were building a significant, substantial, long-term educational program. Additionally, my father, Pat, and Ed were putting reputations they had worked a lifetime to build on the line. Even if it was successful, this school was not going to make them incredibly wealthy, but it could destroy their reputations if it failed.

We were very careful to accept men and women who we believed were smart, qualified, and passionate. Passion was going to be a necessity.

Typical of them was Jack Cush, who was in our second class. "The arc begins with, I really want to be a doctor," he said. "I know I can be a doctor. Then you get amped up when you are told you can't be a doctor. You get your fourteenth rejection letter from a med school. You're told by an advisor your grades aren't good enough, that you have to go to the Philippines, or Guadalajara, or this school in Italy, where you have to learn a new language and go to school for six years." If you didn't get amped up by that, this definitely wasn't the place for you.

"When you start out you had to be idealistic: I want to be a doctor," he continued. "I want to be like the doctors I see on TV, like Marcus Welby or Dr. Kildare. I want to be the Norman Rockwell painting of a doctor, my mother's vision of a doctor. Carrying a black bag and spending your life helping people. That's where it started."

I needed an admissions director to conduct the interviews. It had to be someone I trusted, and who had really good instincts. Andy Belford, my next-door neighbor in Brightwaters and former water taxi captain, was trying to make it as an actor. He was living in a loft he'd designed in Soho while taking acting lessons. He was beginning to have some success and recently had costarred in a Parks Department production of *Waiting for Godot*.

Initially, Andy was very reluctant to accept the position. He wasn't qualified, he told me. We had several long conversations in which I laid out my dream, my concept. I told him I was absolutely convinced—I had seen it—that there were a large number of qualified people who, for various reasons, had not gotten an opportunity to enter medical school.

My goal was to provide that opportunity. We were looking for a special group of students, I told him—smart, committed, resilient, and, admittedly, flexible. And passionate, always passionate. Grades mattered, but so did character. And Andy was a superb judge of character.

Sometimes if you work hard enough you get lucky. I got lucky. Andy turned out to be the perfect choice: He was really smart, compassionate, completely honest, creative, and, perhaps most important, immediately available.

"What would I have to do?" he asked me.

"Admit qualified people," I told him. It wouldn't do us any good to take students who weren't going to complete the program.

The only guarantee he asked for was that he would make the final decisions. He had to live with those decisions, he said, and he would not admit anyone who, in his opinion, would not succeed.

When I agreed to that, he became the—appropriately—acting admissions director. He certainly wasn't the typically older, buttoned-down professional admissions director most applicants were used to meeting. "He looked like a skinny Long Island kid with big curly hair trying to be a '70s bro but not making it," remembered Jack Cush.

Andy accepted the job with the proviso that he intended to be totally honest with applicants. He insisted on telling them exactly what they were getting into, no embellishments. He brought in a few of his friends, among them another taxi dispatcher named Jane Sutter and several of his acting school classmates, to help him conduct interviews. Applicant John Madden remembers being interviewed by a very attractive woman. The question that most perplexed him during that interview was: Is it considered inappropriate to ask the person interviewing you for medical school out for dinner?

In these interviews Andy never misrepresented the school. In fact, he may have been the worst admissions director in history, except he was perfect for our purposes. He often tried to talk applicants out of enrolling. He would make a point of telling them about other foreign medical schools, suggesting if they were fluent in another language, they should consider attending a school where that language was spoken. He advised one applicant, "We're a new school, so if I were you, I would think about going to Guadalajara [Mexico] before St. George's. It's been there a long time, and they're taking a lot of Americans now. They've got an established pipeline to get back to the United States. The main advantage you'll have at St. George's is that it will be taught in English."

Jane Sutter, who was teaching high school history, remembers being given strict instructions. "Tell them we have five courses, we have six professors, one lab, and we use the same textbooks they use at Harvard." Any applicant who was overly concerned about the details probably wasn't right for us. We were looking for people willing to take a chance.

Even as we began receiving applications and accepting students, there were many people who believed this wouldn't work, that it was some kind of hustle. I understood people would have serious doubts that this would succeed. No one had ever done anything like we were doing. It just didn't seem possible, and even relatives were unabashed to say there was no way this could succeed.

A close friend named Jay Wilbur was an engineer, who eventually became head of operations at the school. His father advised him to stay away from me. That's basically what people thought: How could this possibly succeed?

We weren't trying to deceive anyone. We definitely did not accept unqualified students. Admittedly, many offshore medical schools had somewhat lax standards. A school in the Philippines, for example, basically required a $10,000 donation to its alumni fund for admission. From the very beginning we set our standards to be competitive with domestic medical schools, and later, published studies on pass rates proved we succeeded. In fact, a study of our graduates through our first decade showed we had the second-highest pass rate of any foreign medical school—second only to Israel's Sackler School of Medicine.

At a minimum we required an undergraduate degree. We received a lot of applications from students who had done well in college but had screwed up their Medical College Admissions Test. Few people knew how medical schools actually selected students; there were no announced standards. It appeared to be a combination of factors, including grade point average, grades in science-related courses like organic chemistry, a little geographic distribution, being a legacy or a family donation might help, a little bit of luck, and the results of the dreaded MCATs. The MCATs mattered. A student could have a 3.8 GPA but a mediocre MCAT score and be rejected. One bad day or even one bad interview could determine their entire future.

One of our first applicants, Lou Guida, had done very well in college but was rejected by twenty American medical schools. It was, he said, "the worst thing that ever happened to me." In most instances he never learned why he had been rejected, but when he sat down for an interview at one Philadelphia school, the first question he was asked was where he was from. "New Jersey," he replied. That was it, done, finished. The school was not accepting any more students from New Jersey, he was told. He was qualified, he'd gotten good grades in school, and he'd done well on the MCATs. He even tutored students who subsequently were accepted by schools that had rejected him. But he was from New Jersey.

Many of our applicants were as well qualified as Lou. Another man, for example, literally had been the last student rejected by one of the best medical schools in the country. He was told the decision for the final spot had come down to a choice between him and another student. But the other student came from an underrepresented part of the country. That student got the slot. It had nothing to do with qualifications.

Some of our applicants were already working in medicine. They had served as medics in the military, several of them were working as physician associates, as they were then known, or nurses, and some of them were already enrolled in a foreign medical school but were struggling with the language challenge.

Many others had just about given up their dream. Rudy Antoncic was a thirty-three-year-old veteran who had earned degrees from both Clemson and Virginia Tech, then served as a captain in military intelligence during the Vietnam War. He was working in a highly competitive physician associate program at Duke. But that wasn't enough for him to gain admission to Duke's medical school—the program had 9,000 applicants for 120 seats. He was so desperate to become a doctor, he had applied and been accepted to Kasturba Medical College in Manipal, India.

Antoncic had just mailed a check for the $10,000 tuition when a patient asked him, "Why didn't you ever want to become a real doctor?" He told him the truth—he had applied to numerous medical schools and had not been accepted. That patient showed him my ad.

"Where's Grenada?" Antoncic asked.

"I think it's in the West Indies."

He had never heard of it. "You mean it's off the coast of India?" He went to the university library and tried to find it on a globe. Finally, he asked a librarian, "Where's Grenada?"

The librarian patiently replied, "It's the capital of Spain." Actually, the city of Granada is the capital of the Spanish province of Granada, but at least she had heard of it. And eventually she found the island of Grenada in an atlas. "Here's Florida," she pointed out. "There's Cuba, the Dominican Republic, Puerto Rico, and right here"—she tapped a black dot off the coast of Venezuela—"this is Grenada, right here."

Antoncic was interested. This Grenada was considerably closer than India, and classes were being taught in English. He called and spoke with Andy Belford on Christmas Eve. It was pretty late, Andy told him, classes were scheduled to begin January 17. But there was still time if…

Rudy drove to New York and had his interview on New Year's Eve. As he walked into the Grenadian consulate, across the street from the UN, he recalled, "I saw this magnificent logo for St. George's University." That logo was aspirational. At that moment it represented what we intended to become rather than what we were. Andy and Jane Sutter interviewed him for more than an hour. Rudy and his wife, Ruth, had two young children, and Andy warned him we had no provisions for children. Truthfully, we hadn't made many provisions for spouses either. Andy didn't try to talk him out of it, but he did tell him how difficult it was going to be—even without kids. But it wasn't India, and classes were in English. "I definitely want to do this class," Rudy told them. "When can I hear something?"

Fortunately, Andy told him, “The Admissions Committee is getting ready to meet in a few minutes.” He asked Rudy to wait in the outer office. Eventually, he came out and said, “The Admissions Committee has met, Mr. Antoncic. Congratulations, you've been accepted to St. George's University.”

Rudy called his wife and told her they had two weeks to change their life. “We decided to roll the dice,” he remembered. They stopped payment on their check to the school in India and started packing for the West Indies.

We were absolutely honest in these interviews. Without exception. We never made a single promise we couldn't keep. The picture we painted was reality: This is a new school, and there are going to be problems. As I told people more often than I care to remember, “If this is going to be successful, you have to be flexible.” “Flexible” was an interesting word choice—what I meant basically was we knew there were going to be some difficult days, but if you think you can deal with difficulties, this can work for you.

But that didn't seem to matter to most applicants. Danny Ricciardi, for example, had grown up in Brooklyn. He was a street-smart kid with city swagger built into his personality. No one had ever accused him of being shy. Like me, he was Italian; his father had immigrated to America from a small town outside Naples. And like me, he'd inherited a strong work ethic. When something had to be done, it got done.

His father was a produce manager in a supermarket and often reminded him, “If you don't go to college, then every day you got to take the train to the Bronx like me.” A cousin of his had become a doctor. That cousin never took the subway to the Bronx. Okay, Danny decided, I'll be a doctor. After failing to be accepted to any American medical school, he had enrolled in a six-year medical school in Italy. This was at the height of the Vietnam War, and there was a strong anti-American undercurrent among the professors there. After finishing his first year, he had returned to the States and was working as an anatomy/physiology lab instructor at Suffolk County Community College while deciding if he would go back to Italy.

Then he saw my ad and scheduled an appointment. He showed up for his interview with his transcripts and his bride, Peg. While living in Italy, Danny had become friendly with several other American students; most of them were also Italian and had graduated from Fordham University. After Danny was accepted, he called each of them and said, "There's a new medical school opening up, and it's in English. I'm going. You should go with me." Four of them applied and were accepted. "Da Boys," as they became known, were going to medical school together.

David Baras was the child of Holocaust survivors who owned a chicken farm in upstate New York. "My mom had been in Auschwitz and my father had survived in hiding. They didn't have the opportunity for an education, so to them education was the most important thing. My parents made it clear I was going to be a doctor, a lawyer, a dentist, an accountant; those were my options. Growing up on the chicken farm I got to see a lot of veterinarians working, and I always thought that was interesting. So I decided I'd be a doctor. But I did not do well my freshman year at Rensselaer Poly Tech, which meant I wasn't getting into an American med school. I looked all over the world. There was an English-speaking medical school in the Philippines, but they required a $10,000 fee in advance. That was more than my parents could really afford, but it meant so much to them they were still willing to consider it. Then a friend of mine who also wanted to become a doctor showed me the tiny ad in the *Times*, and I responded. I went down to New York City; my grandfather took me to the interview. A week later I was accepted."

Our interviewers asked very general questions. Mostly we wanted to find people who could deal with the hardships that we knew were coming. During interviews with American schools, applicants were asked questions like what their most difficult subject in college had been or if they had a specialty in mind. "What would you do," Gary Oxenberg remembers Andy asking during his interview, "if there was no running water?" That was a real concern at that time. Grenada was transitioning from a British possession to an independent nation. The infrastructure was old and limited, and the country was just beginning to build the modern facilities that exist today. Oxenberg replied that he would do whatever he had to do to survive, suggesting, "I guess I would get buckets of water."

Oxenberg actually thought that was a rhetorical question and continued to believe that until he got to Grenada and discovered there was, at times, no running water. He actually had to fill buckets and carry them back to his room.

The temptation might have been to accept anyone who applied. If we were in this just to make money, we would have done that. I warned Andy about that at the beginning. I had quit my job with the school in the Dominican Republic when I discovered they were accepting students who I had said were not qualified. I hated to see students who likely would not succeed wasting their money, and I was determined we would never put people in that situation.

In deciding who we would accept, grades mattered, but drive mattered more. Because no matter how well a student could perform academically, we had to be certain they were willing to get on a plane, travel to a small, newly independent nation, and deal with often unexpected difficulties. For Andy, in addition to academic qualifications that meant people who had shown some degree of success in anything that required a dedicated effort over a period of time: Do you speak a foreign language? Did you master a musical instrument? Did you play sports on a competitive level? Martin Kane remembers, "Andy was especially impressed with the fact that I had hiked the entire Appalachian Trail. When I told him that, he smiled and told me, 'Hiking in the wilderness was great preparation for this school. I think you're prepared to live in this underdeveloped nation.'"

We received several hundred applications, more than we had room for. While most applications came from the tri-state area in the northeastern US, we also got requests from England, Japan, China, and other countries. It was obvious we had tapped into something larger than even I had imagined. We had no specific criteria. Many of our applicants were older people, several of them in their forties or even early fifties—and life experience mattered too. Basically, if we could convince ourselves this or that person could make it, that was enough. And believe me, we could be pretty convincing.

Unlike the recent college graduates who typically apply to American medical schools, many of our applicants already were established in a career. We got applications from physician assistants, medical researchers, a phlebotomist, EMTs, and several pharmacists. Carrie Zwerdling had a master's in public health from Tulane. Tom Greco was an operating room technician.

We got applications from numerous people already working in other fields as well, including Peace Corps workers, engineers, contractors, teachers, career military personnel, and blue-collar workers. A wealthy middle-aged building contractor gave up his business to pursue his life-long dream to become a doctor. Another applicant was an experienced telephone lineman. An applicant named Moe Horowitz owned an ice cream parlor near the entrance to the George Washington Bridge, which he sold to come to school. Duncan Brown was a roadie for Fleetwood Mac, quitting in the middle of a tour.

Ed Hall was in graduate school, studying for his PhD in psychology while also working as a mental-health associate in a hospital. His wife, Phyllis, was a nurse. He had been applying to medical schools for two years without success. He didn't know why he was being rejected—his GPA was high, his MCATs competitive. A coworker who coincidently was a friend of Andy Belford told him about this new English-speaking medical school opening somewhere in the Caribbean. And his friend Andy, he added, happened to be the admissions director. "Andy was very nice on the phone," Ed remembers, "very pleasant, very friendly. He told me to bring my transcripts and meet him in the city. It was two days before Thanksgiving. We chatted awhile. He asked me a variety of questions: Had I traveled before, how did I adapt to stress, was my wife supportive? He reviewed my transcript and finally smiled and said, 'Welcome to St. George's University, located in Grenada.'"

Ed responded like most people. "Where's Grenada?"

The good news, he excitedly told his wife, was that "we're in medical school." The bad news was, "The medical school is in Grenada. And we have to be there in two months."

"Where's Grenada?" Phyllis responded. Told it was somewhere in the Caribbean—Ed wasn't exactly sure where—she never hesitated. "We'll put everything up for sale," she said. In the next few weeks they sold their two cars, their furniture, she sold some jewelry, and they moved out of their rented apartment into her mother's basement in East Meadow on Long Island. Chasing dreams can be expensive. They agreed Ed would go to Grenada, wherever it was, and get settled, then a month later she would follow.

Over and over and over, we heard the same story: I'll do anything to become a doctor. When Andy asked Lou Guida why he wanted to attend medical school, for instance, Guida replied, "This is my calling. I started carrying a medical bag in grade school. I'll go anywhere and do anything to be a doctor. I don't care how long it takes."

Well, actually not everybody wanted to be a doctor. Chuck Schwartz wanted to be a dentist. "My father was a dental ceramist; he made dental implants, so that interested me. But when I didn't get into dental school, I went to grad school to study physiology. It was a study of how everything worked. There were a lot of labs. 'This is awfully close to medicine,' I remember thinking, 'and it's pretty neat stuff.' And I was good at it. Then my father saw the ad and suggested I consider that."

Another applicant, Nasir Jahdi, had grown up in a small town in Khuzestan Province in southern Iran. As a small child he had been treated by a nurse's assistant in a local clinic. The "doctor," as he was called, handled all medical issues in that town, from strep throat to pulling teeth. The life of the town revolved around the clinic. Jahdi's ambition was to one day become a doctor and eventually director of that clinic.

He attended college in the regional capital, Ahvaz, at times having to choose between food and transportation to classes. After graduation he became a pilot of the Shah's Iranian Air Force, eventually taking a job on Pan Am's ground crew. He applied and was accepted to a community college in Miami, where he intended to study aviation. After landing in Illinois, where he took the English comprehension classes he needed, he got on a bus for Miami. He had become familiar with Miami from American movies, and when he got off the bus, he expected to see palm trees, white-sand beaches, and a beautiful ocean. Instead, he remembers, "I got off in front of a shack in the middle of nowhere. It was like a ghost town from a western movie, where a ball is rolling down the street from one corner of town to the other." He told the bus driver this must be a mistake. "I am going to university in Miami!"

"This is Miami," the bus driver replied. "Miami, Oklahoma."

After spending two years studying and learning English at Northeastern Oklahoma A&M, in Miami, Oklahoma, Nasir decided to pursue his dream of practicing medicine. He had attended both chiropractic school and podiatry school in Chicago, skills that would be useful in rural Iran. "That was only semi-desirable to me," he said, "but it was not being an MD." A classmate in chiropractic school showed him my ad, which we also had run in the *Chicago Tribune*. Within three days he had an application. Several weeks later he was accepted.

I don't know who accepted him. I doubt very much a domestic medical school would have had a seat for him. But Nasir was a perfect fit for us. He was smart, he had done well in school, and he had already overcome so many hardships—it was obvious a few more hurdles were not going to stop him. In preparation for his trip to Grenada, he went to the Greyhound bus terminal to buy a ticket. He showed the clerk his acceptance letter, which included the address of the school. "I want to go to this place," he explained. "I am going to medical school there. How much does this cost me by bus?"

The clerk was an older man with a full beard of curly white hair. He stroked his beard as he looked at the address on the letter: Grenada W.I. "Man," he finally replied, "there's no bus that goes there."

Nasir met every obstacle with enthusiasm. "That's fine. How do I go there by train or my next alternatives?"

The clerk shook him off. "No, you don't understand. You have to buy a plane ticket."

"No. I don't have the money. I have to go by bus or train."

"Well," the man said, "unless W.I. means Wisconsin, you don't have much of a choice."

Nasir went home and, he recalled, "I looked on the geographic map. I looked beyond Cuba for this island. It wasn't there. Then I saw a small spot and said, 'That could be it.' That's when I understood why the Greyhound bus doesn't go there." But he also found the city of Granada, in Spain, which thoroughly confused him.

"I called the number on the letter to make sure they wanted me to go to Grenada in the Caribbean, not Granada in Spain. The person I spoke with made sure I was not flying to Spain with a limitation of money. I sold whatever things I had left to pay for my ticket. I was going to be a doctor. Whatever it required, I was going to be a doctor."

The applications continued to arrive. John Washington was the father of a two-month-old infant when he was accepted. His wife, Sabine, was a social worker. "She understood how important this was to me," he explained. "But this was a family decision. My mom and dad agreed to help with our baby. I knew this whole thing was a long shot. But I decided I didn't want to look back in thirty years and wonder what would have happened if I had taken the chance. My mindset was if it works, great; if it doesn't at least I gave it a shot." He became one of several African Americans in our charter class.

Many years later Jack Cush, who by that time had become an eminent rheumatologist, summed it up well when he compared it to the scene in *An Officer and a Gentleman* in which Lou Gossett Jr. is berating Richard Gere, demanding to know why he is in the navy's officer candidate program. "That's when Gere breaks down and cries, saying, 'I got no place else to go.' That was us." Jack was a local Long Island boy who had decided to be a doctor in his early teens. He had done well at St. John's University and on his MCAT, but not good enough to get into a US medical school. He was thinking Philippines, Italy, maybe Mexico when he went to Bill the Barber's shop in Sayville.

"I bumped into a local lawyer, who asked me about my future. I told him I wanted to go to medical school, and he told me his lawyer father was working at a new English-language medical school in Grenada for some guy who had an office in Bay Shore. After the haircut I drove right to One East Main Street in Bay Shore and knocked on the door, where a young guy with a good tan in khaki pants and a crew shirt answered and gave me an application for medical school. Little did I know he was the chancellor. After the interview I was provisionally accepted first week of August—the provision being I had to get my ass there in the next three weeks. What looked to have been a really bad decision became the best decision I ever made."

A young woman named Beverly Nelson had an especially unusual experience. As part of our charter agreement, we accepted a small number of Grenadians on scholarship. After graduating high school in Grenada, she had gone to live with her mother in the Bronx. She attended Hunter College and then wanted to go to medical school. "But as I got closer to graduation," she said, "I accepted the fact that I was not going to find any money to do this. It was impossible. At that time my husband-to-be, living in Grenada, told me there were some scholarships available from the new medical school and I should apply." Beverly was our only applicant who had to fly from New York to Grenada for her interview with the government's secretary of health—and she became one of our first Grenadian students.

Maybe if I had paused to think rationally about what we were trying to do, I might have been a little more reticent. But I was so busy doing it I didn't have time for that. What was truly astonishing is how many successful people were buying into my vision. My parents, Pat Adams, and Ed McGowan had invested a tremendous amount of time and money. Andy and several other people had accepted the fact that this was going to happen and jumped on board.

Hundreds of students were making sharp turns in their lives. They were giving up careers, risking a significant amount of money, putting relationships on hold, even separating their families because they believed we could do what we were telling them we intended to do.

One reason I had such confidence that the school would succeed was that I knew from experience the value of having something to prove. The people we were accepting were rejects; they had been told by numerous medical schools that they weren't good enough, that they weren't smart enough to become doctors. We really were offering them a last chance. As student Scott Snyder told a reporter, "I'm going to the best medical school I got into. We are underdogs, and so we have to work a little harder." I was banking on the fact that this attitude would enable them to get over the obstacles they were going to encounter. We were offering a viable path: They would be taught in English, using the same primary textbooks as the best medical schools, and they would be entitled to take the boards needed to practice medicine in the United States. It was a different path, but it led to the same place.

The large number of responses we got from that tiny ad reinforced my belief that these applicants were going to make this work. Imagine how desperate these people were to become doctors that they would be willing to travel to a country most of them had never heard of, enroll in a school that hadn't yet started, and be willing to pay a large tuition for the opportunity.

Although my name was on the forms as Chancellor Charles Modica, I actually met very few applicants. It made sense not to let these people know that the head of the "university" was younger than many of them, that my entire experience in the world of education consisted of teaching eighth-grade math, and that rather than being a doctor, I had completed one year of medical school in Spain. Perhaps the wisest decision I made was to enlist older, far more experienced people in every aspect of this project—and then listen to their advice. The biggest advantage I had was knowing how much I didn't know—but finding people who knew it.

One by one we built our first class. We eventually accepted 216 students for the charter class. It was an incredibly diverse group; it included men and women from five countries of different races and religions. We had Orthodox Jews from New York, Sikhs from India, we had Iranians, Nigerians, and students like Linda Klokow, a minister's daughter whose tuition had been donated by the congregation of his Fort Lauderdale, Florida, church.

It was an array of unique people. The only thing they had in common was a dream, the dedication to make it come true, and a slew of rejections from medical schools. That turned out to be an incredibly strong bond. As we discovered, they were the type of people who if asked to build their medical school would have started laying bricks. The fact that so many members of our first classes eventually went on to have distinguished medical careers proved how fortunate we were.

To manage the finances, we set up a rudimentary accounting system. I listed the names of everyone who was accepted on a sheet of lined white paper. When they sent a deposit, I put a checkmark next to their name. When they sent a tuition check, I put another checkmark by their name. We didn't put any money in the bank, not a penny; instead I got another shoebox and put all the checks in there. My father was adamant about that—we didn't touch that money until we were certain we had enough students to start classes. The whole school was in that shoebox.

As soon as it became clear we were going to enroll enough qualified students to open the school, my father hired an accountant. I handed him the shoebox and he took it home. When he came into the office the next day his skin was ashen white. He said to me with a mixture of admiration and rebuke, "Do you realize you have almost half a million dollars in uncashed checks in that box?"

CHAPTER 6

Fishing for Faculty

"We need really smart young instructors like you there."

—Me, to prospective faculty member Vish Rao

At the same time we were recruiting students, we also had to hire a faculty and administrators. We had budgeted for six instructors. That would be enough for the first semester; then we would add faculty members as necessary. I placed a small ad in prominent journals—*Science* magazine, the *Journal of the American Medical Association*, the respected British medical magazine *Lancet*, and two other publications—reading, "A new medical school in Grenada is looking for department chairs and/or faculty members to teach the following courses: anatomy, biochemistry..."

Recruiting was difficult because the academic year was starting and most instructors already had jobs. We had decided to hire PhDs rather than MDs because most basic medical school courses are taught by PhDs. We were not overwhelmed with applications, but we did get sufficient responses to staff the school.

We ended up with an eclectic group. These were qualified, experienced instructors who had reasons for being available. There were complicated marital situations, personal problems, or conflicts at their existing institutions. There also was another category: age. At that time many universities had a mandatory retirement age of sixty-five, and the prospect of teaching on a beautiful Caribbean island appealed to some people who had aged out. My father, Pat Adams, and Ed McGowan interviewed the applicants. It was, as a student in that first class once described it, "A very eclectic group."

I guess I would describe that original faculty as "quirky." Our first hire was Dr. David Brown, a free-spirited and brilliant PhD who had taught psychology at Columbia University and neurophysiology and statistics at New York's Queens College and was now doing neuroscience research at the Albert Einstein College of Medicine. He quickly made Grenada his home. Within two years he was singing the lead role of Nanki-Poo in the Grenada Music Society's production of *The Mikado*. After a stint as our dean of pre-clinical studies program, he actually enrolled, attended, and graduated from the medical school, becoming known as Doctor Doctor. David ended up doing his clinical studies in rural health-care delivery under the direction of a former student of his, Robert Rudawsky, in Truth or Consequences, New Mexico.

The first chairman of our Anatomy Department, Dr. Ajit Dawan, was actually a dentist who had specialized in the head and neck at Columbia. He turned out to be a poor choice; one day in the middle of a lecture about intestinal peristalsis he sighed and suddenly declared, "This is so boring; why don't you just go and read it on your own," and dismissed the class.

Our biostatistics instructor spoke with a thick German accent. Another teacher had come from England with impressive credentials, having worked in a Nobel Prize–winning lab, but had never taught before and struggled with a microphone. He mumbled and faced the blackboard when he spoke, which made it difficult to hear him.

It became obvious pretty quickly that we were going to have to make some changes. Almost as soon as Dr. Dawan got there, he wanted to leave. I dug into my folder of applicants, searching for qualified people who could leave whatever they were doing immediately. Among them was a man named Dr. Vishnu Rao, who had earned his PhD in physiology and neuroimmunology from Banaras Hindu University, a prestigious school in Varanasi, Uttar Pradesh, India. He had done his doctoral thesis, titled *The Reproductive Physiology of the Fish Clarias batrachus (with Special Emphasis on Spawning Using Chemical Inductors)*. Well, that was as close as I could come to anatomy. As impressive as his background was, far more important was the reality that he was available.

It was January, classes had started, and I was desperate. I called him at his home in New Jersey on a Sunday night. As I later learned, Dr. Rao and his wife had arrived in the United States only three months earlier. He actually did have some teaching experience—when he'd left India he had been running a night yoga school for women. He was living with his in-laws in New Jersey; they had encouraged him to come to America because of the opportunities. After arriving he sent out more than three hundred applications for teaching or research jobs. His timing was terrible too—most institutions had already filled those positions, so he'd gotten few responses. When I called he had no idea what job I was calling about. It didn't matter; his father-in-law told him, "Hang up. No one calls for a serious job at seven o'clock on a Sunday night."

"Thank you very much for calling," he told me, but he wasn't interested. And he hung up.

I spent the next week searching unsuccessfully for someone to replace Dr. Dawan. The following Sunday I called Dr. Rao once again. "Last time we got cut off," I lied optimistically. "If you're interested in the job, I'd like to interview you."

He asked me what the job was. "An instructor position," I replied.

"No," he said firmly. "I'm qualified for an assistant professor."

"Okay," I instantly agreed, "an assistant professor position." Titles meant little at that point. We were a start-up, we needed qualified people on our faculty. If that required a title, I was more than willing to discuss it. He was pretty dubious until I suggested we meet "in the delegates dining room of the Security Council in the United Nations."

That was key, he later told me. It meant this was not "a riffraff job."

We arranged to meet at the entrance to the lounge, at the top of the escalator. I got there early dressed in my three-piece suit, which I felt made me appear mature and serious, and waited. And waited. He was late. I was worried he had changed his mind. But I'd noticed one very young man who rode to the top of the escalator every few minutes, looked around, then went down again. Meanwhile, I was going back and forth into the lounge to look around. After we'd repeated this dance several times, he asked me politely, "Are you Dr. Modica?"

"Are you Dr. Rao?"

Vish Rao looked like a serious young student. At most, he was my age. I had been expecting to meet an older man. So had he. Physically, he was a small man with a large mustache that seemed to stretch from shoulder to shoulder. But what was unique about him was that you could see his character. It surrounded him, a gentle, confident aura. As crazy as it sounds, I knew instantly that he could play an important role in building the school. I wanted him.

He expected the chancellor of a university to be much older, he said, and had pictured me bald and fat. We sat in an alcove, and I offered him the job. "What is this job?" he asked. A teaching position at a new medical school in the Caribbean, I explained. He was reluctant. "That's not in the US, is it? That will be far away, won't it?"

"Yes, it's a little island," I replied. In retrospect, it is possible I may have used the word "paradise." Then I reached into my jacket pocket and took out an envelope. This is the definition of optimism. Also desperation. "Here are the tickets. You can go there to see it." I'd prepurchased round-trip tickets to Grenada. We needed him. There were no other applicants for the job. I tried every tactic I could think of. I flattered him: "We need really smart young instructors like you there." I went for sympathy: "We're providing a last opportunity for passionate people and really need your help." I injected realism: "We pay what most other schools are paying. You can get the experience you need while working in a beautiful place." And even total honesty: "The chairman of the Anatomy Department isn't very good, so there's a real opportunity there for you."

Then I handed him an eighteen-page contract. Pat Adams and I had already signed it. "You don't have to sign it now," I told him. "Read it. Take it down to Grenada with you. If you don't like it, there's a return ticket. We'll pay all your expenses too."

"When is the ticket for?" he asked.

"Tomorrow."

Dr. Rao went home and discussed the offer with his wife. They laughed about the irony. "People from the West Indies come to the

United States," she pointed out. "We are going in the opposite direction. We must not be very smart." But perhaps more importantly, Vish Rao remembered an important saying he had learned in India: "It is best if there is a body of water between you and your in-laws."

I think the most important thing I did was not give him a lot of time to think about it. He was on the plane the next afternoon. Maybe the biggest chance I took was giving him a return ticket.

In reality, because of the timing, we didn't really have many options in hiring our first faculty. But when I was searching for an instructor to teach medical writing, I found an application from Professor Harris, a Harvard graduate. I had included medical writing when planning the original curriculum because it seemed to be intriguing. Only one of the top schools included it in their catalog, and I thought it sounded worthwhile, even if I wasn't sure exactly what it was. But when I saw the application from a Harvard grad, I knew I had done the right thing. A Harvard grad! We would be able to list a Harvard grad on our faculty. I believed it instantly gave us a little more prestige. Naturally, when I introduced Professor Harris to our charter class, I made a big deal about his credentials. He's a Harvard grad, I boasted, he even got his doctorate at Harvard! A doctorate from Harvard! And he's come here, all the way from Harvard, to teach you medical writing.

As this young Harvard PhD began his remarks, a large mosquito began attacking him. We watched as he tracked it with his eyes until it landed on his bare arm—and then he smashed it. He brushed it off and told the students, "Thank you for that kind introduction, Dr. Modica, but to be candid, it really doesn't matter where you get your PhD in seventeenth-century French literature."

As I turned red, the entire dome burst into laughter. But not only did he turn out to be a fine instructor, he also ended up running the very popular Sunday morning poker game at a local restaurant. He also was able to teach our students how to translate complicated ideas into easily understood sentences. The charter class and faculty of St. George's University Medical School in Grenada were set.

CHAPTER 7

Opening Day

"Take a key, find a room. Pick your own roommates."

—My father, Lou Modica

Having sold all their possessions, Rudy and Ruth Antoncic and their two young sons landed at Pearls Airport, a one-runway strip in the northeastern corner of Grenada, late on a January afternoon. Cows were grazing alongside the runway. An ominous storm cloud coming over the mountains had darkened the balmy day. The peak of Mount Saint Catherine was enshrouded in fog. As the family started to get off the plane, their five-year-old son held tightly to the armrests, refusing to move.

"What's wrong?" Rudy asked.

"This place is scary," said his son, looking at unfamiliar mountains and what seemed like lush jungle to a small child.

He wanted to go home, he said. It turned out he would not be the only one.

None of our faculty or students had ever been to Grenada. I had been working from our office in Bay Shore. The three founders, who practically had been commuting to the island for almost two years while negotiating the charter, were reluctant to let prospective students, as well as Prime Minister Gairy, know that the chancellor of the university was a twenty-nine-year-old med school dropout. So none of the new arrivals had much of an idea what to expect. That probably was a good thing. The image most people had of the Caribbean was the beautiful beaches and resorts they'd seen in advertisements. This definitely was not that.

There were no direct flights to Grenada. Visitors flew to Barbados, then took a LIAT flight to the island. LIAT, Leeward Islands Air Transport, which became known without affection as "Luggage in another terminal," or "Leave island any time," flew World War II prop planes, DC-8s, and smaller puddle jumpers. It also was known as "the Hope Diamond of airlines," meaning that you took it hoping you would eventually get to your destination. It was really a flying bus service between islands. Most of the students had departed from the tri-state area. To save shipping fees, we wrapped the textbooks they would use in the first semester with twine and asked them to carry them down as hand luggage.

We had chartered two flights from Kennedy Airport to Barbados, one on Thursday and the second flight on Friday. From there students would transfer to the smaller LIAT planes to Grenada. Most of them made it easily. Most of them. The airport in Barbados was sophisticated only in comparison to Grenada. One hundred students left Kennedy on the first flight. Seventy-eight of them successfully transferred in Barbados and arrived on the island. The other twenty-two got stuck on Barbados; a travel agent had screwed up their LIAT boarding passes. Steve Lescowitz was among the "Barbados 22" as they ever after referred to themselves.

After spending the night in a hotel, the students returned to the Barbados airport. LIAT didn't have another airplane available, so we chartered a flight from Tropic Air, which was sort of a second-rate LIAT. "They put us on a twin-engine DC-3," Lescowitz remembers, "and we thought we finally were leaving. The plane taxied to the end of the runway and then the left engine died. It just stopped."

Bill Ventura was also on that flight. "When I saw a DC-3 show up, I thought we were in a Humphrey Bogart movie. The DC-3 had no air-conditioning, and it had to be at least 110 degrees inside the plane. The plane sat at the end of the runway with the sun beating down on us. There were no flight attendants or an intercom system, so the pilots would just lean out of the cockpit and shout information back to us. Several people in our group had never flown before, so when the mechanics took the cowling off the engine and started banging on it with hammers, they got very anxious. Very, very anxious."

Lescowitz continued, "We sat there as they tried to get it started. An hour passed. An hour and a half. The engine wouldn't start. They wouldn't let us off the plane because we were out on a runway. The problem was that a DC-3 has a wheel under the tail. Because only the right engine was working, when the plane started moving back to the terminal it could only go in a semicircle. To compensate for that, every few feet a group of Bajans picked up the rear of the plane and put it back on the runway. Then we went forward several more feet and they picked up the tail again and straightened it out. They literally were carrying the airplane. I remember somebody deciding, 'This isn't good.' We finally made it back to the terminal."

"For several students that was enough," Ventura recalled. "They decided this was a message from God; they wanted to turn around and go home. They finally got to Grenada only because they couldn't get their parents on the phone to arrange a flight home. While we were waiting in the terminal, the second group of students arrived from New York. As they got ready to board their flight to Grenada, we caught up with them. 'Not so fast,' we explained. 'You are not getting there before we do.' We all finally arrived in the early evening."

To welcome the students, the Grenadian government provided a steel band and handed out rum punch. The school was more than an hour's drive from Pearls Airport over rugged mountainous roads. They were so bad Grenadians liked to say their roads didn't have potholes, they had pot ditches.

Arriving students took taxis, which essentially described anything with four wheels and an engine. As Alexander Pollack climbed into the back seat of his cab, he noticed the driver was carrying a sidearm. *What have I gotten myself into?* he wondered. "Don't worry," the driver told him. "Everything's good." When he wasn't driving a taxi, he explained, he worked as a security guard for the prime minister. A taxi driver who also worked part time protecting the prime minister of the nation? Pollack was not reassured.

Jack Cush remembers being halfway over the mountain when his taxi driver suddenly stopped. *Holy crap*, Jack thought, *this is my worst nightmare coming true.* Without explanation the driver opened his door and disappeared silently into the thick brush. "A few minutes later," Cush remembers, "he came back carrying what looked like the largest rat I'd ever seen. Dead. He held it up proudly by the tail for inspection.

"'Yeah, that's great,' I told him. It turned out it was not a rat—it was a manicou, a distant cousin to the kangaroo. He opened the trunk and tossed it in with our luggage.

"It turned out to be a delicious meal. As I was about to find out, as we all were about to learn, few of our preconceived notions about this beautiful island turned out to be accurate."

For many people this trip would be their first encounter with taxi driver Victor Benjamin, a wonderful man who would eventually become our supervisor of grounds and buildings. These first few days were an introduction between our students and the people of Grenada. A testing period. Eventually, as with Victor, we would create a mutually beneficial situation, with literally thousands of Grenadians working at the university.

But Victor Benjamin was first. And he quickly became an essential part of all our lives. Victor drove a small British Ford Anglia, which comfortably seated four people but more often carried as many as ten students. Whatever anyone needed to know about Grenada, Benjamin was the man to see. He offered arriving students important advice, such as, "Don't talk politics with anybody because they could be the opposition, and don't talk religion 'cause there are so many churches here you'll get confused."

We had warned students not to expect very much as far as accommodations, and it is accurate to say that we didn't even live up to that. The buildings at True Blue were surrounded by a wire fence. A painted wooden sign, six feet by three feet, hanging from a wire over the entry, proclaimed St. George's University. At best, it was a makeshift campus.

When Joe Nossiff arrived, he remembers, "I found my buddy, Mike O'Connell, who had arrived the day before, and said to him, 'After lunch you'll have to show me around.' He looked at me with a forlorn expression and waved his hand as if to say, 'Around? This is it.'"

The entire university, as we optimistically referred to it, consisted of the gorgeous beach at Grand Anse and the inland barracks at True Blue. Married students, the five women in the charter class, and faculty members were assigned to the hotel on Grand Anse Beach. Those rooms were euphemistically basic, inexpensive hotel accommodations. They were equipped with a mattress, a pillow, and a lamp. Perhaps the most noticeable thing missing were locks on the doors. It took almost two months before the locks we had ordered arrived and could be installed.

Everyone else got a room at True Blue. True Blue was closer to military boot camp. The grounds were overgrown with grass three to five feet tall, so high that it was difficult to open a car door. There were three people in each room, which contained one bunk bed and one single bed. There were no room assignments; my mother and father, Pat Adams, and Ed McGowan met the students with a box of keys and a truckload of new mattresses. "Welcome to Grenada," my father told them. "Take a key, find a room. Pick your own roommates." Being a founder turned out to be a hands-on job, the three of them literally helping students take mattresses out of the truck and lug them to their rooms.

There was, however, at least one student who appreciated these facilities. Henry Collins had just finished a two-year stint in the Peace Corps. He lived and worked in a very poor area of Kenya and had grown to love the pace of life there. In fact, he had gone through a difficult culture shock after returning to the States. Landing in Grenada was almost like coming home again.

One other group was actually relieved to see the accommodations. By mistake their taxi had taken them to the local police barracks. This was a large, dilapidated clapboard building with holes in the roof, no glass in the windows, and drying laundry hanging in front. So this group was thrilled when they discovered that was not the school. Compared to those barracks, True Blue's aluminum prefab buildings looked sturdy and welcoming. After that there were some suggestions that we arrange to have all of our arriving students stop there first.

Some students assigned to True Blue decided to upgrade. When they learned that married students were living in a hotel on the beach, they suddenly remembered they were married and their wives intended to come down as soon as they were settled. Frank Arbucci, for example, had just arrived at True Blue when Danny Ricciardi, who had arrived the day before, told him, "Congratulations, you're married. Get your stuff, you're not staying here."

Hearing that story actually was gratifying. We knew the situation was going to be difficult. We had tried to enroll students like Danny and Jack and Frankie, people like me, actually, who didn't waste time feeling disappointed but rather set out to make the best of it.

Jack Cush, for example, had ended up in a room by himself, so to keep it that way he invented an invisible roommate. He kept the curtains on the windows drawn and wouldn't let anybody in the room. "I told everybody my roommate was a guy named Bob. What's Bob like? 'I don't know, he's real quiet. We don't talk much.' If they wanted to meet him, he was always either out or in the bathroom. 'You just missed, him,' I'd tell them. 'I think he went to make a phone call.' That lasted six weeks until my actual roommate showed up. I opened the door one day and a man wearing a turban was standing there. But by that point there was nothing that could have surprised me. He was a Sikh, an older man who turned out to be the nicest, most gentle, sweetest roommate it was possible to have."

The truth is nobody was sure what to expect those first few days, especially us. We were trying to do something no one had ever done before, and we were doing it in a country we knew very little about. Our basic plan was to improvise constantly, with everything—solve the immediate problems and put off any others as much as possible.

Everything was new, different, and unexpected. As with any large group, leaders began emerging in the first few days. Having grown up in Brooklyn with the forceful personality he has, it was natural for Danny Ricciardi to take charge. He happened to be at Grand Anse when Prime

Minister Gairy arrived to welcome the students. This will tell you everything you need to know about Danny.…

By that point he had started making friends, among them a musician named Warren Stanton and a woman from Florida named Linda Klokow. How he managed to do this I have no idea, but within minutes the three of them were sitting in the back of the prime minister's Cadillac limousine and being driven to True Blue. Along the way people were stopping to wave and salute the car. Naturally, Danny waved back. As I was to learn, that was typically resourceful, confident Danny. He had been on the island only a few hours and already was being transported around by the prime minister.

I had anticipated a number of students wouldn't be able to deal with the hardships, so I provided for some dropouts in my business plan. Several students didn't even bother leaving Pearls Airport. They immediately decided there was nothing there for them and got on the next flight and went home. Others left as soon as they saw the campus; while new arrivals were getting out of the taxi on one side, others were climbing in the other side to get back to the airport. As Dr. Rao arrived, for example, he was mistaken for a student by someone preparing to leave and warned, "You shouldn't be coming here. This place has nothing."

That wasn't quite true. What we lacked in developed facilities, we more than made up for in determination. We overflowed with determination. Many students stayed primarily because they were too embarrassed to go home. "The first meal provided by the school food plan was a local sausage," remembered Alexander Pollack. "They put this thing in front of me. I had no idea what it was; I'd never seen anything like it. I had one bite and started crying. It was a desperate moment. I really thought I had hit rock bottom. The only thing that kept me there was the fact that I had convinced my parents that this was a good idea. I didn't want to admit to them that I'd made a mistake."

Joe Nossiff stayed mostly out of curiosity. "I told Mike O'Connell that there was a real chance we were going to wake up one morning to see tumbleweeds rolling across the parking lot, but I said it's worth sticking around for a couple of weeks. We've got plane tickets to go back, and no matter what happens we'll have a hell of a story to tell our family and friends one day." Although, he added, most people probably wouldn't believe it.

Fortunately for us, there was only one daily flight back to the States and it left at 6:00 a.m. That meant anyone who wanted to leave had to be on their way by 3:00 a.m. Seventeen students left in those first few weeks. It is accurate to say that a lot of men and women eventually became successful physicians because they couldn't get a taxi.

Other students stayed because they did not want to risk traveling to the airport over a windy mountain road with no guardrails in the middle of the night.

Danny Ricciardi's experience was typical. "When I got down there," he recalled, "I had the same questions as everybody else: One, *Is this thing really going to work?* Two, *Who are all these people?* And three, *What have I gotten myself into this time?*

"The first thing every one of us did was just look around, trying to get some answers. Right from the beginning, though, I was surprised and impressed by my classmates. As a group we were a little older, in some instances a lot older, more diverse, and had more life experience than the people I knew who had gotten into domestic medical schools. I found out really quickly that there were some pretty smart people in our group. We figured out pretty quickly who our whiz kids were—and who had street smarts. We would need both of them.

"Those first few weeks I don't think any of us felt overly confident that the school was going to survive, much less prosper. I can't tell you how many nights I just lay awake wondering what I was doing there and trying to figure out what I was going to do if it didn't work out. It turned out all of us shared that anxiety. But this class consisted of self-selected risk takers and survivors who had only one thing in common: We desperately wanted to become doctors, and we were willing to do anything to achieve that goal. Well, the fact that we were there was proof of that. If we were going down, we were going down together."

In our first student handbook, I had warned students what to expect—couching it in the most positive way. "Students will find their physical and social environment radically different than that of their homes," I wrote. "Many of the diversions taken for granted in America such as television, an abundance of bars, theatres, fast-food restaurants, etc. are either not present in Grenada or very limited..." But, I continued, the good news is "the lack of such diversions does provide an excellent environment for uninterrupted study...

"...the qualities that the student must thrive to develop to successfully begin his medical career at St. George's are tenacity yet flexibility, a sense of purpose yet not without a sense of humor, and above all, maturity."

Especially a sense of humor.

Those first few weeks almost fifty years ago were chaotic. Remembering them, especially knowing what grew out of these early challenges, makes them seem less challenging than they were. Believe me, they were challenging. There was limited electricity and water. Students lined up for basic meals served on paper plates. The only classroom was the open-air lecture hall, and it had no desks, just some uncomfortable folding chairs. Our library had not yet been set up. Goats were strolling free on the grounds. There was only one phone to connect to the outside world. Students improvised: Many of them bought wood and nails in St. George's and, with help from Victor and other locals, built their desks. Later, students would joke they started their medical education by literally building their own desk. But at the time no one thought it was humorous.

Maybe I'm making it sound a little better than it actually was.

Many students stayed only because they had no choice. When Rudy Antoncic woke up his first morning, Ruth was trying to make breakfast for their boys but, she told him, she needed water. Their water had been turned off for several hours. "Look, Ruth," he told her, "this is a mistake. This isn't going to work. Let's just go home and..."

She stopped him. "We don't have a home," she reminded him. "We have no home. We have no jobs." She sighed. "We have no choice."

Ed Hall stood in the phone line for several hours until he was finally able to call his wife. "Listen," he told her sadly, "don't come. I'm coming home."

"You can't," she said flatly. "We've sold everything we had. You just stay where you are and I'll be there in two weeks. We'll figure it out."

"But there's no food. Just these little bean meals."

Phyllis Hall was determined that her husband was going to fulfill his dream. "I'll make up a box and we'll ship it down."

Gradually, though, people began settling in. The sun rose every morning. We provided hot meals. Desks got built. The Grenadian people were welcoming and helped whenever possible. There was great comfort in the fact that everybody shared the same challenges. One afternoon Rudy and Ruth walked down the beach wondering what to do, stay or go home, but then they saw their two boys, about a hundred yards away, shoes and shirts off, running along the beach with their new Grenadian friends. In a half hour their kids had adapted to the situation.

I think it was Danny Ricciardi who summed it up best after the first few days. As he looked around the makeshift campus and saw his new classmates preparing for classes to begin, he decided—in what remains one of the most optimistic comments I have ever heard—"This place has potential."

CHAPTER 8

The Early Days

*"The light is at the end of the tunnel.
But you are going to have to work to get there."*

—Me

I flew down to Grenada the weekend before classes were scheduled to begin. As a realist, I had no expectations, so I was not disappointed. I've always been the type of person who tries to find good in everything, so I saw what was there—but envisioned what was possible.

As makeshift as it looked, this was not something we had thrown together overnight. What started as a good idea had evolved into a relatively sophisticated undertaking—with more than a million dollars invested. It had taken us two and a half years to reach this point, and it was a difficult and often complex process. It started with my good idea, but it had become a serious endeavor with a lot of very professional people involved. It took countless meetings and often difficult negotiations with Grenadian government officials before finally being granted a charter. At every step we'd had to deal with people who doubted it was possible—the concept of opening a medical school just seemed so complicated that it couldn't really be done. But we kept going. I'd spent so many hours dealing with those long lists on yellow pads, learning as much as possible about medical schools, about what was required, about the American medical system. Preparing for this day had been my life.

The students knew absolutely nothing personal about me, just that Dr. Modica, the son of the guy handing out room keys, was the chancellor. A name on a lot of sheets of paper. The governor-general was hosting a reception for students on that first Sunday. I would be introduced to the students there.

That reception was typical of life on the island. Students living in dorm rooms with broken screens and toilets that didn't flush were expected to attend a formal reception. As they arrived, an aide stopped them and asked their name, then turned and loudly announced the arrival of each person. ("Mr. Frankie Arbucci!")

They entered and were welcomed personally by the governor-general. It was at that reception that I met Prime Minister Eric Gairy for the first time. There are many clichés about the leaders of small South American and Caribbean countries. Eric Gairy was none of them. He was, as I would learn, eccentric—he had once described himself as "an instrument of divine forces." But he was actually a strong, smart leader tasked with bringing a country with limited resources into the modern world.

Gairy would become a controversial figure in Grenadian history. I believe it is accurate to say he did many good things for the country but also benefited personally. It also is accurate to say that without him, the university would not have come to Grenada and brought with it literally thousands of jobs, educational opportunities, greatly improved access to health care, and extensive financial investment. Whatever relationships other people had with him I can't comment on, but I can tell you our relationship with him.

Eric Gairy was a tall, thin, good-looking man with always perfectly groomed hair and a small mustache. He often wore a white suit accented with a red tie. "Dapper" would be the most accurate way to describe him. When he walked down the street, people noticed—any street, anywhere. More importantly, he was charismatic and intelligent, and even as he was, at times, heavy-handed with his political opposition, he was dedicated to improving the lives of Grenadians.

Gairy seemed to take a liking to me that first weekend, which made me feel very good…well, at least until my father, Pat, and Ed explained,

"He likes you because you're twenty-nine years old and he thinks he's going to wrap you around his finger. Whatever you do," they warned, "do not agree to anything."

During those first few years, we got to know each other very well. We spent a lot of time negotiating—he was always trying to squeeze additional jobs out of the school. That was his big thing: jobs. "If you want the water to run, you must hire more people to run the water," he would tell me. Jobs and the Evening Palace, the nightclub he owned. In my experience he never tried to make a single deal with the school for personal gain. There were troubling things about him, but never that. I used to argue with my father about his demands: "What's wrong with him trying to create jobs for Grenadians? There's so much unemployment here."

It was hard to argue with my father's answer: "We have a limited budget."

From the very beginning Gairy supported the school as an important economic engine for the island. Whatever his other limitations, to his credit he was the only national leader who saw the future possibilities inherent in this crazy scheme of mine.

I wore a three-piece linen suit to that reception. I always wore a three-piece suit when I met with students. I felt it showed respect for them. It also made me appear more professional. I was twenty-nine, but I looked younger. I had exactly no experience in medical education, and these people had put their trust, their futures, and their money in my hands. The three-piece suit was my uniform, and I had three of them: one dark, one light, one green.

For some reason I wasn't nervous as I waited to be introduced to the students for the first time. The governor-general gave a warm, welcoming speech, then said, "I am pleased to be able to introduce the chancellor of St. George's University, Dr. Charles Modica." I was so caught up in the problems of the students and the fledging school that I was surprised by both designations: "Chancellor" and "Doctor." But then realized that I had a JD and was the head of a university in the Commonwealth.

Hopefully I would grow into my titles, but right now I had to think about my school.

I was greeted with polite, but muted, applause, which quickly became silence as I stepped forward. Whatever they were expecting, I wasn't it. I hadn't prepared a speech, so I spoke to them from my heart. I told them what we all knew to be true—that they wouldn't be standing there if they had been accepted to an American medical school. It meant that somebody sitting somewhere who knew nothing about them had decided that they were not worthy of a seat in a domestic school.

I resented that, I told them; I resented it for them and for myself. I knew exactly how they felt, I continued, because that is exactly what had happened to me. After being rejected from numerous medical schools, I had gone to school in Spain. I offered to show them my *aprovado*, the card that proved I had passed my first year. "If you start your classes down here thinking every admissions committee was right, that you aren't worthy of being a physician, you're lying to yourself. You're putting yourself down."

I spoke with real passion; all the emotions that had led me to found this school just poured out of me. "Do you think the kids at Harvard Medical School weren't rejected by Yale and Stanford and other places?" I asked. "I guarantee every student at New York Medical College had ten or more rejection letters. But they got one acceptance—and therefore they became a US medical student.

"So ten admissions committees felt you aren't worthy of becoming a doctor. I really hope you don't believe that. The reality is they didn't have room. The fact is you're no different than those students accepted by American schools. . . ."

I was rolling now. The American medical system was not working. It was not producing the number of doctors needed to care for patients. And I meant every word I said.

"They accepted sixteen thousand students out of forty thousand applicants, and trust me, there is no difference between that sixteen thousandth student and the very next one in the application pile. Of course, some people should be rejected, but not twenty-five thousand out of forty thousand applicants. No way, that's a lot of malarky. If you don't believe that, then you're not ready to fight the fight. The system is screwed up. You didn't fail; they failed, because they don't have enough seats for qualified US citizens to become doctors. You are good enough. And if you don't believe that, then you shouldn't be here. Because we're going to make that fight, take it to them, and we're going to win it."

I laid it out for them. We knew how poor the facilities were at that moment, but it wasn't always going to be that way. That with their help we could build something wonderful while helping make their dream become reality. "Any of you could leave tomorrow and nobody would blame you. There are a million reasons why you don't want to stay, but there is only one reason that you can succeed, and that is because you're going to do it. You're not going to let anything get in your way, and you believe in yourself."

I made no promises I couldn't fulfill. I knew that if I embellished one little thing, they would turn on me, and truthfully, I wouldn't blame them. In fact, our second class, which started the following June, gave me the "I Never Promised More Than I Can Deliver" award. I promised them only one thing: "I guarantee that you will be able to take the exam that allows you to practice medicine in the United States. I guarantee that. There are going to be problems along the way, but that's the law. If you fulfill all the requirements, then you can take the exam."

And then for the first time I used an expression that the students would hear me say countless times, "The light is at the end of the tunnel. But you are going to have to work to get there."

The other expression I would often use was, "There will be bumps in the road." That was my catch-all that referred to obstacles like limited electricity, limited water, and an abundance of giant mosquitoes. Sometimes I combined them: "We're going to have a lot of bumps in the road, but if you can see the light at the end of the tunnel, you're going to get your MD."

That expression eventually became a class joke. After each of my speeches, they would ask each other, "You see that light yet?" "Nope, not yet. You see it?"

"We all started out as idealists," Jack Cush explains. "Then we got to Grenada and holy crap. This is unbelievable: the pressure, the hours, the learning, the heat, the bugs, the loneliness. Then guess what? Get up and do it again tomorrow. There was no time to think about becoming a doctor. If you didn't already have that passion you were in the wrong place.

"But it turned out it was that passion that made us all take the risk."

At this time that light at the end of the tunnel was only two years away, not four. "A lot of you are going to do well on the boards and you'll be able to transfer out," I predicted. "I think we're going to have a good transfer rate. I think at least 10 percent of you are going to go, and, for the rest of you who don't transfer, I believe completely you're going to do better on the national boards than any other school. You watch, you'll double the national pass rate. I'm not telling you it isn't going to be tough here." (Here it comes…) "There are going to be bumps in the road, and you'll have every reason not to stay here, but, if you really want to be a doctor, you can make that happen. It's up to you.

"Things are going to be tough sometimes. And when they are, ask yourself if they are so tough that you'd rather be learning in Italian or Spanish and possibly spending six years at some of those European schools. We're here, we're teaching in English, we're using the exact same textbooks that every American medical school uses, we've got a dedicated faculty, and I guarantee there is a path to practicing in the States."

There were only three rules we were going to enforce, I concluded. One, you have to buy your textbooks from the school. Two, you have to live on campus. And three, you have to enroll in the meal plan. My reasoning was better than the food: Every parent wanted to be sure their child had a safe place to live, that their child was eating, and that they had the books they needed. Of course, I forgot completely that many of our students were parents.

Danny Ricciardi remembers that first meeting. "I don't remember what I expected Dr. Modica to look like, but that wasn't it. This young guy, he looked about my age, in a three-piece suit. But he talked a good game.

"It was a few weeks later that I had my first one-on-one conversation with him. On the streets you learn how to bullshit, and how to detect it. This Dr. Modica looked me right in the eyes and didn't tell me what he thought I wanted to hear; he told me the truth. There were problems that had to be overcome that he didn't have solutions for—yet. The one thing he emphasized was that he guaranteed I would be able to take all the examinations I needed to practice medicine in the United States.

"I came away from that conversation believing he meant what he said."

The truth is I told them what they needed to hear, which also was what I believed. If we worked together, we could turn this into reality. And I thought they believed me. Ed Hall remembers a friend he had made, a dentist from Long Island, telling him after my speech, "This is going to work out. Hang in there. Trust Charlie." That made him feel a bit more positive about the situation. Two days later he flew to Barbados to meet his wife. When they returned to the island, he found a note on his door from the dentist: He'd gone home.

My father, Pat, Ed, and I had dinner with Vish Rao the night before he was to begin teaching. Although he didn't drink, my mother continued to fill his wine glass. "Drink this," she insisted, "it's good for your health,"

On his way back to his room well after midnight, feeling very relaxed, he met Professor Dawan, who had been recruited to teach anatomy. "I'm leaving on the red-eye special to New York tomorrow morning," he said. "You have to take my lectures."

"What are you lecturing on?" Vish asked.

"The upper extremities."

"Wow," Vish responded, "I just got here. I don't even know where the campus is."

Dawan waved off his complaint. "It doesn't matter, I'm leaving. You must take my lecture. Teach anything you want."

"Okay," Vish agreed, and asked politely, "but may I borrow your anatomy text to prepare?"

"No," Dawan responded. "I don't lend my books to anyone."

This is a problem, Vish realized. He needed to clear his mind. He would take a cold shower, he decided. He turned on the shower. Nothing.

He had been in Grenada only a day, and in that short period of time he literally had become, as he would later love to describe it, a Vish out of water. But the ocean was only yards away. He had never been in an ocean before, but it was water. He splashed around for several minutes, until his mind was clear. Minutes later he realized there was salt in the ocean water, salt that formed a crust on his body that had to be washed off with fresh water. He'd already discovered there was limited fresh water.

In only a few hours the newly becrusted Dr. Rao was going to give his first lecture on a subject he knew little about with no way to prepare. He had no books, no reference materials, no notes. He went next door and knocked. A very large Jamaican student in his underwear finally opened the door. "Hello. I am your professor of anatomy, Dr. Rao," Vish said as if it weren't 3:00 a.m. "I am wondering if I can borrow your textbook."

He spent the rest of the night studying the text. Before he'd left India, his father, a distinguished professor, had given him some advice. Number one: Never go to a lecture unprepared. Number two: Prepare for twice as much time as allotted to your lecture, so if it is scheduled for one hour, prepare for two hours. Number three: If you don't know the answer to a question, tell your students you don't know it but you will find out and come back and tell them. "But most important is number four," he had cautioned his son. "Don't do number three too many times."

Our shuttle system between Grand Anse and True Blue consisted of one car. It was leaving at 6:00 a.m., but when Vish got to the designated spot, it already was full. Three women were sitting in the rear seat, but they invited him to sit on their laps. When he got to True Blue, I was waiting for him. I was in solution mode. "The chairman left," I told him. "Please keep the students busy in the morning for an hour. Tell them where you're from. Talk to them. You don't even have to teach them."

"Dr. Modica," he responded respectfully. "You are the chancellor, but I am the teacher. You hired me to do this job. I will be glad to do it." In that first lecture he admitted to the students that he had not taught in the Western world before and his accent might be difficult for them to understand. "Please," he asked, "if you don't understand, tell me and I will explain to you again." Then he gave the lecture he'd stayed up all night preparing about the upper extremities, in particular the scapula. "They are mirror images," he explained, and to make certain they never forgot it, he pointed out that the right scapula was shaped roughly like India. At the conclusion of the lecture, he received a standing ovation. "That was terrific," I told him. "Now I need you to repeat the same lecture this afternoon."

The lecture hall was so small we had to repeat every lecture twice.

Dr. Rao's second lecture received an even more enthusiastic response. I could feel something happening. The students had gotten the first glimmer that this thing could work. That they could learn sitting under a coconut tree with a textbook. I was seeing the first signs of buy-in. Those students considering leaving decided to give it a little more time. Maybe they were beginning to use their feelings of anger in a good way.

The only problem I had was with Vish Rao. A few days after that first lecture he got sick—he came down with a high fever and a bad case of homesickness. He was very unhappy—he'd arrived in the Caribbean with winter clothes, felt isolated and alone, and finally decided this was not the right job for him. He hadn't even unpacked his suitcase. But as he was preparing to leave, he ran into Danny and two more of Da Boys—Warren Stanton and Frankie Arbucci. They were sitting on a low cement retaining wall leading to the beach.

"What's cooking, Doc?" one of them asked.

Vish took them literally. "Well, I have not eaten yet."

"No, what's happening? What's the good word of the day?"

He told them what he was feeling, admitting he was having doubts this was the right place for him. I suspect every single person involved with the school went through the same thing.

"Nah, don't go back," Danny told him. "Stay here with us; stay in Grenada. We'll figure this thing out."

Apparently later that afternoon, my mother, having heard from Danny that Dr. Rao was considering leaving, knocked on his door. "I was not feeling good," Vish remembers. "I answered the door and there was this lovely lady standing there. 'I am sorry,' I said, 'but who are you?'

"'I am Mrs. Modica,' she told me.

"'Mrs. Modica? You can't be Charlie's wife, because you look older than him.'

"She smiled. 'I am Charlie's mom. I heard that you are not well, so I thought I would bring you some food.' She handed me a basket which contained some fruits, some juice, some banana bread, and a little piece of butter. It was an act of lovely kindness that made me feel welcome. I was about to leave. But my meeting with the students and then this visit from Momma Modica, as I began calling her, changed my mind. Changed my life, actually. I told my wife, 'You must come down here. This is a good place.' With my first paycheck I bought plane tickets for her and our son."

Throughout that entire first year, I was continually plugging holes to prevent the entire structure from collapsing. It was like playing Whac-A-Mole—every time I got one issue settled, two more popped up. The second class, which arrived five months later, had to deal with the same problems and insecurities as the charter class. These "Super Eights," as they referred to themselves, voted to skip all vacations and holidays to become eligible for clinical positions at the same time as the first class.

I traveled back and forth between Bay Shore and Grenada on a regular basis. Whenever another problem arose, here comes Charlie in his three-piece suit to meet with students and remind them about that light at the end of the tunnel. In those meetings I was never Chancellor Modica. I wasn't Dr. Modica. I was just Charlie. My job was to encourage the students by offering help and inspiring hope. I believed that as long as they knew we were paying attention to them and doing our best to respond, they would continue doing their part, which was to learn.

Jack Cush remembers those meetings well. "When things were turning dark, when everything is being flushed down the toilet, you know what happens? Charlie Modica shows up.

"He's the guy with the answers. He's the guy who knows how to fix it. He's the guy there to inspire the masses. He'd show up in his three-piece suit and stay with the class from five p.m. until one in the morning, then go to the airport and be off on a plane. Everyone would say, 'That was great. I feel a lot better about things.' Then after another hour we'd say,

'That son of a gun, he left us. He didn't even answer the main questions. When is he coming back?

"He was a true leader. More than anything, he inspired hope. He told us that there would be an end, that we would fix this. And then we could see it happening. They couldn't fix everything, but they tried. Here's the lesson: When you know someone is really listening to you, and is trying, it makes a huge difference."

I'd meet with students in the open-air classroom from 5:00 or 6:00 p.m. and tell them exactly what we were doing to improve the situation. My stock answer became, "Trust me." Where are our textbooks? Trust me, they're coming. What are you doing about the lack of water? Trust me, we're working on it. When are we going to get cadavers to work on? Trust me, we're getting them. Afterward I would meet individually with every person who wanted to talk to me. I'd often be there until 2:00 a.m., when I had to leave for the airport.

It was in these meetings that Danny Ricciardi and I began developing our friendship. Danny and Da Boys were never hesitant about speaking up when there was a problem that needed to be addressed or, conversely, supporting us when we were trying to resolve an issue. When necessary, he would call me in Bay Shore—collect, always collect—to make sure something got fixed. He stood up for the class.

At times, admittedly, it got contentious. Once, for example, there was a financial problem. It was mostly a miscommunication, but some students believed we were going back on an agreement we'd made. When our director of operations, Jay Wilbur, tried to explain, Danny started screaming at him. When he was finished a classmate said to him, "I can't believe you yelled at him like that."

Danny was also a realist. "You gotta do what you gotta do," he responded. That was Danny, doing what was necessary. He was meeting regularly with other students to sort things out. There was a lot of grumbling. There was no question the fate of the school lay in their hands. They would sit outside and discuss the situation, trying to make each other feel better about the struggles. I'm sure that at times they thought about their contemporaries at American medical schools, every one of which had running water.

Our students were the underdogs, and they knew it. There is something very appealing about embracing the underdogs. It's a recurrent theme in popular culture—but it's considerably more difficult to *be* the underdog, with no guarantee of a movie-like happy ending. There were a lot of difficult days. "Look," Danny would tell them, "the only way this thing works is if we stay here together." He had been to school in Italy and knew how difficult it was to learn medicine in a different language. "It's up to you guys. Do what you want to do, but I'm staying."

I'm staying. One by one students made that decision.

I remember the meeting when I knew for sure that Danny and most of the other students had made the decision to fight with me to establish the school. This took place during the second or third week of classes. We had made a deal with a local restaurant to supply the food for the meal plan. It is accurate to say that it was not a success—meals consisted essentially of poorly prepared limited portions of too few choices. One student began ranting about it, saying with disgust, "I wouldn't feed this crap to my dog."

I didn't get angry. I never got angry. Instead, I listened to him. Much of the time the students were right. And when they were we took steps to change things. We knew the food plan was a problem, and we were scrambling to fix it. In fact, within several weeks we had found a new vendor. In this instance I tried to calm him down, replying, "I'm really sorry you feel that way. But I wish you'd say it a little less harshly."

Then Danny interrupted. "You should sit down," he told his classmate. "That's not the way to talk to him."

Most of the other people in the room agreed with Danny. It was a simple, brief exchange, but to me it was a major turning point in the success of the university. It meant that at least some of the students were ready to fight along with me. The student who complained eventually left the school, pretty much over that issue, but soon after we ceased making the meal plan mandatory. That change proved that we were listening to them, working together to make this work.

During those individual meetings, I was faced with almost every type of problem imaginable, from students having to deal with family issues at home to academic struggles. We continued doing the best we could to solve small problems before they became big problems. For example, students had been informed that tuition payments were nonrefundable after they started attending classes. But one student left after the first week and asked for a refund. He pointed out the problems accurately, including the fact that the anatomy professor had quit. The founders were reluctant to refund his money. We had dealt honestly with our students; we'd warned them what to expect and had every intention of fulfilling our promise: We were going to create the path for them to become physicians in the United States.

But I insisted that we refund his tuition—and after that we extended the refund offer for the first three weeks. You don't like it here? Go home, here's your money. That turned out to work in our behalf, proving to students that our objective was to operate a medical school, not collect tuition money. As we were to see over the next few years, when several other English-language medical schools opened throughout the Caribbean, this was a legitimate fear.

The problems we dealt with were continuously evolving. Each day was an excursion into the unexpected. It was hard to anticipate what we would have to deal with. We constantly found ourselves saying, "What if we do this?" or "How about we try that?" For example, the sun shined so brightly during the day that when instructors using the open-air classroom wanted to show slides, they had to roll down canvas shades to make it dark enough. But because that classroom was not air-conditioned, it became unbearably warm. In response, someone suggested, what if we held classes at night? That seemed like a great idea. We decided to schedule anatomy classes at night for two weeks.

Unfortunately, word spread among Grenadians that the new school was showing bizarre pictures of body parts, and local people would show up for the classes, standing outside to watch. Also, the light from the projector attracted moths, very large moths, which liked to land on the lens. That experiment ended within a week.

Quality-of-life issues were more difficult to solve because we were dependent on the island's archaic infrastructure. Looking at the extraordinarily beautiful sprawling campus today, the equal of any college or university anywhere in the world, it's easy to remember those first few years with some degree of nostalgia. But not when we were living through it. I can say without fear of being contradicted that I never dared tell anyone, not once, "Someday you'll look back on this with fondness."

Even I wasn't sure that was possible.

Lou Guida described it accurately: "Most of my classmates were middle- and upper-class kids from the New York metropolitan area or California, used to pretty comfortable lives. We went down there, and there was nothing. Half the time there was no running water. It was hot as heck, window screens were either broken or missing, and most evenings there was sporadic electricity and no air-conditioning. We had to study by candlelight or hurricane lamps. There was one telephone, and to make a call we had to go downtown and place calls through an operator.

"The first week one of my colleagues spent hours putting screens on the windows. He was fair-skinned, and his backside got badly sunburned. He couldn't sit down for a week—and then he got bit by a centipede. He just looked at me with this sad look and asked, 'Where are we?'"

We adapted. Figured out rudimentary, occasionally ingenuous solutions. To provide transportation between Grand Anse and True Blue, for example, we bought an old bus with a flat roof on it that had once been used to carry chicken crates. "A chicken hauler," Jay Wilber called it. We installed wooden benches so it could carry thirty-five or more students at a time.

The availability of fresh water was obviously a more difficult problem. Years ago, like many developing nations, Grenada simply did not have the ability to pump water to all parts of the island equally. During the dry season especially there just wasn't sufficient water, so periodically they would shut off the water to different areas. Students used to joke that we were all in the same boat—which, unfortunately, was in dry dock.

At times during the dry season there would be no running water for several days or more. Fifty years ago we lacked the infrastructure to deal with that. Students learned to be resourceful: They brushed their teeth with pineapple juice. We posted a sign—Do NOT FLUSH FOR #1—but when it became necessary, students lugged buckets of seawater from the beach to flush toilets…and the salt degraded the pipes, which made the situation even worse.

We adapted. When the water was running, everybody filled their bathtub and every container they had to be used for every possible purpose: "101 Ways to Use Tub Water" they called it. Laundry was done in the bathtub; students would use a plunger to clean clothes, then drape them on the roof to dry. Hot showers were a rarity. At night students would walk down the beach with soap and towels to the Holiday Inn and use its outdoor showers. Grand Anse had a metal roof that heated up during the day, so when it rained students would run outside with soap and towels and shower in the orange water under the runoff gutter. Living on a stunningly beautiful Caribbean island with incredible weather and no chance of ice or snow had its advantages.

When students complained, Dr. Rao would tell them that yoga exercises dictate that you must take cold showers because the autonomous nervous system, especially the parasympathetic system, gets stimulated. Truthfully, I'm not sure that actually helped convince anyone this was good for them. The real problem with cold showers is that they're cold. One of the intriguing questions students had to wrestle with was: What is preferable, a cold shower or no water with which to shower? Many years later, charter class member John Washington told me that after going through this experience, every time he takes a hot shower he thinks of Grenada.

We adapted. Students and faculty would fill hot-water bags—the same type of bags the military used to store a considerable amount of water—and let them heat in the sun. Several enterprising students bought large military-type bladders that they filled before they went to class in the morning and left them in the sun all day so they could take a hot shower when they returned.

The alternative to this, as I found myself telling students, was, "Would you rather be studying medicine in Spanish?"

The freshwater shortage became a serious problem. To mitigate this problem we finally bought an old fire truck in the States and had it shipped down. It would drive up to Grand Etang Lake, a freshwater lake up in the hills, or into St. George's and fill up, then return to campus and pump it into our holding tank. It would make three or four trips a day. One day Marty Kane and several of his classmates made the mistake of going up the hill and looking into the holding tank—and discovering it was filled with dead frogs and live tadpoles.

To make sure Grand Anse had sufficient water, we repurposed the swimming pool, covering it and converting it into a storage tank.

We tried everything. When plumbers repaired the water lines at True Blue, they somehow managed to switch the hot and cold lines. As a result, when we did have hot water it went into the toilets, while the showers remained cold. So for several days we had water literally boiling in the toilets, causing students to boast about their exotic lifestyle: "We even have steam toilets!"

Dealing with power outages was an entirely different problem. Most of the electricity on Grenada was produced by several old military generators in the city. They were not capable of providing sufficient power to the island during peak hours, usually at night when people were home, so just as they did with water, they would load shed. Certain areas would be shut down to keep the system running. We would lose electricity almost every day for at least two hours, but sometimes the outages would last considerably longer. One thing that was certain: Without power there was no light at the end of the tunnel.

There was no way to predict when we would lose power. We adapted: Students kept candles, tinfoil, and lanterns nearby. The tinfoil was used to enhance the candlelight. Flashlights were great but had limited use; a fact of life I learned is that wherever there is a power shortage, there usually is a battery shortage. When batteries were available, they were expensive.

Among our biggest headaches was losing power in the cadaver lab in the middle of a dissection. Dissections had to be completed by flashlight, candlelight, or lantern. At those times it felt like we were in the 1600s. As with every problem, though, the students figured out ways to deal with it. One night, for example, Da Boys were studying for a microbiology exam in Steve Gorman's house when the lights went out. They had been projecting slides onto a white stucco wall, so there was no way of continuing without power.

Even among all the characters in the class, Steve Gorman stood out. At forty-five years old, he was one of the oldest students in the class. He had been a teacher in New York City and had retired on a disability when he saw my ad. As Steve's wife, Martha, has said, "Steve was not the smartest student—but he was smart enough to make friends with the smartest students!"

"Gorman was cherubic. Big glasses, big personality, and," Jack Cush admits, "like me, a little too loud. But he was an amazing person. He would give you his stethoscope and go buy another one for himself. He exemplified why someone should want to be a doctor. His whole being was wanting to help people. And if he wasn't the sharpest knife in the drawer, he knew how to get the job done right. When he needed assistance, he knew who to go to and how to get it."

Steve's experience in the New York City public school system had taught him to be resourceful and gregarious. For instance, he had come down to the island before the other students and rented a large two-bedroom house for his family, a house that came with a maid and—most importantly—a telephone! So that night when the lights did not come back on after a half hour, he called the power company and politely explained the situation. Big test, studying, desperate. "Sorry, mon," he was told. "Can't do nuthin'."

Most people would have seen that as a refusal. Steve saw it as a challenge. Ten minutes later he called back, this time pretending to be a businessman. In his Grenadian accent he pleaded for power, claiming, "My fish are stinkin', mon."

"Sorry, mon. Can't do nuthin'."

Steve was determined. Ten minutes later he called again, this time posing as a professor at the school. There actually was a small leper colony on the island, and Professor Gorman explained that he was taking care of them and they had to be bathed every hour. He asked the person at the power station if he had power where he was. He did. Did he have running water? He did. That's wonderful news, Steve said with relief. "Here's what I'm going to do," he continued. "I'm going to put the lepers on the bus right away and bring them down to you so we can give them a bath."

Electricity was restored within minutes. Gorman wasn't done, though. He called a final time to thank the representative, then told him he was coming there to personally express his appreciation—and was bringing the lepers with him to shake his hand!

Eventually we purchased several well-used auxiliary generators. Although they broke down regularly and had to be repaired, they did make the situation a little better.

We struggled through the first semester. But a survivor's spirit was growing. Dr. Rao, who might have left if he had been able to get a cab, embraced my vision. Students would come to him in despair, he recalled, telling him, "I can't do it. It's too tough for me."

Vish would tell them about his own life, about growing up in a poor area with limited water. "Medical school is only four years long, and the sacrifice you make will only make you stronger. Just hang out one semester. You already bought the books. You have your return ticket. One semester, then you can quit."

He remembers one student whose mind he could not change. He'd had enough; he was going back to New York. "What will you do when you go back?" he asked.

"I was driving a cab before I came down here. I know a guy who has a medallion. I'll start working for him. But I've had it here—I want to withdraw."

Vish shrugged. There was nothing more he could do. The student returned to New York. But two days later Vish got a phone call from the student. "Dr. Rao, I'm coming back. When I landed at JFK I got in a cab. The driver was a little older than me. He just complained about everything, everything is no good. I thought about that, and I finally realized that if I do become a cabbie, that's the person I'm gonna be. I don't want that. I want to be a doctor. I'll be back in a few days."

It would be years before we really were able to mostly eliminate these infrastructure problems. So as with everything else we did, when we were living through them, we tried to find something, anything, positive about it. We began referring to the hardships as "character-building," suggesting to the students that learning how to survive and deal with these issues would prove beneficial when they were faced with the daily pressures of practicing medicine. (Admittedly, most of our students didn't buy that either.)

Maybe the only place these problems were useful was when responding to family and friends in the States who wondered how our students could actually study medicine while living in an island paradise. A lot of people were jealous. Their fantasy was that students were spending their days luxuriating in a hammock on a Caribbean beach, reading their textbooks while sipping piña coladas. As Joan Mack said, "That's when I would tell them how I had to lug pails of water from the beach to my room on the second floor so I could flush the toilet."

CHAPTER 9

Bodies, Bones, Brains

"We're here to take care of this. Everybody stand back."

—Hudson County, New Jersey, sheriff, on the dock with our shipment of cadavers

Opening a medical school brought with it unique challenges: For example, who could provide anatomy-class cadavers?

For a medical school, cadavers are an essential school supply. Studying the human body is a rite of passing for all aspiring doctors. I had promised students they would have cadavers to work on, but I had no idea where to get them.

In our school's curriculum, anatomy was a full-year course—two semesters. The first semester we taught osteology, the study of the human skeleton, how everything fit together. Dr. Rao warned me that he could not teach human anatomy without cadavers to dissect. "They're coming," I promised, and then kept promising, "They're coming!" I knew that if other schools regularly did this, we could too.

Once again, I was in problem-solving mode. It is fair to say that without cadavers the school could not survive. If we couldn't provide them, we could not properly educate our students. We knew it. They knew it. It became symbolic: Getting cadavers was the real test of our ability to succeed. In fact, our first building projects were a library and a dedicated anatomy lab. At one point, to help the students with costs while construction was underway, we even hired several students to help lay the concrete floor of the lab, paying them $25 an hour and putting them in the unusual position of actually building their school between classes.

I was willing to pay anything to get cadavers. There was nothing nefarious about purchasing dead bodies—every medical school in the world did it. In Spain I'd had to buy my own bones. Learning how the human body works is the beginning of learning how to provide medical care. But it is heavily regulated. And it is a sensitive subject. These were human remains, and we had to treat them with dignity and remain respectful.

Somehow, we made contact with a supplier who purchased cadavers for a New Jersey medical school. Admittedly, I had not known there was such a business. They sourced their cadavers from Chicago. This was perfectly legal, and they could ship them to Grenada. "The only problem…" we were told.

I truly could not wait to hear the rest of that sentence. The possibilities were fascinating. Honestly, though, after everything I'd been through, I seriously doubted whatever this was would be the *only* problem.

The only problem was that they couldn't be delivered to the New Jersey medical school for temporary holding. "Well, we're going to fly them down to Grenada," I said. "We have a plane that can leave from Islip Airport [on Long Island]. What do we have to do to prepare them for transport?"

"You just need to keep them in a funeral home," we were told. I have to admit that when I proposed opening a medical school, "a funeral home" was not something I expected to hear. But as I learned, cadavers had to be shipped to a facility licensed to accept human remains, which was pretty much limited to a funeral parlor or a medical school. Luckily, a friend of Rudy Migliore, who was one of my assistants in those formative years, knew someone in the funeral home business. I explained to the owner that what we were doing was completely legal, which I believed to be true. We just needed to have them ready to be shipped a day or so before the flight was scheduled.

The owner was reluctant, but finally agreed. Our cadaver supplier told us he would drive the cadavers from Chicago to New York. This was the way the supplier always transported them. The cadavers were embalmed so they didn't have to be refrigerated. The funeral home owner told me to store them in his building. Because he couldn't possibly know more than a week in advance if he would be hosting a wake or a service at that time, the cadavers would have to be delivered after midnight. And he didn't want the orange U-Haul truck sitting in his driveway. The cadavers would have to be unloaded.

The truck arrived after midnight. I was waiting with a friend from law school. The cadavers were wrapped in dark plastic body bags. They slid the cadavers to the end of the truck bed, and we carried them off. Nothing I had ever done in my life had prepared me to be unloading a truckload of cadavers in the middle of the night. As we carried them inside, he muttered several times, as if to reassure himself, "But I'm a lawyer!"

There were thirty-three of them. The truck returned the next morning and we reversed the process, loading them up for the drive to the airport.

I had chartered an old DC-3 to fly them to Grenada. Prime Minister Gairy had agreed to let us bring them in, but he insisted we do so very quietly and at night. But because we were bringing them in very quietly and at night, Gairy's political opposition spread the rumor that we were actually bringing in military rifles.

The introduction of cadavers to medical students is a solemn event. Our students were taught from the outset how to honor the privilege of using the deceased for the better good of the living. The special challenges of providing the cadavers to our new school made the appreciation for the privilege even more meaningful to all of us. This inaugural delivery was shrouded with sublime reverence, but not without a touch of the surreal.

One difficulty about doing this at night was that Pearls Airport had no lights. So we hired taxis and pickup trucks and directed them to line up along the edges of the runway and turn on their lights just as dusk was settling in. Vish Rao parked his car at the far end of the runway and turned on his blinkers. Several students, including Da Boys, came to the airport with flashlights to help us unload. The plane landed without incident. We put two cadavers in the back of each vehicle and drove in a convoy over the mountains to the campus. The once lovely Grand Anse Hotel had a large walk-in freezer that previously had been used to store perishables. We had built shelves in the freezer and stored these cadavers there. The students unwrapped the cadavers and carried them inside.

As we unwrapped them, we also discovered that several of the cadavers had arrived without heads. When we investigated, we learned that several of the heads had been sent to dental schools, which was not unusual.

Eventually, news that the cadavers had arrived on the island got out. At that time many Grenadians did not know what a cadaver was, causing the *Torchlight*, the political opposition's newspaper, to report that "a shipment of cadavers has come to the island for the new medical school. Unfortunately, they all appeared to be dead."

Flying cadavers to Grenada had been extraordinarily expensive but absolutely necessary to maintain our credibility with our students. Joe Nossiff remembers telling his roommate, "'Let's see what happens at the beginning of the second semester. If we come back and the anatomy lab isn't ready, something's wrong.' When we came back that was one of the first things I checked on. Sure enough, the anatomy lab was ready to go and all the corpses were on the tables. I told him, 'Dammit, they did it. They got it together.' That probably was the first time I really believed this was going to work."

Having solved the immediate problem, we began setting up a system to ensure a steady supply of cadavers for the future. It was, we discovered, far more economical to send them from New York by sea. Shipping cadavers was quite complicated, though. Our second shipment of cadavers, which would be used by the Super Eights, were put in crates marked ANATOMICAL SPECIMENS and delivered to a Brooklyn pier to be loaded aboard as freight. Later I got an emergency phone call in Bay Shore. The longshoremen had contacted customs and walked off the job.

While all of this was entirely legal, it threatened to become a bureaucratic nightmare. Our cadavers were, literally, the bodies of evidence, and we had to get them off the pier before customs and police could detain them. Fortunately, the brother of one of our employees was the sheriff of Hudson County in New Jersey. We contacted him and he raced to Brooklyn to meet a truck we'd managed to get there. Lights flashing, he led the truck onto the docks. "We're here to take care of this," he announced. "Everybody stand back." The cadavers were loaded quickly. And just in time. As the truck pulled away, a convoy of NYPD squad cars arrived.

When the crates eventually arrived in Grenada, our business manager was waiting to pick them up. The problem was that most truck drivers on the island were superstitious and refused to transport cadavers. A well-respected minister on the island, Father Gilbert, managed to convince liquor store drivers that it was safe to transport them. I don't know what he told them, but they agreed to bring them to the campus.

Finally the "anatomical specimens" were off-loaded and brought to the school. When they got there, we discovered that several of them had not been properly embalmed, so in desperation we sent them to a local funeral home, where they were successfully re-embalmed.

We had to learn how to package and ship our cadavers. There were specific governmental regulations, but not a lot of instructions. We learned mostly by trial and many errors.

Out of necessity we developed our own technique for boxing brains. Admittedly, that's another sentence I thought I would never write. Jay Wilber, an engineer by training, figured it out. Driving a water taxi, making containers for brains—he was very adaptable. We all had to be. The story began when we learned the anatomy department of a prestigious medical school was overstocked with human brains and was trying to find someone who could use them. So we purchased them and had them shipped to our office in Bay Shore. When they arrived, we discovered they had been packed in formaldehyde, which was not sufficiently dense to suspend them, so during shipment they had sunk to the bottom of the container. We had to create a way of protecting them when they were shipped to Grenada. Jay designed our own small containers and filled them with glycerin, which is thicker than formaldehyde and dense enough to support a brain. The containers were packed in foam and enclosed in a hard shell.

The problem was these brains had to be transferred by hand from the original packaging to Jay's containers. Jay did that in a large space in the back of one of my father's vacant buildings. He whited out the windows so no one could casually look in. We referred to that space as "the coffee shop" because it previously had been used as a luncheonette. As an engineer, things like picking up brains and putting them in a different container didn't faze him at all.

Bodies, bones, brains—whatever human remains were necessary for any stateside medical school, we figured out a way of ensuring our students would have the same resources to become well trained to serve their patients. Within a few months I had learned more about cadavers and embalming than I had ever wanted to know. Eventually we discovered that an impoverished Caribbean nation suffered from a large number of indigent deaths. People were dying on the streets, and no one knew who they were. That was a terribly sad reality. Someone suggested we set up an embalming facility on the island. This was another one of those decisions that seemed like a good idea at the time.

We were in the embalming business. We built an embalming building. This was not exactly another golden opportunity presenting itself to me, but it did make sense. As might have been predicted, we encountered problems in every phase. For example, until then I had not been aware how difficult it was to get formaldehyde into the extremities. Security became another major headache, and our chemicals and other supplies kept getting stolen. We tried various solutions, but within a year we closed down the facility and got out of the embalming business.

Besides unloading cadavers together, what really bonded the charter class was the note-taking service. Several of our instructors spoke too softly to be clearly heard in the back, so Duncan Brown, the former roadie with Fleetwood Mac, bought an inexpensive microphone and speakers from RadioShack and improvised a viable public-address system.

That helped, but because classes were meeting in the open-sided building, it was still difficult for many students to hear the lectures. Steve Gorman wanted to make certain he didn't miss anything, so he bought a tape recorder and recorded the class. He also bought an old typewriter, and his wife, Martha, transcribed the lectures. Initially this was for his benefit—it was an important study tool—but his classmates wanted copies, offering to pay for them. He rented a copy machine and was in business.

Within days three separate note-taking services were in operation: Danny Ricciardi was marketing Gorman's notes, a group of Orthodox Jewish students from New York had their notes, as did a third group, founded by Rudy Antoncic and calling themselves the "misfits." Ruth Antoncic, Rudy's wife, brought the three groups together into a class-lecture transcription service. The price of notes was about $10 for the semester, but the rule was that everyone who used the notes had to contribute something, meaning you couldn't buy one set and pass them around. It became a class-wide project. Different people taped the lectures, Ruth Antoncic and Martha Gorman, among others, transcribed them, other people ran off copies on a hand-cranked mimeograph machine, and those students with motorbikes or bicycles distributed them. It became a successful business.

When the second class arrived, we allowed charter class students to rent housing off campus. The reality was that we needed their dorm rooms, and the revenue from the transcription service helped several of them pay the rent.

The service grew so quickly it needed to be upgraded. It was taking too long to crank out sufficient copies by hand. Gorman and Antoncic found out that the only electric mimeograph machine on the island was for sale. They went to make a deal. The seller wanted $250, but Steve told Rudy, "When we get there don't say a damned word. Watch, I'm going to negotiate a better price."

To their surprise, when they got to the seller's house in downtown St. George's, three men with military weapons at port arms were standing guard outside. The seller, they discovered, was Maurice Bishop, the leader of the opposition to Prime Minister Gairy. This machine had been used to print the party newspaper. It was no longer needed because Bishop had bought a printing press.

"Steve loved to negotiate," Antoncic remembers. "But Bishop was also tough. He refused to go below $225. They went back and forth. Those guards stood there stoically, holding their weapons in front of them and just staring coldly at us. I decided that the best possible outcome would be getting out of there alive. 'Steve,' I whispered, 'give the man the damned $225.'

"Steve settled, but he wasn't happy. On our way back to the school he grumbled, 'If you'd given me a little more time I could have gotten him down to $200.'"

The business continued expanding. By the second year Danny was also selling sample test questions, which also had to be copied. Ruth was doing much of the work but was underpaid. Gorman had a plan to rectify that. Gorman always had a plan. One morning he showed up unexpectedly at Antoncic's house. Wearing gloves. Without any explanation he began dripping mimeo ink on the floor. The Antoncic's curious dog, Kenobi, began tracking it throughout the house. Ruth started screaming at Gorman, "What are you doing? Are you crazy?" which caused the dog to run faster.

"Watch," Gorman directed. He called Ricciardi. "I'm at Rudy's. We got a problem. You gotta get up here right away." Minutes later a large limo being driven by Victor Benjamin stopped in front of the house, and Da Boys piled out. They couldn't believe the mess. "Ruth's had it," Gorman explained. "It isn't worth it to her anymore." He began packing up the mimeo. "Put this in your car. Take it back with you."

Ruth's pay was doubled that day, just as Gorman intended.

CHAPTER 10

The Ongoing Odyssey: Building a Faculty

"I will not lecture about Sasquatch until I come in here and there is a keg of Carib on the podium!"

—Dr. Robert George

By the time our second class arrived in June, we had settled into a rough routine. The charter class had laid the foundation and the Super Eights began building on it. Among the members of that fourth class was a student named John Windsor, although inside my family his name was John Modica, my younger brother. Neither his classmates nor the faculty knew who he was—because he legally changed his name while attending classes there. John was well qualified, but he didn't want people making any assumptions about nepotism. I had no doubt he would excel, and in fact he passed all of his boards, triple boarded, the first time, and is still chief of Internal Care at a hospital in Connecticut after more than thirty years.

John is ten years younger than me, but we've always been close. He worked for me at the water taxi company and eventually took it over. And like me, he wanted to be a doctor. "It was my mother," John says. "She always respected priests and doctors. My closest friend's father was a doctor, and he became my role model. While I considered following my father into real estate, my first love and my driving force was to become a doctor. I was in premed when my brother told me he was starting a medical school. *That was great,* I thought. It didn't seem the slightest bit unusual to me. I knew what he had been through trying to become a doctor, so somehow this made sense. I never doubted he could make it work; that's what he always did. If Charlie says he can start a medical school, then he can start a medical school.

"It didn't immediately occur to me that I would enroll there. I wanted to go to an American medical school. I had good grades, but not great grades. My brother and Andy Belford told me I wasn't going to be able to get into an American school. So I had what might best be described as an 'informal interview,' although I was not surprised when I was accepted by St. George's."

It was entirely John's decision to change his last name. He just thought it would be easier for him. He picked Windsor because our family lived on Windsor Avenue and it also was his wife's maiden name. He actually went to court and legally changed his name. I never told anyone about it either, and we would only get together at a hotel far away from the school when our parents were there.

The reality of the school was that we were learning as we moved along, while trying to adapt the plan to address every contingency. In hindsight, our plan was more rudimentary than we thought at the time. Our objective was to get established and prove we could do what we claimed we could do: prepare students to take and pass the exact same examinations that American medical school students were taking, and provide the necessary clinical experience needed to become licensed physicians.

But there were no business models to follow, no experts to turn to for advice. What we were trying to do was unique—no one had ever done anything close to this. During this same period the Japanese automotive industry had adopted a philosophy that translated to mean, "Just in time." That meant they did not stock warehouses with parts and supplies in preparation for the time in the future when they might be needed; instead, they got what they needed when they needed it. That's what we were doing: dealing with the daily problems of survival while also engaged in long-term planning. "Long term" meaning two weeks, maybe next month.

We stayed one semester ahead of the students, hiring the instructors we needed when we needed them, and just in time. Some instructors came, stayed a few weeks, then left. It was too much of a hardship: They wanted running water; they wanted dependable electricity. They wanted restaurants in which they could identify what they were eating.

We were able to maintain an unusually small faculty because, unlike American medical schools, the only thing we required of our teachers was that they teach. The faculties of other schools are heavily laden with researchers who also teach some classes. Those instructors are urged to publish the results of their work, which impacts the reputation of their institution. We had streamlined the medical education process, focusing exclusively on medical education.

I continued to plan our future curriculum by looking at the courses offered by the top medical schools. But when I needed to add an additional course, I tried to choose something a little different. I decided we should offer a class on nutrition. I had no real knowledge of that subject, and only one of my go-to schools offered it in their program. It just seemed to make sense to me; it seemed like the world was just beginning to recognize the crossroads between nutrition and health. I didn't discuss that decision with anyone, but I had a hunch it would well serve our students. This seemingly whimsical choice turned out to be by far one of the most important and luckiest decisions I've ever made.

It enabled the school to survive.

I placed an ad for an instructor in several magazines, including *Science* and the *Journal of Nutrition*. It read: "St. George's University is looking for faculty and Chair of the Department of Nutrition." It was a bit of an exaggeration, as the department was in the process of being created. I received several responses, among them a note and résumé from a man named Geoffrey Bourne. This was a year or so before novelist Robert Ludlum introduced Jason Bourne so that had no effect on my choice, but it is accurate to say that our Bourne became as much of a hero to us as Ludlum's fictional character is to many.

Geoffrey Bourne was an impressive man, both in stature and academic achievement. At that time he was chairman of the Anatomy Department at Emory University after having taught at Oxford and the University of London. He also was the editor of the *World Review of Nutrition and Dietetics* and director of the Yerkes National Primate Research Center in Atlanta. An extraordinary man. I had been very happy to recruit Vish Rao, and he was a new graduate living with his in-laws in New Jersey. The only question I had when I looked at Dr. Bourne's credentials was why in the world would he be applying for this position? But I was smart enough not to ask!

We needed him. Adding someone with his credentials to our faculty would instantly increase our credibility. I immediately flew to Atlanta to meet him. He took us to visit the Yerkes Center, where NASA trained monkeys to be launched into space. It also was the home of a chimp named Lana, whom researchers had taught how to use hand signals to communicate her needs, wants, and desires. During our first conversation with Dr. Bourne he asked, in his somewhat formal British accent, "Why in the world would your school be teaching nutrition in Grenada of all places?"

Just imagine that: A man teaching sign language to chimpanzees thought what we were doing was strange.

The correct answer was that I did not have a compelling academic reason. It just seemed like a good idea. Instead, I replied, "I think it's a very important area, and very few medical schools are offering it."

"You're dead right," he said. We hit it off immediately. He was fascinated by the fact we existed—and he was pretty ticked off about academia in general. As I eventually discovered, he was about to age out of his job and viewed us as an underdog, an extreme underdog.

Even more enticing, his wife, Dr. Nelly Golarz, was an associate professor of histology at Emory, and his son Peter was a special assistant for health issues to President Jimmy Carter.

We were definitely competitive, especially because he had no other offers. But he was reluctant. My objective was to convince him that rather than taking a minor position to fill time at the end of his career, this offered him an opportunity to make a difference in the world. "You're just the person who could give birth to a new school," I implored him, meaning every word of it. "I've got two hundred students down there working really hard. A lot of these people have been kicked around by the establishment. When you see what they're willing to put up with to become doctors, I promise you, you're going to be really impressed. You can give the school credibility if you believe in it, and I know if I can get you down there to see it you'll believe in it. I promise, once you meet the students, you're going to want to be part of it."

While he made no commitment, he agreed to visit the island. My problem was that as a result of the success of the note-taking service, lectures in general were poorly attended. Rather than struggling to hear the instructor, students got the entire lecture neatly typed a day later. But I desperately needed an enthusiastic full house to impress Drs. Bourne and Golarz. I began knocking on doors literally begging people to show up. "You guys have got to come to this lecture," I pleaded. "This is the most important event of the school so far. These two professors from Emory are thinking about joining the faculty. If we can get them it's going to make a big difference." I didn't exactly say that their own futures might depend on our ability to attract Dr. Bourne and his wife, although it's possible I might have inferred it.

A few days later I waited anxiously outside the lecture hall, hoping enough people would show up to impress Dr. Bourne. Minutes before class began, people started drifting in. Then they showed up in larger groups. It became a show of support for the school. By the time I introduced Geoffrey Bourne and Nelly Golarz, the place was packed. If we'd had walls, students would have been standing against them. Each of them gave a lecture, and when they were done, they received a standing ovation.

Dr. Bourne was thrilled. "I love your students," he told me later. "They're hungry to learn. I'll take the position of chairman of the

Nutrition Department, but I think what you really need is help running this school from the academic standpoint."

And then he said the words I've never forgotten: "And I'm willing to do that."

"You met the right guy," I said. But what I was really feeling was *I* had met the right guy. This was incredible. Geoffrey Bourne was well known and greatly respected. His presence on our faculty would instantly change the perception of the school. It would put us on the medical establishment map.

"I would do it as vice chancellor," he said. "But I also would like to have final say in academic decisions."

It was like a dream coming true inside my dream. Geoffrey Bourne was exactly what we needed, even though I hadn't realized it. An experienced and extremely qualified academic was offering to take charge of the academics, which would free me to deal with all the other issues.

In addition to Dr. Bourne, Dr. Golarz became our professor of histology, our first female faculty member. Nelly had a no-nonsense personality. She demanded respect. After she had been at the school for several months, she told me that she wanted to be the dean of women students. I doubt we had more than a dozen female students at that time, but she didn't care. That's what she wanted. "Okay," I told her, "you're the dean of women students."

Titles were less costly than raises, so I was open to consider such requests. But obviously they had to be earned. Vish Rao, for example, had proved to be an exceptional instructor. As a visiting journalist described him, "He gyrated on the stage to demonstrate the range of motion of the knee joint. He held the audience spellbound and used slides effectively." Any instructor who can hold an audience "spellbound" lecturing about the knee joint deserved a promotion. He was extremely well liked by the students. We had a lot of administrative positions to fill, so one day I suggested to him, "Dr. Rao, why don't you become the dean of students?"

He shook his head and told me he didn't know what that meant. "What is 'dean of students'?" Apparently, there was no position like that in the British system.

"It means you take care of the students," I explained. "Just like you're doing now. When they have a problem, they come to you for help. You talk to them. You are their advocate." I added, "You'll get a little more money for it too."

The concept intrigued him. "I'm a teacher—I'm supposed to take care of students. You're saying you'll pay me more money if I continue doing what I'm already doing?"

Well, not a lot more money. "That's right," I said brightly. "And you'll also have a title: Assistant Professor and Dean of Students."

"Oh no, Dr. Modica," he said, waving away that possibility. "I'm not qualified for that. You need an older, wiser, balding gentleman to do such things. I'm younger than many of the students."

I was kind enough not to point out that his hair was thinning. "Okay," I agreed, "you can be the associate dean." Our professor of neuroanatomy became dean of students, which was a bit of a problem because he remained very aloof. So, when students had a problem, they still went to Vish Rao.

Building a faculty was an ongoing odyssey. As we admitted in the very first school bulletin published in the summer of 1978, "Recuirting of faculty continues." That embarrassing typo reflected the situation: We were a new school founded on a new educational concept, we were making mistakes, but we were trying to get better. It was hard going. Though we were offering competitive salaries, we had no record. Serious, established academics didn't take us seriously. Others who might have been interested were concerned we were a dead end for their career. We were the antiestablishment, we were in the Caribbean, and most young academics were striving to become part of the establishment.

I also was beginning to discover that those instructors we were attracting often had the same underdog determination as our students. In several instances something had gone wrong in their career, and they were angry about it. They had something to prove. Yale graduate Dr. William McCord, for example, had been the president of the Medical College of South Carolina for a decade, presiding over a massive development program there, before being forced to retire. When he heard about St. George's, he contacted me to see if there was a place for him. Oh, there definitely was a place for him. When he was asked by one of our students why he had come to the school, he replied bluntly, "Those sons of bitches in Charleston fired me." He was as angry about that as our students were about their rejections. So rather than being put out to pasture, he came to the beach to teach. He became our dean of clinical studies and professor of medicine.

Dr. Robert George, who had been teaching anatomy at Brown University School of Medicine, battled an addiction to alcohol. He was open about it. I have no idea if that was why he was willing to give up his career there to join our faculty, but his illness never interfered with his teaching at our school. Everybody knew he drank—in fact one morning some students living in an off-campus apartment were surprised to find him passed out on their couch—but he was an inspiring teacher. Vish Rao always credited him with teaching him how to speak slowly and clearly, how to pause between sentences, as well as how to drink. He was a gifted teacher; students loved his classes. He also was a gifted medical artist and would draw illustrations on the chalkboard to emphasize his point. Students regularly brought cameras to class to photograph these technical drawings, then sent the film home to be developed so they could use the prints to prepare for tests.

But Bob George had an additional passion: Bigfoot. Bob was an expert on Bigfoot, or Sasquatch, the legendary bearlike creature who walked upright and supposedly inhabited North American forests. Students pushed him to lecture about Bigfoot, but he refused—until one day he announced, "I will not lecture about Sasquatch until I come in here and there is a keg of Carib [the local beer] on the podium!"

The lecture was scheduled for the following Saturday night. On a campus with only limited social prospects, on an island with one movie theater, this was the social event of the semester. The lecture itself was sort of mundane, but the keg made it truly enjoyable, and the night cemented Professor George's reputation forever.

Within very few years our faculty included instructors from some of the best universities in America—and Canada.

In late 1976 the New York Yankees had signed free agent Reggie Jackson, and that had made all the difference in their success. Geoffrey Bourne was our superstar signing. He made all the difference. He transformed our faculty from makeshift to world class with one idea: He created our unique visiting professor program, which allowed us to add numerous top professors and scientists to our faculty, people we otherwise never could have attracted or afforded. This was another out-of-necessity concept that we essentially pioneered that eventually became an accepted part of the medical education system.

I described the program in our second annual newsletter: "In most medical schools in the United States lectures have to be covered by the existing permanent staff whether they are experts or not in an area. At St. George's we can bring in an expert to lecture on every area.... Most visiting professors stay one or two weeks and give three to eight lectures...."

The visiting professor program began by coincidence. During the first semester some students relaxing on the beach met Dr. Burton Slotnick, a professor of psychology at American University; he was there on vacation with his family. They talked him into giving a lecture on behavioral science. It was just a casual invitation—"C'mon over and talk to us about what you do." At that time, Dr. Slotnick admitted, he was struck by the "incongruity of serious study in a situation that suggested relaxation and vacationing." He loved the whole idea, education in paradise, and was impressed by the charter class students who had "enormous faith that future developments would produce a complete medical program—even though very little was visible at the time."

Following that, a trickle of other professors came down to lecture, but until Dr. Bourne arrived, it was not any type of organized program. Making the visiting professor program an ongoing extension of our faculty was his idea. He had extensive contacts, he told me, and he suspected many highly qualified people would participate. I grabbed hold of the concept instantly. It made perfect sense for us. I have heard it said we did this out of desperation. I prefer to call it innovation. That's accurate too. I believed in our students. I believed if we provided the opportunity, they would turn it into success. But even with all the problems we'd encountered, I was not desperate enough to do anything that wasn't logical and smart.

We established a program that allowed department heads to bring down as many as six visiting instructors a semester from American schools to teach for a week or two. We had no difficulty attracting top people with our pitch: How would you like to be paid a nice stipend and all expenses to come to a beautiful Caribbean island and give a few lectures to intellectually engaged students?

We hit the jackpot almost immediately. Among our very first lecturers was two-time Nobel laurate Linus Pauling. He and Geoffrey Bourne apparently were old friends. For Pauling, it was the academic equivalent of Gordon Ramsay eating at McDonald's. To us, this was a legend stopping by to say a few words. He gave three lectures on viruses and his primary area of research, the mysteries of vitamin C. I remember a student telling me after one of those lectures, "I can't believe Linus fucking Pauling is here in Grenada in my lecture hall."

"I know," I agreed with equal enthusiasm, "I can't believe it either." At the end of his stay, Pauling told the students, "I am so honored to be down here, and I hope I can come back and be a visiting professor or work down here full time."

I interrupted, shouting out, "I have a contract right here if you want to sign it." I would have written it on a napkin if he was serious.

His presence greatly increased our visibility in the medical education world. By the fourth semester we had thirty-five distinguished professors, physicians, and scientists lecturing about their areas of expertise. Thank you, forever, Geoffrey Bourne.

Among those instructors were the authors of every textbook we were using. I thought it made great sense to have the person whose name was on the cover of their textbooks lecture our students about that subject.

Our students loved the idea: How many medical students could brag they had their embryology textbook signed by its author? My invitation to them pointed out that we were selling three times as many copies of their book as any American medical school because by the second semester we had as many as three times as many students as most med schools.

I also was smart enough to mention that we just happened to have several spots open in January and February. "Your lecture would fit best in February" were powerful words to a professor slogging through snow. Initially those were the only months we could get them to come. This was a perfect way to create a world-class faculty at an affordable rate. Among the early participants were Sir Douglas Black, the president of England's Royal College of Physicians; Sir Richard Bayliss, Queen Elizabeth's chief physician; Drs. Roy Greep and Aubrey Milunsky from Harvard; and Dr. Dennis Kelly from Columbia. They came from the best medical schools in the world, including Emory, Dartmouth, the University of Wisconsin, and Dublin's Royal College of Surgeons. They came from NASA's Ames Research Center and, naturally, Emory's Yerkes Center. They taught their specialties—Professor David Thomas of Scotland's University of St. Andrews, for example, lectured on blood in our histology course.

When they accepted our invitation, several of them later told me, they did so out of curiosity. They'd heard about this new school and wanted to know all about it. But what was gratifying is that after their first visit, almost all of them wanted to come back for a second, third, or fourth time. While obviously the opportunity to have family fun in the sun appealed to them, they also felt appreciated. Students often gave them a standing ovation at the end of a lecture, a response few of them had ever received at their institutions. We didn't ask our students to do that, by the way—it was completely spontaneous. They simply were expressing their appreciation.

Harvard's Dr. Greep told another journalist, "The students are quite a joy to teach.... It just raises the question, what is required for a good medical education? All they get here is teachers, textbooks, cadavers—yet they've got the material!"

University of London anatomy and histology professor F. R. Johnson wrote after his experience, "Not only did we enjoy your generous hospitality in such a glorious and relaxed environment [My note: Apparently some visitors got more running water than others] but I had the personal pleasure of meeting a group of students whose motivation and craving for knowledge made teaching a pleasure." One visiting professor, Dr. Keith Taylor, professor of gastroenterology at Stanford, educated at Oxford, came regularly and—due to his introduction to SGU by Geoffrey—many years later became the second vice chancellor, leading us into a transforming expansion with the development of the School of Arts and Sciences, the Research Institute, and the recruitment of students from across the globe. Another regular visiting professor, Dr. Edmond Fischer, a Nobel laureate in the physiology of medicine, eventually sat on the university's Academic Board for over twenty-five years along with other luminaries, all helping to fashion St. George's into an internationally respected school of medicine.

No matter where these people came from, no matter what they taught or their level of achievement, they all had one thing in common: They taught in English.

CHAPTER 11

Pushback

"We are uncertain about these schools' ability to provide basic science teaching, certain about their lack of hospital facilities for adequate clinical experience..."

—The Wall Street Journal

Several people who first came to Grenada as part of our visiting professor program eventually joined our full-time faculty. One cold December night in 1977, for example, Dr. Steve Weitzman was at home, reading a magazine, when his phone rang. Dr. Weitzman, an internist who specialized in infectious diseases, was at that time teaching microbiology to second-year students at New York's Stony Brook University School of Medicine. A biochemist with whom he worked at Stony Brook said, "Listen, Steve, I just got a call looking for someone to give a review course at this new medical school in Grenada, in the Caribbean. The guy who was supposed to do it got sick. Would you be willing to go down there to give them a crash course in microbiology to prepare them for the boards?"

The Caribbean? A completely unexpected invitation to spend a week in the Caribbean sun in the middle of December in New York, with all expenses paid and a $1,000 stipend for giving a few lectures? "Sure," he agreed. "I'll do it. Why not?"

"You don't have any ethical objections?"

Dr. Weitzman had no idea what the caller was talking about. Who had ethical objections against teaching medicine while avoiding a sunburn?

Steve Weitzman had never heard of St. George's, never heard of Grenada, and certainly had never heard of Charles Modica. And pretty much like everyone else, whatever he anticipated, the reality was less. He and his wife, Nancy, were given a room at Grand Anse, a room with intermittent running water and electricity. When it was suggested they fill a bucket with water in case they needed to use the bathroom, they instead checked into the nearby Spice Island Hotel, which boasted it had twenty-four-hour running water. So much for the stipend.

During his week there he taught several classes, and what surprised him most was the difference in attitude between the students he taught regularly and our students. "At Stony Brook there was a feeling of entitlement among the medical students," he explained. "I was giving an exam once, and I told them it wasn't a high-stakes test. Don't worry about it. They took me literally, and several of them failed. They got mad at me because they had failed, blaming me for misleading them. A female student pointed at me and said angrily, 'Weitzman, you're a real prick.'

"The St. George's students impressed me from my first lecture. They were motivated. They wanted to learn. They were responsive. They asked a lot of good questions. I immediately felt a connection with them. It was such a positive experience I introduced myself to Charles Modica and told him I'd like to stay involved if that was possible."

It was possible. He received the highest possible recommendation. Danny Ricciardi told me, "Modica, hire Weitzman. He knows what he's talking about."

The following year we made arrangements for both our charter class and the Super Eights to spend their fifth semester on the neighboring island of St. Vincent to prepare for their clinical training. That semester was another unique aspect of our program created out of necessity. We asked Steve Weitzman to be part of it. To his surprise he encountered opposition from his colleagues in New York. He was warned, "Weitzman, you're crazy. You're going to ruin your career." Another person shook his head in disbelief and asked, "My God, how could you go there? It's run by a lawyer!" That, I suspect, was intended to be the ultimate insult.

Weitzman paid no attention to those suggestions, instead becoming more involved with the school until his dean at Stony Brook finally objected. "You can't continue doing this," he told him, showing him that school's bylaws, which prohibited employees from working as a consultant without express permission. Permission, he made clear, that would not be granted.

"That's when I decided, I'm out of here," Weitzman recalls. It was a courageous decision—he was opening a small private practice at that time, and this meant giving up his primary source of income. "My practice had a total of three patients. I don't know why I wasn't more concerned, but it was the right thing to do."

Dr. Weitzman eventually became our chairman of the Department of Medicine and dean of clinical studies before serving as our dean of the School of Medicine during two decades of rapid growth.

While the concept of a visiting instructor program wasn't new, no school had ever used it as extensively as we did to complete our faculty. "Our physiology course was taught by a parade of visiting professors," remembers Philip Lahrman. "Month after month they would come down, one after another, teaching that segment in which they were expert. Once we got used to the concept it worked really well. We were learning from the same teachers as students at America's best medical schools. Most of the teachers were excited about being there and took nothing for granted."

Many schools frowned upon their professors participating in our program, but the lure of sun, sand, and teaching excited, engaged students in midwinter was tough to fight. These visiting instructors became our best ambassadors. They would return to their institutions and tell their colleagues about this pugnacious new school on a tropical island, where classes were taught in English and the students were welcoming, smart, and serious about learning. As a result, we began getting inquiries from other instructors asking for an invitation. Our list grew quickly.

Obviously not every instructor was great. There were people who considered this a free vacation and didn't take it seriously. Some of them didn't even bother showing up for their scheduled classes or labs, and, as Danny told us, there also were some "pet rocks." Overall, though, the quality was high and the instructors were professional. Within two years we had a waiting list of well-qualified teachers, and we actually were turning down the majority of requests.

Not surprisingly, John Cooper, the president of the Association of American Medical Colleges, attacked the concept, complaining publicly about our "circuit-riding professors" as opposed to the traditional "large resident faculty." I understood that; he had to protect his member schools with well-paid professors who taught one or maybe two courses a year.

Two years after essentially starting the program, Burton Slotnick returned, this time as a scheduled lecturer on medical psychology. In that brief time the school had grown significantly. The first time he was there we had five buildings, histology classes were taught in a converted hotel laundry room, and we didn't have an anatomy lab. When he returned we had a new state-of-the-art neuroanatomy facility with twenty-one tables. We didn't have a library then—we didn't need one because we only had about a dozen books—but I'd purchased a sixteen-thousand-volume medical library from a New York medical institute that was going out of business and constructed a building to house it. The library was our first new building.

On Slotnick's first visit, transportation between True Blue and Grand Anse was haphazard, meaning basically either get a bike or remember that walking is good for you, but since then we'd set up a reasonably reliable shuttle service between the two sites.

Dr. Slotnick admitted he was surprised that the program had not only been sustained but had grown significantly in both numbers and quality. He said he was especially pleased we were using the same textbooks as the best American medical schools rather than the easier alternatives. And finally, he agreed with our philosophy: It required only a relatively small faculty to present a solid medical education—if all the faculty members did was teach. The first two years in Grenada, he said, were as good as some schools in the States—and better than many.

"The school has everything in hand," he concluded.

If he only knew.

When we accepted our charter class, the American medical establishment had ignored us. If they even recognized our existence, they considered us nothing more serious than a yawn, assuming we would disappear quickly without leaving any evidence of our brief existence. But as we established our footprint, they had to pay attention to us—and how the deficiencies in the system were now being overtly exposed.

They had spent decades telling the American public their paradigm that educating doctors was a highly complex process that of necessity had to be limited to very few selected students. Now this upstart school on some island nobody had ever heard of somewhere in the Caribbean was pulling back the curtain. And they were not happy about it.

The fact that some of their best professors were bringing attention and the prestige of their institutions to St. George's made the situation even more troublesome. It's impossible to determine precisely when the American medical establishment first considered us a challenge to their long-held beliefs and began its effort to contest our model. As soon as our visiting faculty program took hold, for example, the Association of American Medical Colleges circulated a memo to all medical schools warning instructors against being exploited by "a number of medical schools of questionable quality." This memo urged academics to verify the legitimacy of a school before agreeing to lecture there, without defining "legitimacy." It certainly was a fair warning, but the implication was clear: While we weren't specifically identified, the fact that this was done just as our program was taking hold made it obvious why it was done. The result was that several professors who had accepted our offer canceled their scheduled lectures.

In addition, just as Stony Brook had done to Steve Weitzman, some institutions were prohibiting faculty members from participating in our program. I understood that too; in many cases they were paying these people significant salaries, and we were using their association with these institutions to greatly enhance our own credibility. We didn't have Harvard's faculty, obviously, but in our bulletin we could—and did—identify our lecturers as members of Harvard's faculty, or any of the other prestigious schools.

But it was difficult to understand their animosity. We certainly weren't a threat to them; we were accepting the students they had already rejected. In fact, Andy and I told everyone who applied, if you can get into an American medical school, go there. Run there. The path to a career in medicine is much easier.

They attacked us by claiming St. George's graduates were less qualified. That was ridiculous: To practice medicine in the States, our students had to pass exactly the same examinations as any other foreign applicant, the same exams all those young doctors from Europe and India working in hospitals had taken and passed. A representative of the AAMC, speaking about the proliferation of Caribbean medical schools that had sprung up after us, told the *Wall Street Journal*, "We are uncertain about these schools' ability to provide basic science teaching, certain about their lack of hospital facilities for adequate clinical experience…"

Those are legitimate concerns. Admittedly there are medical schools all over the world, including in the Caribbean, that should be questioned. But they failed to differentiate us from them. They bunched all foreign medical schools together, spreading the inaccurate impression that our standards were less than American schools and our students were somehow inferior.

That was unfair. I came to believe that they actually were more concerned about the competition than the quality. Some so-called experts were predicting there would be a glut of physicians within a decade. To prevent that, the number of available clinical positions in hospitals already was limited. As the American Medical Association's assistant director of undergraduate evaluation and standards claimed, "It appears there will be enough American-trained doctors for our needs, although there is a problem with their geographic distribution. The number of first-year [hospital] residencies is rapidly being filled by American graduates…." In other words, they were concerned our students would take clinical slots reserved for their graduates, while at the same time admitting an uncomfortable reality—rural communities were already having difficulty attracting young doctors.

They could not have been more wrong. The reality is that forty-plus years later, according to the AAMC, the United States has a shortage of doctors. Even they admit the country needs somewhere between 90,000 and 130,000 more physicians.

In fact, the pushback was a lot about control. The medical establishment had established the medical system and maintained absolute control of it. That establishment liked things just the way they were and didn't want to be challenged. They took whatever steps necessary to protect the member schools. The possibility that a new medical school located on a Caribbean island could educate and graduate qualified physicians, doctors often every bit as good as those American schools were producing, seemed incredible to them. The fewer people who could work outside the system, the better it was for the system. In part these attacks on us, as I told a reporter for *Newsday*, "was about control of the supply of doctors."

Among the first of the many legal challenges we had to deal with came from the New York State attorney general's office . The AG suggested we had committed fraud by listing all members of our faculty, both full-time and visiting instructors, in our first student handbook without differentiating between them. That was true, I had done that, but it was an unintentional oversight that we quickly corrected in a newsletter published several months later. But the AG's office opened a fraud investigation, literally writing to every faculty member listed in our first student handbook asking about "the nature of their participation." When they received almost unanimously positive responses, they quietly dropped the investigation. No charges were ever brought against us.

But the conflict between St. George's and the American medical establishment was just beginning. We would disagree with them over many issues in the future. And we had yet to graduate our first doctor.

CHAPTER 12

Island Life

"We're working on it."

—Me, a lot

There was one trait that every one of our students had to have in common—you really had to want it. I was depending on that. Grenada is an island paradise and a wonderful place to vacation, but at that time it was a hard place to go to medical school. When students complained, I would tell them in my usual optimistic manner, "It makes you a lot tougher. It prepares you for dealing with unexpected situations you're going to encounter in your career."

The truth is, it did. It definitely was character-building.

Jack Cush tells this story about one of the nine women in his class. While the practice of medicine at that time was not exclusively male, female doctors were still a rarity. And the profession was much tougher on women than men. "There was one woman who was very shy when classes began. She was a passive person who rarely raised her hand in class. I don't think I ever heard her raise her voice. We became friends. She occasionally expressed doubts about her ability.

"Fast-forward seven years. We were in our third year of residency in the same hospital. I was chief resident—imagine that? Chief resident from a brand-new, wacky idea of a medical school outside of the country! And she was senior resident. I rounded a corner one day and there she was. She looked very professional and very sharp—and she had a surgeon pinned against the wall. She was poking him in the chest, telling him loudly, 'You are going to do that damned biopsy or I'm going to have your ass. And don't you dare tell me no. . . .' The transformation was unbelievable. I've always attributed that to the time we spent on the island."

One giant hurdle that I hadn't been able to solve during those first few years was how to place our students in hospitals for the last two years of their training. Without that experience they couldn't be licensed. I was up front with our students: I couldn't guarantee they would get a clinical slot in the States. They had nothing but my promise they would be able to take the American licensing exams.

I never stopped working on it, trying to figure it out. Meanwhile, I continued meeting regularly with them in my three-piece suit; it was my light-at-the-end-of-the-tunnel period. My go-to answer about most questions and complaints continued to be, "We're working on it." But still, those students would warn other people planning on coming down from JFK in New York, "Just don't look back. If you do you may stay there."

Living in Grenada was an adventure. Not always a good adventure, but always interesting. It's important to remember how many decades ago this was, when formerly dependent colonies were emerging as independent nations. Whatever preconceptions anyone had about being on a beautiful Caribbean island, with magnificent beaches and balmy weather, were quickly discarded. Only someone like Henry Collins, who had worked in a poor third-world village in the Peace Corps, had anything to which it might be compared.

In reality, other than a few incidents the island was actually quite safe. Violent crime is just not part of the culture. In fact, periodically the police would put groups of prisoners to work cutting the brush. Demonstrating how different this culture was from the States, the police supervising them would be unarmed—while the prisoners were carrying machetes.

The first two classes shaped the future of the school. It started with housing and food. We lacked sufficient dorm space for more than one class, so as the second class arrived, we let the charter class rent their own housing. As one student admitted, "It wasn't bad. I went from a bedroom in my parents' house to my own shack on a Caribbean island."

There actually was a lot of housing available on Grenada. Property owners were happy to find tenants. I leased several small cottages around the island, which I then rented to students basically for whatever they could afford.

Believe me, I didn't make any money on this. In some cases, if I knew the student was struggling, I had to negotiate down. Rudy and Ruth Antoncic found a small cottage that had been built as temporary housing years earlier, temporary apparently being defined as meaning "still standing." Instead of windows it had wood shutters. Running water consisted of a pipe coming out of the ground just outside the house. There was a mudhole in the yard infested with worms and maggots. Ruth had put up with a lot the first semester, but this was too much. "I don't think that's good," she told Rudy, referring to the maggot-filled mudhole. But the rent was only $150 a month. They didn't have much choice.

When I heard about it from one of Rudy's classmates, I offered them one of the small houses I'd rented in a middle-class community. The rent, I told them, was whatever they felt was fair. They offered $300 a month. I turned that down, telling them that I would not take a cent more than $150. But I also insisted on a guarantee that Rudy would stay and graduate. That's what we settled for. I thought it was a good deal for us; I considered it an investment in the future of the school. If we were going to survive, we needed to send people like Rudy into the medical world to prove we could educate doctors.

Students found housing all over the island. While much of it was small and shabby, there also were villas overlooking the harbor, places with pools and other amenities. Grenadians were living there on only a few dollars a day, so nothing was extremely expensive. Frankie Arbucci and several of Da Boys rented a place called L'Anse Aux Epines Estate, essentially an eight-acre estate with a beautiful fieldstone house at the tip of a peninsula. "When you opened the front or back doors," he describes it, "you were looking at the ocean. We had a fifty-foot swimming pool. Sundecks on the roof. A driver, a gardener, and a cook. The prime minister lived down the road. The whole thing was $350 a month." With running water.

Another group got a similarly good deal. A reputed gangster from New Jersey supposedly had embezzled millions of dollars and built a beautiful house on top of a mountain with a commanding view. Which I suspect was essential. The group that rented it referred to it, perhaps appropriately, as "the Big House."

Those few great houses obviously were the exception. Most students rented considerably smaller places. Paul Vallone, for example, lived in a place called "the Flamboyant Arms," which was, as he explains, "quite an exaggeration. It was anything but flamboyant. We didn't even have a front door. Literally. One day I came home from class and found a cow, an actual cow, in my living room. Local people would let their cows and goats graze on the grass, and this cow obviously had wandered into the house and sat down. But by then we were so used to unusual things happening that we just shrugged it off and accepted the fact that there was a cow in our living room.

"We just couldn't let something like that fluster us. When I went back to the States, my friends would kid me about how tough it must be to study on a beautiful beach. I'd ask them, 'Don't you want to hear about the cow in my living room?'"

Several students rented apartments from the Bishop family. Maurice Bishop, the leader of the opposition political party then—who unbeknownst to us was actively planning a coup—would come around personally to collect the rent.

Some students survived by couch surfing. David Baras and Mary Jo Koestner, who was in the Peace Corps working in Grenada as a nutritionist at the hospital, met and fell in love but couldn't find a suitable place to stay. "We carried all our possessions in a duffel bag each," Mary Jo recalls. "That made it easy to move around. Our classmates were very obliging; they'd let us sleep on a couch or in their garage. When diplomats left town some of them allowed us to use their place. We were the go-to house sitters. Somehow it worked for us."

Off-campus housing not only was necessary, it proved very beneficial for the school. It forced our students to live among the residents. Rather than being an isolated outpost, the school and our students became part of the community. The trust and bonds that eventually made a difference in our success were created. And so were jobs. Lots of jobs. In addition to the people directly employed by the school and the money we put into the island economy, students could afford to hire local workers to clean and cook for them since wages on the island were so low.

While in most instances that proved mutually beneficial, on occasion there were culture clashes. Ricciardi and his roommates came back to their rented house one afternoon to find their housekeeper, Clydie, with a broom in one hand and a wet cloth in the other, forcefully sweeping the ceiling as if trying to knock off bugs. But there were no bugs. The next day they came home and she was doing the same thing. When they got home the third day, they found her sitting in a chair in their driveway, surrounded by several people as a local priest pronounced incantations.

It was an exorcism. Apparently, she had been seeing apparitions in their house. Ligaroo, a werewolf; Anansi, the spider; and La Diablesse, the devil-woman, were all part of Grenadian folklore, although why they were in Danny's house was never determined. After that day, though, it was Clydie who never returned. Admittedly this type of thing was rare. The practice of voodoo had taken root in Haiti, and there were pockets of it on other Caribbean islands, but few people on Grenada took it seriously. Clydie was one of the few. It figures that she saw the apparitions in Danny's house.

It also took us some time to figure out how to feed our students. For several years the phrase students would use to describe the situation in Grenada to family and friends was a grim, "They don't even have a McDonalds." Well, we also did not have a Dunkin' Donuts, Wendy's, Arby's, Red Lobster, or any other popular chains. What might charitably be described as our "cafeteria" was on the True Blue campus, which meant that those students at Grand Anse had to travel a couple of miles for every meal. Those meals were supplied by a local company, and if good intentions were edible we would have done fine. Unfortunately our students preferred actual food.

Meals consisted of local foods few of our people had ever seen before. If you liked callaloo soup, for example, you would have been happy, but most people saw it as a kind of green, lumpy mystery. Some of those students, probably accurately, optimistically described our meal plan as a "weight-loss program." Chuck Schwartz remembers going home after the first semester having lost twenty-five pounds. "My mother took one look at me," he says, "and started crying."

Martin Kane recalls that blood sausage was served at one of the first meals. "It was big, fat, and greasy. It came out on a plate with some strange fruit, or maybe it was a vegetable that none of us could identify. No one ate it. I take credit for starting the infamous food fight. What we learned that day is that the best thing about blood sausage is that it travels well airborne."

There was an outdoor cooking area at Grand Anse; it previously had been the hotel bar. It had two ovens, one of them reserved for the use of our Orthodox Jewish students—the God Squad as they called themselves—to keep kosher, and a pit with a grill over it. Students would cook on this grill every night, and then, amazingly, when they came down in the morning, the grill would be sparkling clean. The students assumed housekeeping was cleaning it every night.

We didn't have housekeeping.

That comforting thought disappeared very early one morning when a student went down for coffee and discovered two cats happily licking the grill clean.

The mandatory food plan caused a lot of unhappiness. Ironically, though, the food fight—which was rapidly assuming legendary status—had released a lot of frustration and helped bond the class together. Unfortunately, it bonded the class together against me. At one of my first meetings with the students someone said to me, "An army travels on its stomach. How are we supposed to study when we're not getting fed food?"

"We're working on it" was the best response I could give them, and that was true. When I began reminding them once again about the light at the end of the tunnel, someone shouted out (I believe it was Ricciardi), "Hey Dr. Modica, nobody cares about that light unless you can eat it."

That rule about having to participate in the meal plan disappeared pretty quickly.

Looking back on it today, from a sprawling modern campus on an island offering all the facilities and amenities available anywhere else in the region, it's amazing what those first classes were able to accomplish. Grenada was a new nation, still recovering from its former status as an often overlooked member of the British Commonwealth. The school was among the first businesses to make a serious commitment there, and we grew together.

"We shared everything," Jack Cush said. "That's what made it work. Everybody was homesick together; everybody was miserable together. It was like the Billy Joel song: We all stand together. We were in this battle together. In that brotherhood we found the strength and support we needed."

But there was a lot of room for growth. While there were some very good restaurants on the island, the most comfortable places catered to tourists and were prohibitively expensive for most of our students. It was amazing to watch our people improvise. I wasn't kidding when I claimed living on the island would teach students how to problem-solve. TV's MacGyver would have been happy there. Students often got together in study groups, or sometimes party groups. One student, for example, found himself cooking pasta for about twenty people. Pasta was very popular because it was inexpensive and filling. He had everything going just right until it became time to drain the water. He had no strainer, no implement for draining it. He came up with a unique solution. He poured the several pounds of pasta into a pillowcase, waited for the water to drain out the bottom, and put the pasta back in the pot—and none of his guests ever knew about it.

The few wives that had come down with their husbands took responsibility for feeding a lot of people. "Family-style eating," they called it. It required a lot of sharing. They baked bread and pizza from scratch. One of them made a yogurt culture that was left outside, and wives would take a small sample and grow their own yogurt. There is no doubt that without the support of these women, several of our students would not have made it through. They were an incredible group, as much a part of our success as their husbands.

But it was especially tough on these women: Several of them had left thriving careers—and they expected to be able to find employment on the island. The problem was that the government would not permit them to work; they didn't want them taking jobs away from Grenadians. That made some sense, obviously, but for many couples the lack of that income was an additional hardship, and it left the wives with a lot of time on their hands.

Some of that time was spent food shopping. Shopping was an event. They would walk several miles back and forth to a local grocery store, which might or might not have what they needed. Ruth Antoncic had grown up in a large family in rural Wisconsin and took great pride in being self-sufficient. "In Wisconsin we bartered with farmers or grew what we needed in our backyard," she recalled. "I thought I would be able to do that when we got to Grenada. I knew it was a tropical country, so I assumed I could grow what we needed. I can have a garden, I thought, that'd be wonderful.

"It didn't work out that way. Where we were was like a desert. It was very dry. We ended up scratching for everything. There were times we couldn't get eggs. We couldn't get tomatoes. Sometimes it made no sense: This was the land of sugarcane, and we couldn't get sugar. How could that be? Those items we could get were very expensive because it had to be shipped from Canada or Australia. We definitely ate a lot of rice and bananas, coconuts, and fish. When I was fortunate enough to buy a box of green bananas, we would eat them in every possible way for a month. I fried them like potato chips. I boiled them like potatoes. Our Grenadian neighbors taught me how to cook all the local dishes."

We were on an island, so fish was readily available. All types of fish prepared every possible way: fried, fileted, broiled, grilled, spiced. Also, although we know better now, we ate the local favorite, turtle eggs. Some students claimed they had never eaten healthier in their lives; others claimed that after two years there they would never eat fish again.

Many students received "care" packages from home, and anyone coming back to the island from the States would bring back "delicacies" like peanut butter, canned white tuna, Kraft macaroni and cheese, and cereal.

Americans had to get used to living without a market or bodega on every corner. Once a month, for example, a local butcher would take an ad in the paper announcing that he intended to slaughter a cow. People would rush to the place to be there early in the morning. A long line outside the local food fair generally meant a load of potatoes had arrived.

Maybe the best way of describing our food plan is to state, flatly, nobody starved. Somehow, it worked. Although no one was happy about the situation, they all got nutrition. Basically, people ate what was available. Henry Collins remembers his first date with the woman he eventually married: "I made dinner for her. We had poached eggs on crackers with some cheese. I went outside and cut a lime off a bush and squeezed it on the cheese. That was it."

There also was not a variety of entertainment options to fill their free time, which wasn't much of a problem because students didn't have a lot of free time. "When we wanted to take a break," Ed Hall remembers, "there were very few things to do. The library got a few newspapers. Getting the Sunday *New York Times* two weeks late was a big deal."

For some students religion played a role. We had a group of Orthodox Jewish students, and we made whatever provisions for them that we could. At Passover they hosted seders and invited classmates to join them. Many did. For several students, like Jack Cush, the church became an important place to find some peace. "I wasn't religious. I hadn't gone to church on a regular basis at home. I was Catholic more by birth than by practice. There was a Catholic church in Grand Anse, and going there made a difference for me. It gave me the opportunity to sit quietly and think about what was important, about what mattered. I was on this island and I was homesick, and I would go to that church and the Mass was familiar, the structure was familiar, the words were familiar.

"And the music was unbelievable. There was a steel drum and maybe two guitars, once maybe a piano. They sung; some of the songs I knew, some of them I learned. It was uplifting. I would bring my roommates. It made a difference."

It was remarkable how dedicated these students were. Part of that, undoubtedly, was the awareness that the better they did on the tests, the more opportunity they might have to transfer into an American medical school. That was a major goal, and we encouraged that. We wanted them to transfer to the same schools that had originally rejected them. That was proof of our founding principle: These students were every bit as qualified as the selected sixteen thousand.

We also knew that the more of our students who were able to transfer into those schools, the more desirable it made us as a starting place. Come here, go there. So, they studied. As one student admitted, "My biggest problem had always been not being focused enough. Fortunately, on Grenada I could have been as unfocused as hell and still got six hours of study in every day."

As beautiful as the beaches are, there was a limited amount of time people wanted to spend on them. There was a drive-in movie theater not far from the school, but because few students had cars it became a walk-in theater. They would go on a Friday or Saturday night with beach chairs, blankets, and cold beer. Most of the films were British and often more than five years old. At times the projectionist would show the reels in the wrong order, which in some cases resulted in a very different story. One movie that was especially popular was *Star Wars*. As Martin Kane described it: "As I sat there on a bench, the screen and the sky and the stars above and around me all blended together, reinforcing the universal theme of the movie. It was surreal." But the drive-in was popular; it was a pleasant escape for a few hours…except for the bats of course.

Bats were attracted to the bright screen and would dart back and forth in front of it. Eventually we all got used to it. We got used to everything.

There was no television available from the States, so I bought a twenty-one-inch TV and we created a TV room. Every time I went down, I'd bring a video of the latest *Saturday Night Live* with me. That TV room was so small we had to schedule viewing sessions. Radio was the background music of our lives, the connection to home. The most popular stations were "the big RA!"—Radio Antilles—and FM Radio Trinidad, which played American music. RT carried Casey Kasem's *American Top 40*. The Grenadian radio station played local music and news, but the programming wasn't very sophisticated. For example, the wife of one of our students, Mary Jo Koestner, hosted a daily five-minute program on the station during which she offered nutritional tips. Among its most popular programs was the late-afternoon obituary show, on which they reported who had died on the island and told listeners a little about them.

Several students had shortwave radios and would sit outside at night listening to superstations in New York, St. Louis, Chicago, and Canada. When a major event was taking place in the States, students would run speaker wire up the flagpole in the center of the True Blue campus and attach it to a transistor radio. That enabled them to listen to the World Series or the Super Bowl. Armed Forces Radio broadcast two NFL games each weekend, so naturally one of our students created "the Mango Bowl," a betting pool on pro football.

Radio also was the primary source for world news. Iranian Nasir Jahdi, for example, was listening to the BBC one afternoon when it announced the shah had been deposed and mullahs had taken control of his country. "It was very difficult sitting there on this beautiful island so helplessly as this was taking place. Every afternoon I was tuning in that radio to hear what was happening in my home: which generals were being executed, which senators were being executed, what was happening to people I knew." The remoteness of Grenada could be a blessing or a curse for students, depending on what was happening at home.

The weather made it a great place for physical activities. Students would go hiking, jogging, and sailing. They would swim, surf, snorkel, or scuba dive. I had a small powerboat and would take a group of them waterskiing in Secret Harbor.

There were two beaches near campus named for their proximity: the Five Minute Beach and the Twenty Minute Beach. The Caribbean was so crystal clear that Chuck Schwartz was able to find his wife's diamond engagement ring after she dropped it in waist-high water.

Almost by definition this was a competitive group—some students competed to see how many mice they could catch—but mostly they participated in sports. Tennis was popular, and the students semi-organized basketball, baseball, soccer, and even rugby leagues. When the Cubans arrived after the Grenada Revolution in 1979, Cuban workers would join the baseball and basketball games. The baseball field was laid out in a cow pasture, which became a bit of a problem because it was a cow pasture. Which meant it was shared with cows. Someone had brought hockey sticks, and (mostly) Canadian students played street hockey on the tennis courts. Some of our people ran in the Grenadian marathon and competed against the Grenadian national water polo team in the harbor.

Joe Nossiff remembers running in one race and as he got near the finish line, he realized he was running neck and neck with a nine-year-old. "With about fifty yards to go, I began sprinting as fast as I possibly could. I finished way back in the pack—but at least I beat the nine-year-old." Our ping-pong table was continually in use. People converted empty paint cans into weights. Here's something I didn't know—a one-gallon paint can filled with sand weighs about three pounds, but filled with concrete it becomes a twenty-pound weight.

Music filled a lot of gaps. One of Da Boys, Warren Stanton, had real talent. On many evenings he'd sit on the low cement retaining wall between the beach and the dorms at Grand Anse playing his guitar. Danny Ricciardi had grown up in Brooklyn with music producer Jimmy Iovine, who was working as a recording engineer for artists like John Lennon and Bruce Springsteen and later founded Interscope Records and signed Tupac Shakur. Danny arranged for Stanton to audition for Iovine in his Central Park South apartment. Warren sang several love songs he had written. The next day he and Danny laid down six tracks at Iovine's Jersey City recording studio. Perhaps because Stanton was far more serious about medicine than music, nothing came of that. But he did make news among his classmates: Late one night he was driving his motorcycle back to campus. He was on a dark road and for some reason did not have his headlights on—and became the first member of his class to collide with a cow.

Stanton was only one of several members of the charter class who actually had talent outside of schoolwork. Or who believed they had talent. Among the most popular shows on American TV at the time was *The Gong Show*, a program on which people mostly without talent performed sometimes bizarre acts until the judges banged a giant gong, ending their appearance. It was hosted by Chuck Barris, so naturally our David Baras staged our own version in the dome. It was a very big deal.

First prize was a case of Carib beer. Second prize also was a case of Carib beer. And third prize was a case of Carib beer. The lighting and effects were created by Fleetwood Mac roadie Duncan Brown, so the show looked professional. It attracted about five hundred people, almost the entire school, with the profits going to a fund to help pay for heart surgery for a Grenadian child. Among the memorable performers was Emmitt Cox, one of our African American students with a deep, beautiful voice, who was backed up by several dancing girls.

Our *Gong Show*, which became a staple of student life for many years, and increasingly became an uproarious roast of members of the faculty and administration, added to the growing camaraderie among the early classes. Initially they were in survival mode: They lived together, studied together, shopped and sang songs together. They established a structure and pioneered traditions like the Sand Blast, a large beach party at the end of the semester. They were survivors taking advantage of a last chance.

The only thing they had in common was the fact that they had been rejected by multiple medical schools, and that was a sensitive issue. In fact, in the middle of the first semester, the charter class had a conference to talk about that. As Robert Rudawsky remembers, "We decided as a group that we would never be known as medical-school rejects; instead we were international medical students in the English language. It was an organized, conscious, dedicated effort to brand ourselves as something different than what everyone knew we really were, which was American medical-school rejects."

The first classes also were bound together by pranks and near tragedy—among them the creation of the legendary Caribbean Cowboy. Duncan Brown always wore a cowboy hat. Always. That was his personal style. He had returned to the States for Christmas break. While he was back home, several people who stayed behind, among them Francis McGill and Tim Ashby, apparently had too much free time. They circulated a professional-looking press release announcing that Clint Eastwood and the famous actor Duncan Brown were coming to Grenada to film a new movie, *The Caribbean Cowboy*. It was supposed to be a little joke played on their friend Brown. The local newspaper got a copy of the press release and printed it. Unfortunately—there's that word again—a government minister read it and believed it. Always looking for ways to promote the island, completely unannounced, he went to Pearls Airport to meet the LIAT flight on which the famous actor Duncan Brown was arriving. He also had organized a small welcoming committee. This was a big event for a small country.

Also meeting that flight were Ashby, playing the role of the governor-general, and Fran McGill, playing the character "Lady Delise," wearing a long dress and quite large hat. Another student, Bob Bryden, was filming the famous actor Duncan Brown's arrival. They also had recruited several Grenadians, who were carrying large signs welcoming the Caribbean Cowboy; they had been instructed to cheer when he got off the plane.

Apparently, there also was a horse involved.

It was supposed to be a little prank, just a bunch of our kids having some fun. No different than the type of stuff that happens on every campus. Duncan Brown knew absolutely nothing about any of this. Neither did I, at least until I received an angry phone call from the government official's office. As a general rule, it is never a good idea to get an important official involved in a prank. He was upset, very upset.

"What do you know about this?" he demanded.

"Nothing," I said honestly.

I was warned in very clear terms that nothing like this must ever happen again.

The near tragedy took place one afternoon when Emmitt Cox, the singing "star" of the St. George's *Gong Show*, and two other students were riding their bicycles back to Grand Anse from True Blue. Emmitt was married, and his wife was eight months pregnant. The bike riders turned a blind corner to see, according to the local newspaper, a Toyota HiAce commuter minivan "traveling in the opposite direction at a high speed." Two of the bikers swerved out of the way, but Emmitt was hit head-on. News of the accident spread rapidly throughout the school.

Joan Mack, one of the few students who had a car, raced to the scene with Linda Klokow and Rudy Antoncic. Incredibly, Gary Lombardi, who was a passenger in the minivan, had been one of New York City's first paramedics before becoming a student. Rudy had been a physician's assistant and Joan had taken anatomy courses in dental school, so they knew how to triage.

They went to work tending to the injuries so Emmitt could be transported to the hospital. They then gently lifted him into Joan's Ford Escort and raced to St. George's General Hospital. Two members of our faculty, our Grenadian associate dean of clinical studies Dr. Ethelstan Friday and Dr. Morrie Alpert, assisted by John Madden, who had been a physician's assistant in New York, operated for three hours. They successfully stabilized him, though it was a difficult operation. When Madden ordered an array of X-rays so they could determine the full extent of Cox's injuries, he was told by a nurse, "We only have three or four X-ray plates." He decided to get X-rays of his neck, pelvis, and chest. Without the additional X-rays, they had to guess the extent of his fractures. They splinted his extremities.

It was clear we needed to get him to a better-equipped hospital.

There were few phones on the island, but Joan found one and called me. We arranged for an air ambulance to fly Emmitt to Miami as soon as possible.

When Emmitt's classmates heard about the accident, many of them gathered at the hospital to lend support. The following morning Alpert and Madden flew with him to Florida. During the flight Madden had to give him two units of blood. Emmitt was in very bad shape, but he indicated to Madden that he needed to write something down. Madden handed him a pencil and the paper wrapping from inside sterile gloves.

Emmitt scrawled a message for his classmates: "I'll be back."

I'll be back. After several months and numerous operations in a Miami hospital, he was transferred to UCLA. Eventually he recovered and continued his medical studies in California, becoming a noted orthopedic surgeon. His accident helped the class unite and reinforced the growing school spirit.

Following that, though, we did require our students to have health insurance. We also began a program to significantly upgrade St. George's General Hospital. Our first two years there we donated more than half a million dollars in modern equipment, including two hundred hospital beds, a spectrometer, surgical instruments, microscopes, and a new X-ray machine—and lots of X-ray film. No one would ever again be denied X-rays because of a film shortage.

With our assistance a completely new hospital facility opened in 2002—and every citizen of Grenada today has more options than ever for their health care.

But this was taking place in an essentially undeveloped paradise. In whatever free time our students did have, they found time to lead a social life. This definitely was not a party school—nobody went there to have a good time—but there was so much stress on students to succeed that when an opportunity to relax presented itself, they took advantage of it. So there were parties that ended with unexplained footprints on ceilings. Friendships and relationships, many of which have lasted a lifetime, were formed. Other relationships broke up.

There were so few women in the first classes that the men looked elsewhere for companionship. Actually, everywhere. Some students dated Grenadian women. Cruise ships arrived twice a week and Air France had several flights weekly, so students dated women working on the ships or flight attendants. Wives and girlfriends would visit regularly. Life happened: One student's wife came down to be with him and left with his roommate. Raz Giliberti met his future wife when she came to Grenada with her best friend to visit her friend's brother.

Pressure is what turns coal into diamonds, and medical students into good doctors. Added to the normal stresses of medical school, our students had to deal with a lack of predictability. Would the school stay open? Was the education they were getting sufficient? Would they be prepared for national tests? Would they even be allowed to take those tests? And always, what happens next? Would they be able to get residencies in the United States? When is the electricity going to be turned back on? Was all of this just an expensive waste of time?

That stress put a lot of people under a lot of pressure for a long time, and the inevitable result would be many diamonds, but stress can also create cracks. Even under the best circumstances, when you bring two hundred or more people together, many of them will not get along. That happened. There were fights. A few marriages did break up. We had exactly the same problems that will occur whenever you bring together a large group of people, then added the stress of a start-up medical school.

Without question the students' children enjoyed the lifestyle most. Unlike their parents, they had no basis for comparison. There weren't many of them, and we hadn't made arrangements for them, but the kids proved to be far more flexible and resilient than their parents. They adapted. Older children either attended Grenadian schools or were homeschooled, while younger kids led what they later described as a Mad Max existence. "My brother and I were like two mongooses," Josh Antoncic recalls. "My mother likes to remind me that I would always complain when we went shopping. 'Mom,' I explained, 'I was four years old and we had to walk two miles carrying groceries.'"

But kids are kids. Among Josh Antoncic's first memories is setting the hill behind their rental house on fire. That became a problem when his parents discovered they didn't have a working hose. Fortunately, their neighbors were able to hook up a hose and extinguish the fire. "Life for a kid there was wonderful," he recalled. "I never thought about putting on shoes. For lunch we would go out back and pick a mango off a tree. I was in the forest one day and I saw someone hunting iguanas with a bow and arrow. 'I'm getting lunch,' he told me, then killed one right in front of me. He cooked it right there. Imagine being that kid and living that life."

One of the things kids liked to do was go frog hunting. There was never a shortage of frogs. During a hunt one afternoon, five-year-old Josh tripped and fell into the deep end of the empty swimming pool. He hit his head and was knocked unconscious. Fortunately, several students were right there to lift him out of the pool. While not close to the severity of Emmitt Cox's accident, he obviously required medical attention. He could not have been in a better place for that: When he opened his eyes, six anxious medical students were hovering over him ready to practice what they had learned.

Josh lived in Grenada for a year before returning to the States, and after that experience, as he admits, it took him some time to acclimate: "When we finally returned to Pittsburgh, my mother took me to a local grocery store. I looked around at all the different brands of cereal and thought Pittsburgh must be the wealthiest place in the world."

CHAPTER 13

Island Politics

"You are going to lose. Just try not to lose too much."

—Grenada prime minister Sir Eric Gairy

We strongly urged our students to stay far away from the politics of the island. We were guests there and desperately needed the cooperation of the government, so nothing positive could come from getting involved in local politics. For example, we asked them to stay out of bars like the Sugar Mill, Clancy's, and the BBC because at that time those were opposition party hangouts.

Prime Minister Eric Gairy had made his presence known. St. George's was as important to him, both economically and politically, as his support was to us. No one in Grenada deserves more credit for the success of the school than Gairy. He deserves credit for bringing the school to the island, and with that came jobs for Grenadians and a growing economy.

Days after the school opened, he came to the campus to address the students. He arrived in his limo, flags flying from its bumpers, a motorcycle escort in front and behind him. He was dressed formally, in what looked like a tuxedo with tails, wearing a sash and an array of medals. He also was accompanied by his bodyguards, a security group known as the Mongoose Gang. It wasn't threatening, but it was a reminder. Gairy was a wonderful speaker. He welcomed us to Grenada and reminded us that we were guests there and had to respect the laws and customs of that country. Among those rules, he added casually, was that students could not wear blue jeans.

Well, that was a surprise. Jeans were the uniform of young people in the States.

There was a local dress code: women wore dresses and men wore black pants and, usually, a white shirt. This was traditional. Jeans and shorts were not common. We had told our students to be respectful when they went out and about, but we did not realize that there was a serious interdiction on jeans for American kids studying. Jeans ended up being a political statement. It turned out the opposition political party, led by Maurice Bishop, all wore jeans.

As Gairy concluded this serious welcoming speech, he had one more completely unexpected request: "Does anybody here play tennis?" He loved tennis, we found out, and had courts at his official residence. When John Washington responded he played regularly, Gairy invited him to play in what became a weekly game.

Gairy visited the campus annually for the next few years to repeat the speech he had recently given at the United Nations. Attendance at these gatherings was pretty much mandatory. His aides handed out copies of his speech.

I got to know Sir Eric very well. In addition to being prime minister, Gairy was head of the national labor union and owned several businesses, among them the Evening Palace. The Evening Palace was a popular nightclub/bar not far from Grand Anse. Imagine those exotic and sensually subdued nightclubs from the great 1930s black-and-white movies, with soft romantic music playing in the background.

The Evening Palace was the exact opposite of that.

"Think cinder block," as my sister Lorraine once described it. "I don't even think it was painted. It was small and dark, like a basement."

The prime minister regularly invited members of the faculty to receptions there. Almost weekly, personalized gold-embossed invitations were hand-delivered by a government employee requesting "the honour of your presence" at a reception honoring the West Indian cricket team or a visiting dignitary or whatever he could think of. Administrators and faculty members were expected to be there most Saturday nights. We used to refer to it as a command performance. "Women were expected to wear long gowns," remembers Jane Sutter. "It was sort of weird to be in this kind of dingy place dressed in a gown you wouldn't even wear to a wedding in the States."

We learned quickly that if we went there on a Saturday night, the following week went better. It was guaranteed that at some point during the evening the prime minister would suggest joyfully, "Let's celebrate with champagne!" Two or three or sometimes more bottles of cheap champagne would suddenly appear on our table—and the next day a bill for that expensive cheap champagne would arrive at the dean's office.

I understood that Gairy was in a difficult position as the leader of a newly independent country with a poor economy—Grenada had 40 percent unemployment—and a relatively uneducated population. He really was trying to lift the people out of poverty, and we were potentially a source of a lot of jobs. I had been warned by my father and Pat Adams that Gairy was going to try to take advantage of my youth. They were always wary of him, fearful he would be able to manipulate me. He certainly did try—although I never knew him to be dishonest. For example, during one of our first meetings in his role as a union leader he told me, "You need to hire lifeguards for the school."

Lifeguards? We had one empty swimming pool. "Why is that?" I asked.

"I understand from the guards that your students are swimming at Five Minute Beach. We don't want to have a drowning. The school is doing well so far." He suggested we hire four lifeguards so they could work in shifts. I got it: My grandfather had been a union organizer and was always trying to find jobs for people. That's all he was doing.

Five Minute Beach was, naturally, a five-minute walk through mud and trees from True Blue. It was not easily accessible. Gairy was right, though—it actually was potentially dangerous. It was secluded and the beach was shallow for several yards, then took a sudden dip and got very deep. It was like stepping off a shelf. But I recognized this as a test to see how easily and how far I could be pushed. "You know, Mr. Prime

Minister," I responded, "what we'll do is tell the students they're not allowed to swim there unless they're strong swimmers, but we just can't afford that right now."

I also pointed out that the hotels didn't have lifeguards on the beach. He dismissed that, explaining, "That's different. They were here before."

It was a test for both sides. The founders wanted to make sure I didn't fold. Gairy wanted to see how hard he could push. I concluded diplomatically, "I don't think we need them right now. But I'll think about it."

When I told this story to my father, he just rolled his eyes. I knew what he was thinking: Here we go, he's trying to milk us of everything he can get. I actually thought that was the wrong attitude: What was wrong with the prime minister trying to create jobs for Grenadians? And Gairy was fine with my decision. I had passed the first test. Believe me, he won his share of these battles in those first years. Once, I remember, he asked me to hire a driver named Courtney Whitney. When I asked him why, he explained, "Because he has access to water." Simply put, if we wanted a steady water supply we had to hire him.

We did. Our problem was that he was a daring driver. He would race up and down Grenada's often steep, winding, and rocky roads, constantly shifting, slamming down on the accelerator. As Jane Sutter reported, when driving with him, "Our stomachs would get all concerned!" Finally, one day I said to him, "Courtney, you know what I love about your driving?"

In his lovely island lilt he asked, "No, Dr. Modica, what might that be?"

"You drive like you have an egg underneath the pedal."

His face lit up in surprise. "I do?"

"You definitely do," I said, "and I want you to remember that." He did too; well, most of the time.

Within a year we had established an economic presence. We employed about a hundred people as secretaries, maids, maintenance workers, groundskeepers, and, of course, careful drivers. But no lifeguards. There was no way of calculating how many jobs we had indirectly created, from bus drivers to restaurant workers, but it was at least another hundred.

The government paid considerable attention to the new medical school. Very little happened on the island that Eric Gairy did not know about very quickly. He had seen the possibilities of this new venture—and unknown to us he was monitoring the effects of his vision. In fact, when the school opened the only methods of communications between Bay Shore and Grenada were telephones and our one telex machine. There were only fourteen telephone lines into Grenada, and when making a call an operator had to physically plug in the connection.

We were certain the Grenadian government was monitoring those phones and the telex, which would give them an advantage when we had to negotiate. So to maintain privacy we created a code. Admittedly it was not very sophisticated: We bought two identical orange pocket dictionaries. When we wanted to send a coded message, we would telex a phony purchase order using a key word in the title to alert the recipient this was a coded message. Names and numbers led the user to a specific page and word in the dictionary. It was rudimentary, but it worked.

That code became especially valuable during the revolution just a few years later. At times it was surprising how much the government knew about the school and our students. Nasir Jahdi, for example, had arrived in the country with a new, gorgeous yellow Ford Mustang. His sister and her husband bought it to use when visiting the States and had left it with him. He shipped it to the island from Illinois, intending to sell it and use the money for tuition and expenses. There was not another car like it on the island. It attracted a lot of attention. The rumor started spreading that Nasir was the nephew of the shah of Iran, who had come to Grenada to escape the revolution there.

Nasir was a medical student, but because he had been through podiatry school and chiropractic school—which included courses in anatomy and physiology—like many graduate students in domestic universities, he also earned a few extra dollars working as a tutor in osteology and human anatomy. Not surprisingly, the government had heard the rumor that a professor at the school, who possibly was related to the shah, had brought an unusually beautiful American car to Grenada. Several weeks after the car arrived, Nasir was invited to appear before the cabinet. The entire cabinet assembled to question him about this car. Where did it come from? What was his plan for the car? Who did he intend to sell it to? It was obvious that the prime minister wanted this car. Eventually, though, Nasir sold it to a retired Czech pilot who owned a popular restaurant.

Gairy and I developed a mutual trust. He liked me, I suspect, because I was respectful, I was honest, and I remained adamantly nonpolitical. We would meet or speak weekly. At times he would invite me to cabinet meetings to discuss an issue. Whatever the issue, he was going to make the final decision, but he liked to present it to his cabinet to allow them to pretend they had actual power. During those meetings he would use me to demonstrate to his cabinet how tough he could be when necessary. He'd lecture me, he'd warn me, he would remind me that we were there as the guest of the government. Although later he admitted to me that much of the time the whole thing was a performance. "You are going to lose," he suggested. "Just try not to lose too much."

But he also invited me to meet privately with him at his home. These meetings were very different. Rather than a show of strength for his cabinet, they were productive working sessions during which we exchanged ideas. There was no chest-pounding; he never raised his voice. After listening to whatever I needed to discuss, which might have ranged from requesting better electrical connections to the price we were paying for fresh water, he would ask his cabinet members afterward for their opinion. And then he would tell them what their opinion was.

But there was one day I knew he finally had come to trust me. Late in the first semester he invited me to his home on a Saturday morning. We were sitting in an outdoor porch off his bedroom. He was dressed in pajamas, a bathrobe, and slippers, which was not unusual—we'd met this way several times previously. What did make it unusual was that he began this meeting by dismissing his aide, who until that morning had always joined us whenever we met.

Whatever he wanted to talk about, he wanted to keep it very quiet. "I guess you're wondering why I have asked you to come here today," he began.

"Yes, of course. I'm hoping that perhaps you have some good news for the school."

"Today will be a very important meeting in the history of this country," he said. "But before I discuss anything with you, I need to have your absolute confidence that you will not share this meeting with anyone."

"Oh no, Mr. Prime Minister, I would never…"

He stopped me midsentence. "I mean no one. Not even your partners." He waved his finger back and forth. "No one. You have to promise me that. Otherwise I can't go into it."

He certainly had my attention. I agreed that I wouldn't tell anyone about whatever it was he was going to tell me.

"I'm going to go into my room and bring out something to show you. We're going to talk about it. I need your help." As he rose he again cautioned me, "But you can tell absolutely no one about this. It's too important for this country."

A minute later he returned carrying an old crumpled brown paper bag that looked like it might have once contained a take-out order from a New York deli. He set it down on the table with a thud. "You know what's in this bag?"

I shook my head. "No, Mr. Prime Minister. I have no idea."

He pointed at it. "The future of our country may be in that bag." Gairy was given to drama, but I had no idea what he was talking about. "I need your connection with the scientific community in the United States to give me an analysis of what's in this bag."

"I'm very happy to help you if I can."

He reached into the paper bag and pulled out a large sparkling rock. It was about half the size of a water glass and had what appeared to be gold speckles in it. He looked me right in the eyes and said firmly, "We may have discovered gold in Grenada."

The rock was sparkling. Maybe he was right; I had no way of knowing. "Oh my God," I said. "Wow. I can see what you mean about the future of the country."

He tapped the rock. "This is a sample. It may be nothing more than a shining rock, but on the chance it's real I need to investigate."

I suddenly understood why this had to be kept secret. Gairy was well aware how crazy this whole thing sounded. Gold discovered in Grenada?

We both knew the chances of that being true were slim. But if people found out about this inquiry, his reputation could easily be tarnished. He couldn't take that risk. But on the slim, slim chance it was real, he had to find out.

"I need to know what this is before I do anything more. I don't know about these things, but you must have scientists you deal with."

I wanted to help—if this was true it was a wonderful thing—but I didn't know what I could do. Gairy assumed I had better connections in the scientific community than I actually did have. "Well, we teach medicine," I said. "But I can try to help you."

"Good. I need to know if this is gold and, if it is, the percentage of gold in this rock and its value. Then we can make the decisions that need to be made."

"I'll do my best. I'm going back to the States in a couple of days. I'll get an analysis and call you right away."

"Oh no," he said quickly. "You mustn't call." He didn't acknowledge that operators were listening to conversations, but that obviously was his fear.

"Well, I don't know exactly when I'll be coming back down here or how long it'll take to get this analyzed."

He considered that. "I have an idea," he said. He took a blank sheet of paper and drew a line down the middle dividing it into two columns. "Let's make believe this is the sample I'm giving you. You can call me. If this sample has 10 percent gold, I want you to tell me that the soil sample I gave you would be best for growing more nutmeg." He wrote down 10 percent in the column on the left and "nutmeg" on the same line in the column on the right, nutmeg being a major crop grown on the island as well as being drawn on my mother's kitchen wallpaper. "If it's 20 percent gold, I want you to tell me that the soil would be best for cocoa." He went down the list: bananas, avocados, mangos, spices, and fruits up to 90 percent. "So you'll call and tell me what crop would be best to grow in that soil sample."

We each took a copy of this code. I brought the rock back to the States with me. I managed to contact a geologist at the University of

Minnesota and sent it to him for analysis. A few weeks later I received a spectrograph measuring the percent of various elements in that sample. None of them were gold. It was mostly pyrite, fool's gold. My problem was that somehow I had to report this to the prime minister. The only thing I knew with absolute certainty was that I was not going to refer to it as "fool's gold."

I called him. "Mr. Prime Minister," I began, "remember those soil samples?"

"Yes, Charles?"

"Well, I got the report back. I don't think any of the crops we talked about would grow in that soil."

"I see," he responded, considering that. "So perhaps it's between nutmeg and cocoa?" he asked hopefully.

It suddenly occurred to me that in our code we had neglected to make a provision for the most probable outcome: zero. "Um, no, Mr. Prime Minister. It would be below the nutmeg."

There were a few seconds of silence as this news sunk in, then, "How much below?"

I tried to find a way to report the bad news to him. "Actually, there aren't any crops that can be grown in this soil."

"No crop?" he asked, finally grasping it.

"No," I said. "It didn't contain enough enrichment to grow any crops. Do you follow what I'm saying?"

"So then you're saying there is zero percent chance of any crop?"

"I'm sorry, but that's right."

He was not surprised. If anything, that shared secret brought our relationship closer. For all his quirks and eccentricities, Eric Gairy's decision to bring our school to Grenada turned out to be far more valuable than gold. And it took real courage to make it. There were many people in the country who did not support the school, wondering if it was a political move by Gairy to increase his power. But even with all his craziness about gold mines and his fascination with UFOs, he was a visionary. He was first and deserves credit for that.

CHAPTER 14

Establishment Wars

"All they do there is go scuba diving and sit on the beach all day."

—Association of American Medical Colleges official to a reporter

During our first few years, as we struggled to get established, the medical community had considerable doubt about our academic standards. That was not unreasonable—we were new, and we were attempting to transform the long-accepted process for educating physicians. An entire mystique had been created around this closed system. Few people questioned it, and even fewer challenged it.

We had to prove ourselves. So it was not surprising that from the day we opened, the medical education establishment did everything possible to question our legitimacy. At every opportunity they warned potential applicants about us. The impression they tried to convey was that we probably accepted just about every person who applied and likely provided an inferior education, the inference being we were in it only for the money.

The first objective of any establishment is to protect the establishment itself. The American Medical Association and the Association of American Medical Colleges essentially control American medicine. Foreign medical schools had traditionally supplied an acceptable number of American physicians. When I published the first edition of my *Foreign Medical School Catalogue* in 1972, it was estimated as many as one-third of all practicing doctors had been educated outside the United States. The vast majority of those people, though, were foreign nationals drawn to this country by preferential immigration policies, then encouraged to stay.

While that supposedly filled America's need for more doctors, it also created a very controversial "brain drain," especially from third-world countries. We were, and in many instances still are, taking the best graduates of government-subsidized schools in foreign countries. In India, for example, the government pays most of the tuition for medical students, but many of them come here to do their residencies—and end up staying.

Even though compensation is less than it was in the 1980s, US physicians still have the highest income level in the world. To try to slow down this brain drain, in 1976, just as we were about to welcome our charter class, Congress made changes to the Immigration and Nationality Act that tightened regulations governing foreign-trained physicians. What that legislation actually did was increase the system-created shortage of doctors. That was the void I knew we could help fill.

The numbers of Americans who studied abroad and trickled back was always small enough to be easily absorbed into the system without causing any problems. Unlike the vast majority of foreign-trained students coming to the US to practice, these people were coming home. They didn't need visas or green cards; they just needed to pass the same examinations as students from American schools to be accredited.

St. George's University was the first school established specifically to educate American students studying abroad so they would be licensed to practice in the United States. For that, we were immediately perceived to be a threat. These schools had done a fine job convincing the public that being admitted to an American medical school was the ultimate academic achievement, that it was the top of the educational pyramid, an almost sacred thing. Then this thirty-year-old opened a medical school on an island with ten faculty members, and within a couple of years our students were outscoring theirs on national exams. That did not fit their view of reality. It was a public relations nightmare. After all, back in the '70s, physicians were pretty much at the top of the food chain. Their reputation was lofty and respectable. My son, the doctor!

They had succeeded in assuring themselves and everyone else that what they had done—medical school and residency—required enormous talent and intelligence, reached only by a select few after an arduous journey through the sacred and arcane pathways set out by the AAMC: But we were on the front lines of medical education. We had learned all about the process, the expenses, the testing, the enormous stress—but on a daily basis we also saw the difference that dedication, desire, and passion made. Our students loved medicine, they loved working with patients, and they proved over and over they were the academic equal—and sometimes better—of almost all domestic students. We were so raw, transparent, stripped down to the essence of learning medicine that our existence was appalling to them. Things were working just fine for them; there was no need to change.

By existing, we threw doubt on their entire paradigm, and they began attacking us. The first line of attack was the fact that we were a for-profit school, suggesting that money was more important to the school than providing an education. To be honest, that was not completely irrational. But what was forgotten was the fact that originally every American medical school was set up as a profit-making business. That includes Harvard Medical School. That system had begun changing in 1893, when Johns Hopkins opened its nonprofit medical school. By 1900 about a third of the 155 existing American medical schools were not for profit. What also is interesting in this dynamic is that since the opening of St. George's, as of this date, more than 25 percent of hospital systems in the US have become for-profit, and that number is growing.

The most significant change in medical education occurred in 1910 when the Carnegie Foundation reported that too many medical schools were "mercenary concerns that trade on ignorance and disease." In other words, too many of them existed as profitable businesses rather than places of education. As a result of that report, the government began establishing uniform standards and our highly structured medical educational system took shape. Entrance requirements were raised, and a model curriculum emphasizing the scientific method, clinical exposure, and laboratory research was devised. Within a few years about half of the existing medical schools had gone out of business. That eventually evolved into a system in which almost all US medical schools became nonprofits contractually aligned with universities. With very few exceptions, that was the situation when we welcomed our first students to St. George's in January 1977.

The fact that we were for-profit made it easy for them to criticize us. The inference was clear: American medical schools are altruistic, bringing the brightest young people into a noble profession, while we were in it for the money. They implied and probably suspected we were only preying on desperate people. But the biggest difference between domestic medical schools and St. George's was that American schools required students to do research while we specialized in educating them. Here's why: American medical schools are expensive and have limited enrollments. In most of those schools, the ratio of staff to student is about 1:1.9, while we have six faculty members for every two hundred students, a 1:33 ratio.

The fact is that the 1:1.9 ratio has nothing to do with educating students. The faculty of American medical schools also conduct research and are expected to publish studies. Many members of their faculties have limited interaction with students. God bless them, that is vitally important, but it has nothing to do with the quality of the education students are getting. Our students see their instructors in the classroom or lab. We have never required our instructors to do anything other than teach.

In their budgets, research is lumped with teaching, which inflates tuition and all the associated costs. I recognized that I could provide a better quality of medical education by focusing on teaching rather than research. If I hadn't spent so much time learning about the system, I probably would have questioned the quality of education St. George's could be providing too.

Aerial of True Blue campus in 1977.

MEDICAL STUDIES
BRITISH WEST INDIES

The St. George's University, School of Medicine, is pleased to announce that applications for admission from American students will be considered commencing with the 1977 class. For further information on the 4½ year English Programme post a written request (please do not phone) to:

ST. GEORGE'S UNIVERSITY
School of Medicine
c/o Consulate General-Francis M. Redhead
Grenada Mission to the United Nations
866 2nd Avenue Suite 502
N.Y., N.Y. 10017

September 1976 advertisement in the *New York Times*, following the approval of St. George's University by the Grenadian Parliament.

Paul Ringiewicz and another student at campus entrance, 1977.

Andy Belford, first Director of Admissions, arriving at Pearls Airport circa 1977.

"Da Boys" of the Charter Class. *Left to right:* Danny Ricciardi, Frank Arbucci, Quentin Giorgio, and John Lorenzetti.

First campus restaurant.

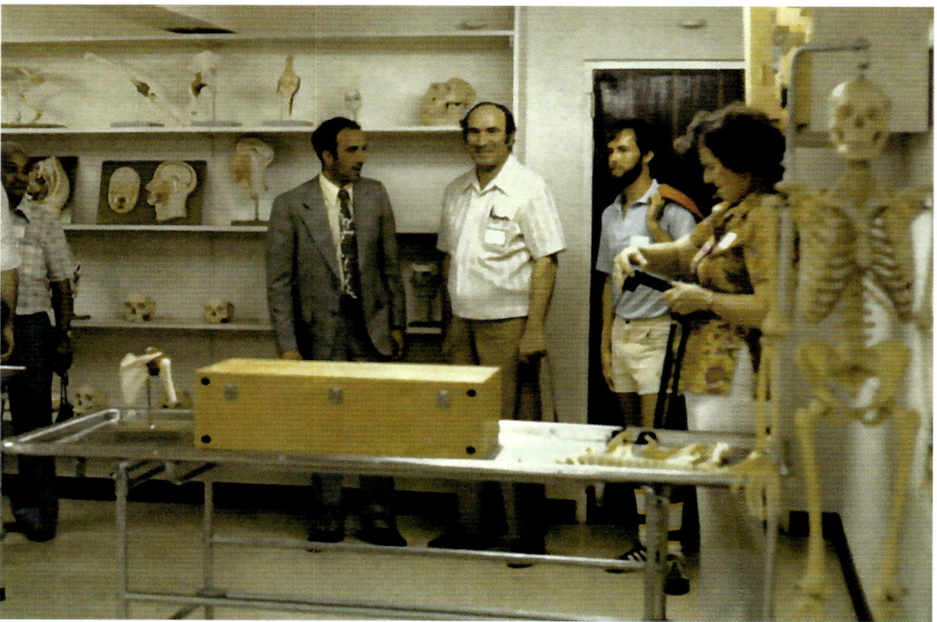
Earliest campus Anatomy lab.

Prime Minister's Residence, 1970s.

SGU's first Vice Chancellor, Geoffrey Bourne, and his wife, Nelly Golarz, Dean of Women.

Morris "Morrie" Alpert, MD, Dean of Kingstown Medical College, and John Madden (SGU '81) at SGU's campus in St. Vincent in 1981.

Chancellor Modica and Vice Chancellor Bourne at a Joint Government Monitoring Committee, circa 1978.

Students playing volleyball on campus, 1978.

Charter Class lining up for the first graduation ceremony, May 1981.

Charter Class at Graduation, May 1981.

Charter Class Graduation, May 1981. *Left to right:* Jane Sutter, Registrar; C.V. Rao, Associate Dean of Students, Charles R Modica, Chancellor; Geoffrey Bourne, Vice Chancellor; Andy Belford, Director of Admissions.

Students posing on beach, 1981.

Raz Giliberti and Jack Pasquale with Morrie Alpert.

Charles Modica flying the school plane.

David L Brown, MD, PhD, Professor of Behavioral Science and the first Dean of Faculty.

Maurice Bishop, Prime Minister of Grenada, speaking to a student, circa 1982.

Early Alumni Association. Left to Right: Fran McGill, Bernie Katz, Jack Cush (Chair), John Madden, Bob Fleming, and Terry Palatt (All SGU '81).

U.S. helicopter during the U.S. intervention of 1983.

Chancellor Modica and Professor CV "Vish" Rao, after the 1983 evacuation.

President Ronald Reagan on campus after the 1983 US Intervention, greeting Chancellor Modica with Vice Chancellor Bourne.

President Reagan and Chancellor Modica at the White House in 1984.

John "Jack" Cush (SGU '81) lecturing at Alumni CME Conference on SGU campus.

Chancellor Charles Modica, Dean Morrie Alpert, and Charter Class Alumnus, Danny Ricciardi, at 1989 campus Alumni CME Conference.

Charles Modica and Morrie Alpert at Morrie's 80th birthday party.

Discussing the massive campus building campaign in 1995. *Left to right:* Anselm LaTouche, President of Creative Design and Building; Andy Belford, campus architect and visionary; Keith B Taylor, Second Vice Chancellor; and Lauriston Hosten.

Groundbreaking for the WINDREF Research Foundation. *Left to right:* Findsley St. Louis, Minister of Health; Calum Macpherson, Founding Director of WINDREF; Keith B Taylor, Vice Chancellor; Prime Minster Rt. Hon. George Brizan; Carlisle Glean, Minister of Education

President Jimmy Carter on campus in 2004: *Left to right:* Peter Slinger, Associate Professor; Donna Weber, Registrar; Jimmy Carter, former President of the United States; Ted Hollis, Professor; Vice Chancellor Peter Bourne; and Anthia Parke, Assistant to the Chancellor.

Peggy Lambert, founder Louis J. Modica and his wife, Marian Modica, at the University's 25th Anniversary celebration.

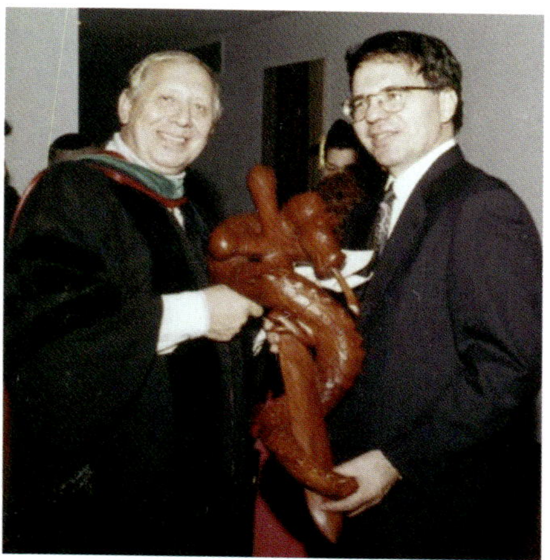

Provost Allen Pensick and Dean of Medicine, Stephen Weitzman, at SGU Graduation.

SGU's Academic Board: *Back Row:* Frederick King, Craig Burrell, Sir Malcom McNaughton, Edward Fischer, Jack Cush (SGU '81), Robert Blanc. *Front Row:* Sir Kenneth Stuart, Paul Cutler, Charles R. Modica, Keith B. Taylor, Dame Hilda Bynoe.

The Founders of SGU: Edward McGowan, Louis J. Modica, Patrick F. Adams, and Charles R. Modica.

Front Row: Theodore Hollis, Dean of SAS; Courisse Knight, Premedical Director; Raymond Sis, Dean, SVM; Margaret Lambert, VP/Dean of Enrolment Planning, Allen Pensick, Provost, Vish Rao, Dean of Students

Middle Row: Glen Jacobs, Vice Provost; John Madden, Director of Career Guidance; Robert Jordan, Sr. Dean of Basic Sciences for UK; Robert Ryan, Dean of Admissions

Back Row: Rodney Croft, Dean, UK Clinical; Calum Macpherson, Dean SGS; Colin Dowe, Associate Dean of Admissions; Andre Havenga, Chair DES

2018 Graduation at Lincoln Center. SGU Administrators Peggy Lambert, Dean of Enrolment Planning, Associate Dean of Enrolment Planning, Robert "Bob" Ryan, Executive VP Clinical Affairs, and CV "Vish" Rao, Dean of Students at Lincoln Center meet some very proud and happy family members from Nigeria.

SGU's administrators enjoying the SGU dream. Left to right: Bob Jordan, Andy Belford, Peggy Lambert, Vish Rao, Al Pensick, and Keith Taylor (seated).

Dedication of the Charles R. Modica Campus in 2025: Chancellor and Lisa Modica with Dame Gloria Payne-Banfield, who served as Grenada's Permanent Representative to the UN.

Signatures of the Charter Class Graduates.

Dedication of the Andrew J. Belford building in 2018 for our first Director of Admissions then Campus Designer. *Left to right:* Vish Rao, Charles R. Modica, Peggy Lambert, and Andy Belford.

On paper, medical schools are money-losers for universities. That's a significant reason why the number of available spots in medical schools has not kept pace with population growth or need. Between 1982 and 2003 the population of the US went up 28 percent; at the same time older doctors were retiring, more women were entering the profession, and both the health-savvy and the aging population were demanding more care.

Incredibly, as the demand for doctors increased, the number of first-year medical students actually decreased slightly. It was all about maintaining the status quo. If a medical school wanted to add seats it had to find donors to pay for them. Want to add ten students? Raise a million dollars.

In addition to their own education, American medical students are paying the salaries of professors they will never see in a classroom. That structure was costing even a small school like New York Medical College three to four times what students were paying in tuition—but those schools had no choice. If a school wanted to receive accreditation by the Liaison Committee on Medical Education, which was required to make students eligible for federal loans, it had to follow the regulations. It had to ante up.

It was a comfortable club they were running, and an effective way of keeping us out of that club. While the accomplishments and credentials of esteemed professors might affect the reputation of the institution, it does not necessarily impact the quality of education students are getting. But the result of it all was that there were too many applicants for too few spaces, resulting in me going to medical school in Spain.

The system created the need that we tried to fill, then tried to prevent us from succeeding. The only way we could survive was by doing things differently. I don't know where my ideas come from, but I have always had an ability to find solutions for problems. That's my business survival instinct. Part of that, I suspect, is that I didn't simply accept the existing systems. I didn't assume that because things were being done in a certain way, that must be the best way to do them.

One of the first significant decisions I made, for example, was to bring in two classes a year rather than one, as medical schools had done for a century. I had to ignore what the established schools were doing and instead ask, "Why can't it be done this way?" I'm sure there was a reason it had always been one class a year, but whatever that reason was it no longer made sense. Two classes a year was innovative but logical. We literally doubled the size of our student population without drastically increasing the size of the faculty or affecting the quality of their education. The primary difference was that the faculty was teaching the same course twice a year.

Bob Jordan was an associate professor of anatomy at the Medical College of Virginia, one of the oldest medical schools in America, when he became a visiting professor at St. George's. Three years later he joined our faculty teaching anatomy, eventually becoming department chairman. "When I was a professor at both the University of Cincinnati and Virginia," he explains, "I was required to conduct research as well as teach. Doing research takes time, effort, and money away from teaching. I loved the fact that in Grenada all I did was teach. We could easily condense year-long courses in the States to six months, and I could teach two classes a year without having to worry about not being promoted because I hadn't published any research papers."

Carlos Pestana, a dean at the University of Texas, San Antonio, described our philosophy in his book *The Rejected Medical School Applicant*: "There are no academic ladder games to play," he wrote. "...But because acquiring a reputation or getting the Nobel Prize is not in the cards at Grenada, the teachers who go there are the ones who enjoy teaching." He had discovered the true core of St. George's University—teaching and learning.

In fact, Pestana was so impressed by that concept—and our students—that two years after publication of his book he joined the faculty as a visiting lecturer.

As it became increasingly difficult for the American Medical Association to simply dismiss us, they had to address and emphasize the doubts swirling around any innovative endeavor. "All they do there," an AMA official told a reporter, "is go scuba diving and sit on the beach all day." They wrote in their newsletter that the emerging Caribbean medical schools were of dubious quality, and unless action was taken there would be a proliferation of inferior medical schools. As a general statement that was not unreasonable, but it was outrageous and unfair to group us with those other schools in the region.

Speaking for the Association of American Medical Colleges, the head of the Indiana University School of Medicine told *People* magazine, "They shouldn't even be called medical schools." And in a widely circulated position paper entitled "Foreign Medical Graduates," the American College of Physicians suggested, "Much disappointment, as well as time, effort and expenses might be avoided if ways can be found to advise American students before they embark for a foreign medical education of the unlikelihood they will ever successfully qualify as a physician in the United States."

Again, at the time that paper was published, close to a third of all doctors practicing in America were considered foreign graduates—which included all of the United Kingdom, France, Germany, Spain, Italy, and India.

These attacks on our credibility even extended to Japan. One afternoon Andy Belford saw a film crew wandering around Grand Anse Beach looking confused and went out to help. When he found out their issue, he was amazed. Apparently, a former Miss Japan had been accepted, this crew was there to "expose" the school, and they were frustrated because they couldn't find any students "studying on the beach." They needed that kind of video to reinforce the point they had already decided to make.

Andy politely told them they would usually find students on the beach after final exams but before the plane ride home—if they were willing to stay there for a few more weeks.

The same presumptive and biased investigation by organized medicine began soon after the charter class arrived. In October 1978 the medical establishment convinced NBC News that this small school on this small island somehow was posing a threat to the entire American medical system. It smelled enough like an exposé to interest the network: They could claim to be the good guys, protecting their viewers.

It was a setup: NBC sent a crew to the island in the middle of the summer when the campus was closed and the students were back home. There were only a few administrators on campus. This crew snuck around, shooting footage through louvered windows. They had no idea what they were looking at, but they filmed it anyway. They took video of an osteology closet in which boxes of bones and full skeletons had been stored and mistakenly identified it as "the anatomy lab." It certainly looked questionable.

It was initially supposed to be a five-minute segment on the *Nightly News*, but because they believed it was an important story, they instead gave it to *The Today Show*, which promoted it as an investigative report. I found out about it when an NBC crew pounced on me at my parents' home.

I think I surprised them by not running away from their camera. Rather than getting angry or fighting with them, I asked for an opportunity to respond to their claims. I wasn't afraid of the truth being reported, and I knew we hadn't done anything wrong. But I did a smart thing: Even though I wanted to go on the program and personally refute their charges, I realized I was just thirty-one years old and had no serious medical or educational background.

Geoffrey Bourne had gravitas. Geoffrey Bourne had a distinguished career in academics at prestigious institutions. He needed to speak for the school. Unfortunately, he was in England. We asked him to take the next Concorde back to New York. That was a huge expense for us, especially as NBC would not commit to putting him on. But the existence of the school was at stake.

Tom Brokaw hosted the segment. John Cooper, founding president of the AAMC was there, ready to expose what he believed existed. I was sitting backstage in the green room with a churning stomach. In the next few minutes, more people would learn about the existence of St. George's than all the people who had heard about it since my first ad appeared. It was five minutes on national television that could determine the fate of the school.

They began the segment by showing the edited footage. It was an unprofessional hit job. It showed an essentially deserted, run-down campus with locked buildings and bones piled in boxes. The film was shot to make it look like an undercover exposé, through half-shuttered windows and seemingly concealed cameras. It portrayed the school as a complete sham. I was outraged, horrified, frustrated, and, frankly, a little bit scared. If it had been an accurate representation of what we were, we would have been dead. And we probably should have been.

But it wasn't, as just-off-the-plane Geoffrey Bourne patiently and politely explained. He had sat quietly as the film was broadcast. When it was over Brokaw turned to him and asked, with some astonishment, "Dr. Bourne, you were chairman of the Anatomy Department at Emory University Medical School, director of the famed Yerkes Center, and the editor of *Nutrition* magazine. Now you're the vice chancellor of this school. How could such a distinguished academic associate himself with a school like this?"

Geoffrey Bourne was the perfect gentleman. If he took any offense at this, he didn't show it. "Thank you, Mr. Brokaw," he said. "I appreciate your comments, and yes, I have done a lot in my life. And now I'm associated with a school that is nothing like what you've presented."

Go, Geoffrey, I was practically cheering. You tell 'em.

"I'm proud to be associated with this school," he continued. He corrected several of the misstatements in the story, doing so without raising his voice even slightly, and then threw his own punch: "Frankly, Dr. Cooper's AAMC has been against the school from the very beginning. I know there are jealousies because we have taken students who should have been accepted to medical schools in the United States, offered them an opportunity, and they are doing exceptionally well."

I just sat there thinking, *This is the luckiest day of my life*. I wanted to run out there and kiss him. He had successfully put Cooper on the defensive. Cooper repeated his usual complaints, but Geoffrey boxed him with facts.

The establishment continued its attacks on every possible front. The Department of Health, Education, and Welfare suddenly reneged on an agreement we'd reached allowing our students to participate in the federal student loan program. After receiving our charter we'd been approved for federal loans up to $5,000, but without warning HEW secretary Joe Califano informed us that our students were no longer eligible. Among the reasons cited for this decision was "a shortage of cadavers," a problem that had already been rectified.

Pat Adams, who had negotiated the original agreement, was irate. As I said, this was an indication the establishment was scared of us

HEW denied it had succumbed to pressure, naturally. But whatever the truth, it was another potentially devastating action. Many of our students depended on that money, and we were depending on our students to get that money. We realized we had no choice—my father agreed to personally fund a tuition loan program.

It was a huge risk. We offered no-interest loans for the first nine months after graduation. While there were some problems, some misunderstandings, and a few angry words—money does that—those loans made it possible for many charter class students to stay in school, enabling the school to survive. Eventually only one student failed to fully repay his college loan.

Long term, though, we couldn't survive without access to that loan program. We knew that, so somehow we had to get it reinstated. I had learned to deal directly with unexpected problems while running my water taxi company. The key was remaining calm and focused on a solution. In those days we'd had dispatchers falling asleep in the middle of the night, boats running out of gas. One night one of my captains met a female passenger, docked the boat, and went home with her. I listened as another of my dispatchers calmly stated, "Roger that," to a "May Day! May Day! I'm sinking" call by a captain whose boat was indeed sinking. I had learned to expect the unexpected and deal with it.

To get student loans reinstated, I began a long and complicated relationship with regulators, legislators, lobbyists, and influencers in Washington, DC. It would be impossible to guess how many meetings

I've had with legislators and government employees since then. Both medicine and education are highly regulated fields, and combining them multiplies the potential problems. It was often like wandering in a maze within a maze.

The first member of Congress I dealt with was Mario Biaggi, a conservative Democrat from the Bronx. My father was a Republican from Long Island—in fact he ran for Congress in 1980 and was defeated. But like every successful developer, he had forged relationships with public officials. So when this problem began I reached out to Biaggi. There was no political gain in this for him, although a few of his constituents may have been enrolled, but his office was very helpful in getting the situation resolved.

While eventually we were able to get reinstated, the subject of loans remained a problem for a long time. At one point several years later, for example, the Department of Education reported having loaned more than $9 million to about three thousand students attending medical schools in the Caribbean. In response the American College of Physicians wondered how the government could justify spending American tax dollars to support medical education or residency training for graduates of these schools—several of which were not accredited.

But in that same paper the ACP admitted that ending that program "could cause severe problems for those teaching hospitals that rely on foreign medical graduates for the provision of patient care services. Many of those hospitals are located in urban centers and serve predominately poor and underserved populations."

That last sentence reinforced the fact that domestic medical schools were not providing enough graduates to serve those people and places who needed them the most. Graduates of American medical schools were not encouraged to enter primary care in underserved areas. Our students, and those of other Caribbean schools that followed us, were filling that need.

Over decades, so many attempts to make seemingly small legislative changes that could have a large effect on us have been made that we got used to fighting back. Very few senators or members of Congress knew anything at all about foreign medical schools. And what little they did learn often portrayed those schools as profitable scams. As a group we had very little power.

The AMA made it sound like a good issue for a politician. Who could be against protecting constituents from being hurt by unqualified graduates of terrible medical schools? And if those politicians could pick up some campaign donations from the AMA and similar organizations, all the better. It has always been an uphill battle for us. Even today, despite our graduates having gone on to fill at least some of the shortage created by organized medicine, they are still harping on the old canards of our innovative medical school.

In 2005, then Alabama senator Jeff Sessions introduced a bill to cut off federal loans to Caribbean medical schools, claiming we were essentially diploma mills "created to serve American students who cannot get into American medical schools." While this bill was aimed at genuine diploma mills, it was deceptive since those schools had not undergone the intense review by the DOE and students in those schools could not get US-backed loans.

The DOE has protections for their loan program built into the intensive approval process. This fact is usually ignored when they are on the attack. The substandard schools in the Caribbean are brought out and touted—even today—when organized medicine wants to attack St. George's University. We had to derail this bill. The Republicans, who held the power in Washington, were not especially friendly to us. So instead of trying to lobby individual members of the Budget Committee, we decided to meet with Sessions and plead for our life.

In preparation for this meeting, I asked our office to get me the names of any students from Alabama. Instead of trying to convince him with cold statistics, we wanted him to meet his constituents. We wanted him to understand how his bill affected real people. There were six Alabama residents enrolled, four men and two women. Three of them were in school in Grenada, the other three were doing clinical work in the New York metropolitan area. We invited all of them to join us for this meeting and provided transportation. We scheduled it for a Friday so they would miss only one day of classwork. We told them that our objective was to influence Senator Sessions; we asked them to personalize the school. "Just tell him the truth about your own experience," I said. "We just want him to learn more about the school."

The meeting was southern cordial. As I introduced each student to the senator he asked politely, "Where'd y'all go to school?" Most of them had done their undergraduate studies in Alabama. But when I introduced the sixth student, a woman named Misty Bass, he perked up. He asked, "Are you any relation to John Bass, the famous fisherman?"

Although John Bass was one of the best-known fishermen in the world, I didn't think she would have the slightest idea who Senator Sessions was talking about. Instead, she smiled and admitted, "Yes, he's my husband."

I sat there stoically, knowing it would be in poor taste to leap out of my seat and scream, "Yea!"

"Really?" the senator asked. His whole body language changed. He leaned forward, dropping his defensive posture. Suddenly he was engaged. He started a real conversation with our students, asking them about their Alabama schooling, their GPAs, their ambition. Two weeks later I was attending a fundraiser for the senator because our lobbyist had told me, "He gets it."

While that encounter did not end our ongoing debate with the medical establishment, it added to the growth of our reputation as being regarded as a worthy medical institution.

CHAPTER 15

Showtime!

"We really didn't know how good our education was compared to other people until we took these standardized tests."

—St. George's University fourth graduating class member Leo Rotello

The years of preparation, the hurdles we'd faced and overcome, the futures of the school and our students came down to one test. This really was the light at the end of the tunnel time.

Everything we'd done, everything we'd accomplished—setting the curriculum, creating the physical facilities, recruiting classes, finding and hiring a faculty, supplying the necessary equipment from toilet paper to cadavers, the loans—it all came down to a simple question: Could our students pass the standard examinations?

Until we proved that we were providing a competitive medical education, nothing else really mattered. I believed in them. I felt confident in their ability. I believed they wouldn't just pass those tests, they would excel.

Until the beginning of the twentieth century, medical education had been scattershot, lacking uniform standards and training. Essentially people could buy a medical degree. Any student who paid his full tuition—most of which was split among lecturers—would be licensed to practice medicine by a board often consisting of those lecturers. Basically, you paid your money, you got your license.

It wasn't until 1907 that all the states began giving licensing exams, although each state created its own process. In 1915 the recently created National Board of Medical Examiners began giving a licensing test to all medical students. But it wasn't until the late 1940s that all the then forty-eight states accepted the results of that test to issue a license to practice medicine.

When we founded the school, we were relying on the law that guaranteed graduates of any medical school approved by a country in which it is operating, meaning listed with the World Health Organization, the right to take the required US licensing examinations. But taking the tests and passing them are quite different. It would be impossible to attract future students if we couldn't provide the promised path to practice medicine in the United States.

The first competitive test our students took was the National Board of Medical Examiners (Part I) administered by Coordinated Transfer Application System (COTRANS), which was given at the end of the basic sciences—the end of the second year. This test was taken by students both in the United States and throughout the world. Everybody took the same test. It was a measure of progress—but it also provided a path for students outside the States who did well on it to transfer into American schools.

I had spent two years preaching to our students, telling them over and over they were going to do better than their peers in the States. This test was going to either prove that I had been right—or perhaps put us out of business and our students out of their deserved future. In dramatic terms, it was…showtime!

I was a lot more confident than anxious. I knew what our students had sacrificed to come to Grenada. I knew how hard they had worked. I knew how serious they were about becoming doctors, and believe me, I was well aware of all the problems they had dealt with. For them, this was, as Larry Adams described it, "my last ditch effort to become a doctor. It was the bottom line."

Foreign medical schools at that time had an initial pass rate of about 33 percent on this examination. I had been consistently bold about my predictions. I told our students they probably would double the world pass rate and a substantial number of our students would be able to transfer into domestic medical schools.

Very few people took me seriously, assuming I was just promoting the school. They were wrong—that wasn't hyperbole; I believed it in my heart. There was no reason we would not excel. We were teaching in English with the same textbooks being used in the top schools. Our visiting professor program allowed us to attract some of the better teachers of specific subjects in the world, and maybe most importantly, we had a student body with something to prove—to themselves and to others. They had been knocked down, sometimes numerous times, and gotten back up.

I was depending on that attitude.

There were some people who believed we would discourage students from taking this test, knowing that a good performance would enable them to transfer, meaning we would lose their tuition. Actually, the opposite was true. I wanted them to transfer; I preached that. I told them if you can get accepted by an American medical school you should absolutely transfer. In fact, providing a viable opportunity to transfer was one of our core objectives.

But equally important for us, if we could demonstrate that our students could transfer into the same schools that had rejected them, we would attract far more people than we would lose. I believed those students who were able to transfer would be our best ambassadors. They would spread the gospel of St. George's.

The COTRANS was given once a year. Because our second class had raced through their classes, the first two classes took it together. The test was given at the New York Coliseum.

It was very exciting, but admittedly nerve-racking. This was the first opportunity our students had to test themselves against their sixteen thousand peers who had been accepted by domestic medical schools. "That was a critical exam," Leo Rotello recalls. "We worried about it because we really didn't know how good our education was compared to other people until we took these standardized tests."

We waited patiently for the results. Maybe we didn't exactly hold our breath, but there were anxious moments.

When the results were announced we were stunned. Thrilled. Overjoyed.

As our second annual newsletter reported, "Chancellor Modica said the COTRANS results were far better than even our most optimistic supporters could have ever hoped for…these results plus the overall passing rate placed St. George's well above the averages of other foreign medical schools."

We had a 79.8 percent pass rate. As I had predicted, our pass rate more than doubled the rate of most foreign medical schools. US schools averaged about 90 percent, but only one foreign school, Israel's Sackler School of Medicine—which had only a few US students—had a higher pass rate than we did.

But most startling was the fact that one of our students, Jeffrey Schultz, earned the highest score of any student studying medicine "throughout the world as well as every medical school in the United States." That was an incredible achievement, the highest score of any student studying medicine anywhere in the world. As *Tropic* magazine reported, "Like most Caribbean-bound students, Schultz had been rejected by many American schools." The world of medical schools opened to him, of course, and he transferred immediately to one of the best in the country. That was the best possible advertisement for us. In addition to his results, three other St. George's students scored in the ninety-ninth percentile.

Geoffrey Bourne was euphoric. He had been criticized in academia for lending his academic prestige to this potential scam school. This gave him the opportunity to boast, "All these results demonstrate that the caliber of our students and the level of teaching at St. George's is as good or better than any medical school in the world."

As good or better than any medical school in the world. I liked the sound of that. Take that NBC!

Within a few months, seventy-four of our students were able to transfer into American medical schools. Henry Collins, for example, transferred to Northwestern, the school his grandfather had attended that had rejected him. "I was walking four feet above the ground because I had gotten into a great school. So I hadn't suffered any hardship going to Grenada.

"I remember thinking how primitive it had seemed—we took pharmacology classes in a vacant building next to a grocery store—but finally realizing it doesn't matter if your school is some big stone edifice with ivy on the walls. What mattered was what's in your brain, who's teaching you, and, maybe most of all, how hard you work."

Almost without exception our students performed well in their new programs, validating our claims. Until those results were published, there had been doubts about our grading system. Was an A in Pathology at St. George's the equivalent of...of what grade at NYU or any other school? Those first transfer students proved they were getting a quality education.

During our first two years, we were second only to the University of Guadalajara, Mexico, a school that had been established in 1935, in students transferring to US schools. Eventually we had the highest transfer rate of any foreign school in the world; many years, literally one-third of our students were able to transfer. One year we achieved an almost unheard of 50 percent transfer rate. Another year we had twenty-eight students transfer into New York Medical College. The University of Miami began accepting so many of our students that Bob Jordan would visit there annually to assist in the transfer process.

Personally, I loved, *loved*, watching students like Bob Stroud being offered a place at the University of Maryland Medical School—which had rejected him four different times. As Geoffrey Bourne said, these transfers "underline the excellence of our teaching program and highlight the inadequacy of the US schools' selection process."

Exactly.

Given the fact that we were still unloading mattresses, depending on the fire department to deliver water, and fighting with the power company to keep the electricity on, our success in the COTRANS was a monumental achievement. We actually outperformed several fully accredited US medical schools whose students had completed their first two years.

These results surprised—and scared—the medical establishment. They couldn't believe this start-up had outperformed established schools.

As the respected British medical journal *Lancet* wondered, "If so much can be achieved by setting up a proprietary medical school in a distant West Indian island…and at modest cost, what might be achieved in the US itself when all sorts of academic buildings are standing vacant…" The article concluded with the medical establishment's worst fear: "Perhaps…the proprietary medical school may come back."

A staff physician at St. Michael's Medical Center, New Jersey's state medical school, told a reporter that St. George's educates its students economically, admitting, "These results raise questions about the expense of US medical education as well as the admissions criteria."

We obviously had created a problem. One of our visiting faculty members from Harvard told us that "[Harvard] President Bok chided his medical faculty as to why their highly selected students are doing poorly on the National Board exams." The answer, this professor suggested, was that because they had been accepted to Harvard Medical School, they "assumed they already knew what they need to know."

I learned firsthand the level of disbelief at our results several weeks later. I was in Chicago to attend an AMA meeting. I went there hoping we finally could start talking about who we were. We wanted to be part of the establishment. We wanted to work with them to achieve the mutual goal of educating doctors. Instead, I stepped into an elevator and within a floor found myself listening to a conversation about the test results. These men did not mention the school by name, and they didn't know who I was, but there was no doubt they were talking about us. Clearly, they were dumbfounded by our success. One man said flatly, "I think they must've gotten hold of the exam."

"Nah," the second man replied. "How could they have done that?"

"I don't know, but there's no other logical explanation."

There were a lot of people like that man in the elevator, who were suspicious of those results. They had been hopeful that the national boards would expose us, that a massive failure would prove them right in their disdain and put us out of business. When that failed, they held out hope it was an outlier, that our students had prepared for that first challenge and would not be able to repeat it. However, they were not willing to see it play out.

The AAMC obviously was shocked by our performance. Its spokesman casually dismissed our success, telling a reporter, "Just because one or two have done that well is not indicative of the quality of the program." And then they reacted: They changed the testing system. Literally changed the system. Maybe it was a coincidence; maybe it had nothing to do with our success. But suddenly, foreign medical school students were no longer permitted to take the national boards.

Instead, a new test was created solely for foreign students, the Medical Sciences Knowledge Profile. This would make it impossible to compare our scores with US schools, and the results were not published. They were not going to have surprising comparisons to American school students again.

Since students attending foreign medical schools were no longer allowed to take the national boards (COTRANS was the first part of the boards), a new test was created specifically for international medical graduates seeking to be certified to do a residency in the US, a necessity in order to practice medicine in the country. And rather than taking it after completing the first two years, it was given after completing medical school.

Our first results under the new test were equally impressive. The charter class had a 96 percent pass rate, second only to Sackler again—although we had ninety-nine students taking the test while they had ten or eleven. The world average was 39 percent. Guadalajara had a pass rate of 49 percent. I would like to think our students' superb performance on this "foreign students only" test is what led to today's testing, in which all medical students, both domestic and foreign, must pass the same exact licensing exams.

Those results were far better than our most optimistic supporters—me, for example—could have realistically hoped for. We were proving the established medical education system was not the only way to produce quality doctors. And just to make certain those people protecting that system were aware of our accomplishments, I placed an ad on the front page of the *New York Times* Education section listing the results—with St. George's number two. This was it, the big kahuna, the actual light at the end of the tunnel. On the first attempt, 96 percent of the graduates of this upstart medical school were certifiable by the Educational Commission for Foreign Educational Graduates and could obtain residency training and then practice medicine.

Each time we were attacked, a reporter would call me for a combative comment. In response I'd repeat my standing offer to any medical school dean who believed our school shouldn't exist, who believed our graduates weren't as qualified as their graduates. Each of us would pick ten graduates who would compete in any type of examination—oral, clinical, paper tests, anything they wanted—but not let the people doing the testing know which students were from which school. I guaranteed they would not be able to tell where the competitors had attended school. In fact, I was sure they would be embarrassed. Not surprisingly, no one ever took me up on that offer.

CHAPTER 16

The Caribbean Gold Rush

"Don't give up. I'm here...."

—Me, with my team

Another result of our success was competition. We had created a viable path for Americans to attend an English-speaking medical school and eventually become licensed physicians in the United States. And while those first few years we were barely breaking even financially, it was apparent this could become a very good business. A lot of entrepreneurs were watching with great interest to see if we could do what we were promising. Once it became clear that we were legally, academically, and economically viable, other people jumped into this new world. Without intending to, without wanting to, I had created an industry.

When *New York* magazine reported that Bob Ross's Ross University School of Medicine on Dominica had made almost $1 million profit in 1981, the real Caribbean gold rush began. Entrepreneurs raced to the region, trying to find a hospitable island. Many of those island nations, seeing the positive impact we had made on Grenada, welcomed them. Schools popped up on Montserrat, Antigua, Aruba, and Anguilla; on St. Lucia, Barbados, Trinidad, and Jamaica; on Dominica and Grand Turk; in the Dominican Republic; on St. Maarten, Nevis, and St. Kitts. By 2017 there would be more than one hundred different schools, seventy-five of them qualified to offer certification, meaning they were recognized by the government of the country in which they were located. In the previous decades many others had opened and shut down.

Many of those schools were substandard. They rented space anywhere possible. One was located over a bar, another was near an open sewer, still others were in abandoned Quonset huts. Some of those schools had as few as thirty or forty students—who were required to supply their own microscopes.

We had uncovered a large, underserved, sometimes desperate reservoir of young people who dreamed of a medical career—and there were many unscrupulous people ready to take advantage of them. Two "schools" were caught selling bogus diplomas; they were shut down, and several administrators were sent to prison for falsifying documents. This was terrible for us—it fed into the narrative being spread by the AAMC that all Caribbean schools were inferior and students who graduated from those schools were not qualified to practice medicine. "The present situation can generally be described as chaotic," the prestigious *New England Journal of Medicine* reported. "They are lacking in any guiding philosophy, dubious in its equity and dangerously uneven in professional standards." Unfortunately, and inevitably, we got thrown in with them, and it damaged our reputation. "Guilt by association," Geoffrey Bourne lamented.

These schools were opened by a fascinating array of people, among them some unusual characters. That included businessmen, physicians, con men, and even the brother of a Nigerian chieftain living in Chicago.

Our first significant English-speaking competitor in the Caribbean was Bob Ross, who founded what became the Ross University School of Medicine. And we were responsible for that too. I eventually got to know Bob pretty well. A man named Robert Rosen had essentially created the flamboyant character Bob Ross. "The new Marco Polo," as *Time* magazine called him, had earned millions of dollars by building trading partnerships with mostly isolated countries behind the Iron Curtain—countries like Bulgaria, Poland, and Romania but eventually including Russia and mainland China. He had learned about us from his partner, a man named Jerry Berenson, whose son had utilized the pipeline I had set up to enroll qualified students in the Dominican Republic. He recognized the potential and opened his own placement agency to send students to foreign medical schools, among them St. George's.

His fee for a successful placement was, I believe, $1,000. In our first few months we accepted several of his clients. But one day a couple came to my office in Bay Shore. They were from Merrick, a nearby community. Through Bob Ross's placement company, their twin sons had applied and been accepted by St. George's. For his work they had paid Ross $2,000. "We didn't know anything about the school," they told me, "and he did. But we don't think it's fair that we have to pay separate fees. We wanted to pay him only $1,000." I thought this was simply a dispute about that fee, but then they said something I will never forget. "When we asked him about it, he said he had to keep the whole $2,000 because he doesn't get it all. 'How do you think we get these kids into school?' he told us. 'We have to take care of the admissions people.'"

I was stunned. Speechless. "We have to take care of the admissions people"? Paying them? This was the kind of story that could destroy our school. It would reinforce claims that admissions were for sale. I was irate. Andy Belford, my close friend, was our admissions director. "What?" I said incredulously to the parents. "Well, I grew up with the admissions director. I don't believe that for a second."

Andy was working in his office. He came back to my office and listened to this story. In all the years I'd known him I couldn't recall ever seeing him so angry. "We would never do that," he said. "Never. I guarantee you that nobody here got one dime. Not a penny."

I phoned Bob Ross. We'd spoken several times, but I didn't really know him. I told him who was sitting in my office. "These people told me they had to pay a double fee. I didn't even know they used your agency."

He backed off. "We didn't exactly say that."

"That's what they just told me." After a brief conversation I said flatly, "You really have a lot of nerve. I don't know who told them that. Their kids are in school, but I expect you to refund $1,000 to this family."

"We can't do that," he said equally firmly.

"That's up to you. But I guarantee that unless you give them a refund, we will never accept another applicant from your company."

He didn't back off. Not an inch. Eventually we met face-to-face in his office, and he tried to justify those charges. "We have expenses," he said. He pointed his index finger at me. "And you are not telling me what to do with my own agency."

Bob Ross was just about twice my age, but I was not afraid to stand up to him. Not when my school's reputation was on the line. "Well, I am telling you something. I'm telling you we're never going to accept another student from you."

"Okay," he responded. "I'll start my own school. You'll see."

Admittedly, I did not take that threat seriously. Who knows if he had already been making preparations to do just that? But eight months later the University of Dominica School of Medicine opened on Dominica, just months after that country gained its independence from Great Britain. Its charter class had eleven students. Three years later, at the request of the island's government, the name of the school was changed to Ross University. Ross University eventually became our main competitor and through the years has accepted students we certainly would have liked to have enrolled. Bob Ross always watched what we did, then tried to emulate that—and sometimes even go further. For example, we had two entering classes each year, so he increased it to three new classes annually, in January, May, and September.

Bob Ross was a physically large man, and boy, did he love attention. While I was known for wearing conservative three-piece suits, he often sported a ten-gallon hat and a full-length beaver-skin coat. On the walls of his office he had photographs of himself with, I believe, six former American presidents. We certainly were in competition, although there was an abundance of qualified applicants to fulfill both our enrollments.

I think Bob took the competition a bit more personally than I did. For example, at one point the nation of Grenada honored me by appointing me its ambassador-at-large. Although that honor meant a lot to me, the extent of my boasting is that at times I will wear a Grenadian flag pin on my lapel.

Soon after, Bob expected the same recognition from Dominica—and got it. Ambassador-at-Large Ross then affixed small Dominican flags to the front of his limousine, which gave him an official-looking boost as he drove around New York City.

Among those areas we pioneered at St. George's was obtaining clinical placements at American hospitals. That was an uphill battle. Maybe an up-mountain battle. While getting that program established, I became acquainted with Abdul Islami, the vice chairman of St. Barnabas Hospital in Livingston, New Jersey. Dr. Islami was also an executive officer of the Educational Commission for Foreign Medical Graduates and the leader of the state medical board that had to approve St. George's right to place students in clinical positions in New Jersey. It had taken us a tremendous effort over a prolonged period of time to finally get approved for clinicals in New Jersey. But he was always an honest broker. We demonstrated the high quality of our program and earned his respect by being transparent in what we had already achieved and our willingness to improve the program in any way the board determined might enhance the program. Eventually one of his relatives attended St. George's. Few, if any, other foreign schools who applied to conduct clinical placements received this approval.

Undoubtedly the most unusual character I dealt with was Eddie Antar, and the character he had created was Crazy Eddie. Antar transformed one electronics store in Brooklyn into a forty-three-store chain with low prices and a legendary ad campaign. An actor named Jerry Carroll became well known for screaming at viewers, guaranteeing to beat any legitimate price on TVs and stereos—often while objects like bananas and cherries were being thrown at him—while reminding them, "Crazy Eddie! His prices are innnnn-sane!" The commercials were so widely known they were parodied on *Saturday Night Live*.

It's difficult to understand how selling stereos translated into founding a medical school. In the lawsuits that followed he claimed he had been scammed. Actually, opening his school was not difficult. Many Caribbean nations wanted to repeat Grenada's success. There was no shortage of doctors ready to spend several winter weeks in the warm sunshine with their families in exchange for teaching a few courses. And few people were better at advertising or promotion than Crazy Eddie Antar. It didn't matter what he was selling—a color TV, a medical school education—he was a great salesman.

His University of St. Lucia School of Medicine was founded in 1980. The school operated mostly out of rented hotel rooms—and still managed to attract about a hundred students. It had no facilities, no books, certainly no "fresh cadavers" (as described in later lawsuits), and, ironically, no televisions. When students wanted to watch the World Series, they had to pay the only person on the island with an antenna able to pick up a signal to turn it in that direction.

I learned about Antar's school when I saw a half-page ad in the *New York Times*. My heart stopped. We were still struggling to survive, and this ad made it sound like the school was being founded by Harvard professors. I hadn't been overly concerned about the other schools that had opened because they were taking students we had not accepted; the only advantage they had over us was lower tuition. But this? If this new school offered a competitive education at a lower price, that would be a problem. We had no idea who the people were behind this, but the ad made it appear they had sufficient financial support to actually do some of the things we could only dream about.

A friend of mine once said that the key to success in American business is being the first to be second. Meaning let someone else do the hard work of creating the path, pay attention to their mistakes, then once the market is proven to exist, go in bigger and better. If someone had done that while we were still developing, it would have damaged us and maybe even put us out of business. Reading the ad, I was concerned that this might be that effort.

Several weeks later I learned Eddie Antar, *the* Crazy Eddie, was the owner of this school. The rumor was that his brother-in-law couldn't get into an offshore medical school (it may have been St. George's), and the business model attracted him. So, like Ross, the brother of a Nigerian chieftain, and others, he got into the business. I certainly was concerned;

maybe he didn't know anything about medical education, but every time I turned on my TV, I was reminded that he was a master marketer.

For many different reasons Antar's school was a dismal failure. Early in its second semester, we got a phone call informing us that he was considering selling it and wanted to meet with us. I spoke with each of our founders, and they were unanimous: Are you innnnn-sane! They weren't the slightest bit interested in meeting with him. I always like to explore possibilities, so I was finally able to convince them to at least have a meeting. *What harm can it do?* was the essence of my argument.

The initial meeting was held at the famed Sardi's restaurant in Manhattan. We didn't know what to expect: Antar was reputed to be one of the toughest negotiators in a business legendary for tough negotiators. Supposedly, he had a hundred-pound German shepherd that was known to lick the ears of distributors during negotiations, causing an executive of a consumer products company to once complain, "If you don't like dogs, you learn to act like you do."

Sardi's was an upscale restaurant, tie and jacket required. I went to this meeting with my father, Andy Belford, and Pat Adams. We arrived and waited. We knew we were not meeting the shouting pitchman from TV. Instead, the maître d' came walking toward us trailed by a short, kind of stubby man wearing a dark-colored jogging suit with a thick gold chain hanging loosely around his neck.

This was Eddie Antar. He was alone—there would be no ear licking. He'd gotten into the medical school business because he thought it was a good idea, thank you, he said, but he was concerned about the future of his school. So he had decided to sell it—to us.

We actually had rehearsed for this meeting. The one thing on which we had all agreed was that we would not buy his school. I went carefully through all the reasons why we would not buy it, then asked him exactly what his goal was. To his credit, he replied, "I'd like to get back some of the money I invested, and I want to make sure our students are taken care of." It turned out he really was concerned about those students. The way he expressed it was classic Antar: "These students aren't retail merchandise. I can send stereos back. I can send tape machines back. But I can't send students back."

There was a potential upside for us. At least some of his most qualified students would stay at St. George's. I told him, "We'd be happy to take your students as transfers." But we certainly were not going to pay him anything. "Maybe what we can do," I suggested, "is give them free tuition for the time they spent with you."

When you're charting a path through new territory, you have be extremely careful. We hadn't graduated our first class. If we suddenly accepted a large number of transfers, it might appear that we had very low standards. We also knew that at least some of these students were rejected by St. George's, and a few of them had actually flunked out. Some of them didn't even have undergraduate degrees. As financially enticing as this pot of students was, we could not jeopardize our accreditation by accepting them.

My father was a tough businessman.

He wanted something in return for accepting even well-qualified students. I knew Antar wasn't going to pay anyone to take his students. He was closing the school because he was bleeding money. The two men negotiated back and forth, back and forth, without reaching an agreement. At the end of the meeting, Antar looked at me and said, "You know what, Charlie? The apple doesn't fall far from the tree." Whatever he meant, I took it as a compliment.

But it was my father who responded, telling him, "In this case the tree was on a big hill."

When we met a second time, Antar told us that Bob Ross had offered to pay a certain amount for each student and accept their credits without requiring them to retake courses. "We can't do that," I told him. "I was trying to meet you in the middle. You're putting those students at risk. We can't offer anything more than I told you. We can't even take all of your students. But I'll tell you what—we will take your faculty because we need additional teachers anyway. Then at least you won't have to worry about their contracts."

Antar eventually accepted our offer, which was better for his students but probably worse for him. Bob Ross was furious. He demanded to know what I had paid Antar. The only thing I would tell him was, "Less than you were offering." He couldn't accept that. It was beyond his understanding that someone would take less money.

These negotiations with Antar had taken place very quietly. He did not want St. Lucia's government to know he was shutting down. After we made the deal I flew to that beautiful island with Andy Belford, Vish Rao, and several other staff members. The students were in class, but they were asked to assemble in a central meeting point. An announcement was made that the school was closing immediately. People gasped, then started crying. They were in shock. They were watching their dream end. I understood that. I did think, for an instant, that had things gone differently, that could have been our students. It hurt.

As the news settled in I introduced myself as the chancellor of St. George's and told them, "Don't give up. I'm here with our director of admissions, our dean of students, and some of our colleagues. We'd like to try to get as many of you as possible to St. George's..."

There were 127 students enrolled in St. Lucia. We outlined a path for every one of them to attend St. George's. Those who had the entering qualifications and good grades were accepted on par, right where they were in their studies. Some of them were accepted into the first term; others were given a provisional acceptance based on their going back to school to complete our academic requirements and an interview—but we made sure every single student had a pathway to enter SGU if they wanted it.

We also set up a program with Barry University in Florida that enabled some of those students to earn a dual degree, a bachelor's degree in medicine and a master's in biomedical sciences. It wasn't a perfect solution, but it was very good. We did this, I explained, because I believed we had an obligation to ensure students who had come to the Caribbean—like those on St. Lucia—were not exploited.

There are always going to be people trying to take advantage of others. I was concerned we would be thrown in with them. To survive, to succeed, we had to not only be better than other offshore medical schools, we had to be as good as most domestic schools. We worked extremely hard to establish our reputation—and we have always fought hard to defend it. The reality is the medical establishment has continued to fight offshore medical schools, even while the shortage of physicians continues to grow. In 2020, for example, the AAMC predicted the nation would face a shortage of between 54,000 and 140,000 doctors by 2033. And because a significant number of domestic graduates continue to pursue the higher-paying specialties, the already-existing shortage of primary-care physicians will become even more acute.

As we learned during the COVID-19 pandemic, that lack of front-line physicians can be devastating. But that hasn't stopped the AAMC from taking positions that restrict access for our graduates. Primary care is a disaster in 2022. One of our early graduates recently told me that he would love to cut back his workload—but it's impossible. "There's no one who can take my patients," he explained.

A position paper issued in 2017 quoted an article in *Academic Medicine* warning, "U.S. medical education today faces a threat similar to that leading up to the [1910] Flexner Report [which led to the introduction of national medical school standards]. Although this time the schools that do not meet the training standards necessary to ensure public health are outside U.S. borders. A dire emergency is approaching that could compromise American medical education…"

While warning of this impending "emergency," and even after decades of proof that our graduates are in every possible way the equal of domestic school graduates, the establishment continues to lump St. George's, Ross, and several other long-established Caribbean medical schools that graduate fully trained and highly qualified students into the larger group of all Caribbean schools.

And yet, with more than twenty thousand graduates, Grenada ranks second only to India in the number of internationally trained physicians licensed to practice in America.

I am extremely proud of that. And dedicated to catching India!

CHAPTER 17

The Battle of St. Vincent

"I know this is a crazy idea..."

—Me again

The practice of medicine is learned in a clinical setting. That's where medical students are transformed into doctors. Generally, after completing two years of classroom study, students spend the next two years working with physicians and patients in a clinical setting, while taking additional courses that expose them to a variety of specialties. By passing the first part of the national boards, our students had qualified for clinical training. That was a huge deal—it meant they were going to learn medicine in a hospital setting. It meant they were going to become doctors.

I'll never forget how one of our students responded after learning he had passed the exam: He proudly brought flowers to his mother's grave to share the news with her.

I knew from the beginning that finding clinical spots for our students was going to be a difficult problem to solve, so I put it off while dealing with the more immediate challenges—like providing food and water. But eventually I had to deal with it.

Finding clinical slots in hospitals was vital. Without that two years of training our students could not complete their medical degrees or be licensed to practice medicine in the States. But almost all the available positions in teaching hospitals were already being filled by students from domestic schools.

The two-hundred-bed St. George's General Hospital was located on the top of a bluff. The view was spectacular; the hospital was not. Though we had helped upgrade its capabilities, it was far from a modern health-care facility. Its wards were segregated by gender, and signs directed patients to FEMALE MEDICINE. Some patients brought their own sheets with them. The staff, while dedicated, practiced medicine as it was practiced in Caribbean nations—they did as much as possible with the limited equipment they had.

Following a tenet of the British model of medical education, our students were taught how to conduct thorough physical examinations of patients at this hospital. We even instituted a graduation requirement that our students had to pass a final oral examination bedside with real patients observed by four physicians, all of whom had to give a passing grade. Later on, we switched to the method pioneered by US medical schools of using mock patients (standardized patients) who were given scripts of medical problems to present to the students. We felt validated when we learned later that the ECFMG adopted a similar requirement for all foreign medical school graduates. Looking back, especially from the viewpoint of a modern medical school offering students cutting-edge facilities, I take great pride in the fact that we were able to produce so many fine physicians with those limited resources.

It was a challenging situation. One day a woman came to the hospital showing a large growth. A breast cancer tumor was literally emerging from her chest. "My God," one of our students remembers thinking, "this is what cancer looks like." There was nothing the hospital could do but send her home to die.

So it was obvious we were going to have to find some way of getting more clinical spots. That was our Holy Grail. As it happened, in 1978 I attended a meeting of all the Caribbean ministers of health, which was held on St. Vincent. I had been asked to attend by Grenada's health minister essentially so I could brag about the school. We had been in operation for only slightly more than a year but already had made a measurable impact on the country's economy. These other people could see what was possible and wanted to get involved. So naturally I was the center of attention at the meeting.

At a cocktail party, St. Vincent's minister of health, Randy Russell, who also owned the local Pepsi bottling company, took me aside and surprised me by asking bluntly, "Could you start a school here?"

In business situations, whenever possible I begin with a yes. No can always come later. Several days later I repeated that request to the three founders, telling them we had an opportunity to open a second school. "Why would we want to do that?" they responded. "We would double our costs. And if we do that, every island in the Caribbean will want us to open a school."

True. And just imagine what we could have built if we'd done just that. But I was concerned that if we did not do something, St. Vincent might find someone else who would open a competing school on that island. We had drawn the blueprint. As we had seen with Bob Ross and others, following it was relatively simple.

But as I thought about the possibilities, the wheels began turning. I was a firm believer that my wild ideas could be transformed into reality. It suddenly occurred to me that we could satisfy St. Vincent while solving the biggest problem we were facing.

One of my biggest advantages was being young enough not to be weighed down by experience. Rather than thinking of these problems as challenges, I saw them as opportunities. My solution was to create something that no one else was doing, something that as far as I knew had never been done: We would hold a transitional semester on St. Vincent.

I told Russell, "You know, we really don't have the wherewithal to open another school, but I think I can engineer something that would work for both of us."

It was enough to catch his curiosity.

I continued, "We'd need you to give us a charter for a full school, but with the understanding that for the time being, and maybe forever, we're only operating one semester on the island. What we want to do is add a fifth semester to the curriculum. It would take place between the two years of classroom study and the two years of clinical work in a hospital, and prepare them for the clinical work." This would allow us to provide the hands-on preparation our students needed before beginning their hospital rotations. They would learn how to properly use a stethoscope.

What I was also doing was protecting our turf. We were completely dependent on the whims of Sir Eric Gairy. Having a second charter would give us a landing spot if Grenada suddenly tried to change the equation. If necessary, we could pack up the whole school and operate on St. Vincent. I told the founders, "I know this is a crazy idea"—maybe I should have said *another* crazy idea—"but I also know we don't want a competitive school opening on St. Vincent. This will be great for St. Vincent and for us. It'll be that fifth semester we've been talking about, preparing our people for clinicals."

They embraced the concept. "Could we grant a degree from that school?" Pat Adams asked. Just in case? Absolutely.

My plan satisfied multiple needs. In contrast to Grenada's main hospital, St. Vincent had a 250-bed, reasonably well-equipped hospital capable of taking X-rays and conducting basic laboratory tests. The St. Vincent government eventually agreed to establish an affiliated institution, the Kingstown Medical College, which I named after the capital of St. Vincent, just as St. George's was the capital of Grenada. While we would be chartered to conduct our full program there, in actuality our students would move there for a fifth semester emphasizing preclinical preparation. We were thrilled.

Sir Eric was not thrilled. In fact, his response might accurately be described as "furious." The school had proven to be a great boon to Grenada's economy. It was his job to protect that. He "invited" me to answer questions in front of his cabinet. "We understand you're thinking of bringing part of your program to the island of St. Vincent," he said.

That's true, I admitted. "I was going to talk to you about it. But the program is nothing like what we have here. What we have here is working beautifully. We love what we have here." Maybe I embellished a bit, claiming we had always planned to conduct this portion of the program in the States but it would be considerably easier in the islands.

This was a very difficult meeting. We needed those clinical slots in the hospital on St. Vincent, I explained. It doubled our clinical capability. But, I emphasized, "We're only promising to have the fifth semester there."

With that, Prime Minister Gairy SLAMMED! his hand down on the desk. "You shall not go to St. Vincent!" he shouted. "We will consider this a violation of your charter. You are dishonoring Grenada. That is not going to happen!" With that, he got up and stomped out of the room.

Well, that certainly had not gone well. Maybe it was a good thing I hadn't told him we also had contacted Trinidad and Antigua to see if they would consider letting us conduct a clinical program in their hospitals. Given Gairy's response, it probably was a good thing they had turned us down.

I called my father in New York. I had to be careful with my words, assuming someone was listening to our conversation. "The prime minister doesn't want us to go there," I told him, adding, just in case anyone was listening, "Of course I understand that, but the main thing is to get more clinical spots lined up. If we can't get these clinicals in the United States, then we need to get them down here."

I also told our students about the decision to open a facility on St. Vincent, hoping to get their support. I told them anything positive I could think of: This will help us get more hospital spots. It will give you an entirely new experience. It's good culturally. It'll make you a better doctor and "qualify you as a doctor to serve in any part of the world." I pointed out that for more than two hundred years, Oxford and Cambridge had taught preclinical subjects on their campuses, as we did in Grenada, but then sent their students to hospitals in London for clinical experience, as we wanted to do on St. Vincent.

None of it seemed to matter. Whatever I said, our students were as strongly against it as the Gairy government. They were settled on Grenada, they had their housing and routines—they did not see the purpose in being uprooted.

I had always been honest with our students. I never, ever claimed we would be able to secure clinical spots in the States. What I did promise was that we would find places that would enable them to fulfill the licensing requirements they needed to practice domestically. I was confident I could secure those spots in the States. That's what I was working toward. St. Vincent could help us—at least temporarily—fill that gap. I refused to give up hope. There had to be a way, I just hadn't found it.

I also did not want them to get involved in the politics of the situation.

Gairy finally agreed to meet with me privately. In that meeting I emphasized that getting additional clinical positions was absolutely essential for us. "Is there any way around this?"

He shook his head. "I cannot see any."

A few days later I was told the local labor union called a strike against the school and walked out. Coincidently, the head of the union was Eric Gairy. The workers demanded a wage increase and other benefits far greater than anything we could afford. It didn't shut us down, but it definitely slowed us down.

While I was in New York, Gairy decided he needed to address the students. He circulated a letter telling them, "The government views with great concern the move by the authorities of the St. George's School of Medicine to set up a programme of clinical studies in St. Vincent and is aware that that these students are unwilling to go to St. Vincent." He added that our charter "does not extend to St. Vincent and no student of this school can be expected to go there unless the Act is amended."

He did not mention that he was the only person who could amend it.

He was using our students to apply additional pressure and visited the campus to make a speech. Eric Gairy never traveled silently. He made a grand entrance, arriving in his flag-flying limousine, accompanied by a motorcycle escort, dressed in full regalia. Our students were asked to assemble in the lecture hall. There was absolutely no implied threat, but the curiosity factor was off the scale. Gairy was a wonderful performer. The students always enjoyed watching him. More than three hundred students from the charter and Super Eight classes crowded together.

He mounted the stage carrying a closed box. He set it down on the podium so the audience could see it. They knew from its presence and placement it obviously contained something important. But what?

He had their curiosity, and therefore their attention. "The school wants to move one of your semesters to a neighboring island," he told them in his booming voice. "This government does not support this. We think this is against your interest. It is my position to defend the best interests of my country. I have spent my life doing that."

With that, he finally opened the box. He reached into it and withdrew a brightly colored medal. He held it up high and explained how he had earned it. Then he did it again with a second and then a third brightly colored medal. Finally, he asked, "I want to know. Do you want to go to St. Vincent now knowing this?" They did not. They saw no value in spending several months on another island.

I was furious. He had outsmarted us. But I also was an optimist. He had outsmarted us…so far.

I certainly had come a long way since law school. I was trying to negotiate the settlement of a workers strike at my medical school on a Caribbean island. But I was completely aware that Sir Eric was manipulating events. We finally met about a week later.

"This is very unfortunate, Mr. Prime Minister," I said. "We have this ongoing strike, and you're angry about St. Vincent. How can we deal with these problems?"

"I have two hats here," he responded dramatically. "I am the union leader and I am the head of this government. I will not talk about both of these issues together. Which shall we talk about first?"

"Maybe we should talk about the union first," I suggested. I understood the political aspect of his problem: If he allowed us to go to St. Vincent, he had to get something in return. I had my fingers crossed that he was going to lead us out of this mess.

"All right," he agreed, waving his index finger back and forth, "but we will talk only about the union issue. These people need raises." We went back and forth, back and forth. I asked him if we could balance his request with the second issue. "No!" He was emphatic. "We can discuss only one issue at a time. I am wearing my union hat now. We must have an increase in salary." He then paused, as if thinking about it, deciding, "We will accept a one-third increase."

That was the price. His workers had to receive a 33.3 percent wage increase in addition to other small benefits. I knew I was going to get lambasted by the founders, but I didn't see any other options. "All right," I said, "I'm going to give you an agreement on that. It's going to be tough for us, but we'll do it. Now can we talk about the other thing?"

His eyes opened wide. "Oh, you mean my other hat? I have to put on my other hat, my prime minister hat." He shifted in his chair and took a deep breath, as if we were starting a different meeting. "I understand your desire to go there," he said. "But I am concerned. You must promise me that you are going to have only one semester there. I don't want students spending a whole year there."

I was thrilled to agree to that. "Grenada is our home. That won't change." I gave him my word, and he trusted me to keep it.

I called my father to tell him I'd settled both issues. I told him how important this was for the future of the school, how it gave us a fall-back position if we couldn't secure enough clinical slots, and then finally mentioned, almost as an aside, "Oh, by the way, we have to increase salaries a little bit."

The Kingstown Medical College opened in spring 1979. At that time St. Vincent was considerably more developed than Grenada. It had been discovered and named by Christopher Columbus in 1498. Since 1763, with a few minor bumps, it had been a British colony. In 1979, several months after we opened the campus, it became an independent nation. There was a so-called active volcano on the island, La Soufrière, which had last erupted in 1902, so we were not overly concerned about that.

There was no chance it would erupt again. No chance.

The first thing we did after receiving a charter from the St. Vincent government was build a modern 250-seat lecture hall—with walls and windows that could be closed! The island had an established middle class. There was a large bakery just outside the airport, so when arriving or departing you were overwhelmed by the comforting aroma of fresh-baked bread and rolls. There was more housing, easier availability of supplies, a casino, and perhaps the key to civilization, imported Budweiser beer.

That actually became a selling point for our students. A taste of home! Not only couldn't you get American beer in Grenada, at times they would run out of beer bottles and students would have to buy a keg and reuse old bottles. Once, I remember, the local brewery actually issued a request on the radio that people return empties so they could be refilled.

During those early years I was constantly trying to improve our faculty. When I heard about a qualified professional who might be available, I did everything possible to lure him or her to Grenada. I learned somehow that Dr. Morris Alpert, a well-respected and very popular professor of surgery at Albany Medical College, was being forced to retire and was not happy about it. Our kind of guy. I flew to Albany and minutes after meeting him knew I wanted to hire him. We didn't know where he fit, but we knew we wanted him.

Dr. Alpert flew to Grenada to meet with Geoffrey Bourne. Geoffrey also wanted to hire him to do something somewhere. Alpert agreed to join the faculty but wanted a senior position. "You know," I told Geoffrey, "when we open the second campus on St. Vincent, he'd be a great choice to run it."

One of the jackpot decisions I made—like hiring Geoffrey Bourne—was hiring Morrie Alpert. Morrie reminded some people of the cartoon character Mr. Magoo; he was short, bald, and cantankerous, and he often seemed to be fumbling. But anyone who approached Morrie as if he were anything like fumbling soon became aware of his true temperament—strong, irascible, honest, intelligent, and forthright.

If you're truly lucky, on occasion a person will show up in your life at the precise time they are needed with the skills required to accomplish the task. It happened to me. Twice. Geoffrey Bourne and Morrie Alpert. Morrie created the program on St. Vincent mostly out of dreams and wishes. He successfully integrated the basic sciences the students had spent two years learning with their clinical correlations—the practice of medicine. The first two years on Grenada were bookwork, lectures, and labs. Students could do that anywhere. In a shaded parking lot. In a converted laundry room. On a magnificent beach. Our visiting professor program guaranteed a flow of excellent instructors. But clinical experience, hands-on medicine, had very different requirements. We still weren't quite sure how we were going to make that happen. The semester on St. Vincent was designed to prepare students for it. Wherever "it" would be.

While I was struggling with securing clinical slots, students never panicked. They were amazing. As Joe Nossiff remembers, "We didn't have anything at that point; they were still trying to cobble together a plan. But for some reason we weren't in a panic about it. I think by that time most of us had faith in Charlie that he was going to figure out a way."

Morrie Alpert created the fifth semester structure. There was nothing like it, as far as we knew, at any medical school in the world. Other schools did not have that transition—they went right from books to clinicals. He began by personally conducting rounds, taking the students around the hospital on St. Vincent, teaching them to be doctors. But he also had made countless friends throughout his distinguished career and began inviting them to the Caribbean. Every two weeks a prominent oncologist or hematologist or ophthalmologist or whatever specialty was desired would arrive from Brown, Harvard, Georgetown, McGill, Northwestern to teach the clinical correlation of the basic sciences—how to use the information students had been taught in order to treat patients. Coincidently, Chuck Schwartz's wife had attended Albany Med School. He noted, "It turned out that many of the same people who had taught her were there teaching me."

It wasn't an easy semester—Morrie made sure of that. He was a disciplinarian, and he was demanding. Raz Giliberti remembers, "Attendance at all lectures was compulsory. He didn't want his guests lecturing to a half-filled auditorium. We could not miss a class. We could not be late for a class. If we were, he would find us and drag us in. I remember him dragging me out of the casino, telling me, 'Giliberti, come with me. You've got cardiology in the morning.' We loved him for it."

"He was always yelling at us," Jack Cush recalled. "Do it right, do it right, whatever we were doing. Do it right. When we got to St. Vincent, we didn't know very much. We were starting from textbooks. It was like a cooking teacher holding up a spoon and telling people who read cookbooks, this is a spoon. He was constantly correcting us. 'You're on the wrong side of the bed. You're using the wrong hand. Get out of the way.'"

After all the complaining, the first classes enjoyed living on St. Vincent considerably more than they had anticipated. It was more developed than Grenada and had more of the amenities they desired. There were quite a few homes and apartments for rent at reasonable prices. There was dependable running water and electricity. Supermarkets delivered. Did I mention the Budweiser? The beaches were nowhere near as beautiful as Grenada, but there were beaches. And instead of Gairy's Evening Palace, the major distraction was the Emerald Valley Casino in Kingstown, where croupiers rotated to the island from London's Playboy Club International.

In terms of medical education, the students agreed it was extremely beneficial. It was, in various ways, their first finishing school. "We had an extra four months of intense lectures in the various medical specialties, neurology, cardiac, pulmonary, diagnosis, all of them," said John Modica.

The semester was sixteen weeks long. Half of each day was spent in a classroom listening to lectures on clinical application, how to put knowledge into practice; the other half of the day was spent working alongside doctors in the clinic.

This was the first time many of our students had actually treated patients. It was, as they described it, their opportunity to learn their anus from their elbow. Or as it also was referred to, Introduction to Medical Embarrassment. Jack Cush once made rounds with a practicing physician and a group of his fellow students. "One of my classmates was a big, tall, very cocky guy," he recalls. "We stopped at the bedside of an emaciated young man. He was suffering from malnutrition. He had a tube down his throat and several IVs inserted; he was not looking good. As the attending physician was explaining in detail how his body was shutting down, I glanced at my classmate. He was standing at the back of the group. I saw his eyes roll up in his head and this redwood tree of a man went straight down. He hit the floor hard. That was the end of rounds for the next hour."

In so many different ways, our students began learning the practice of medicine. John Washington used to get a ride to the hospital from one of the residents. As they drove to work one morning, he remembers, they passed a man walking on the side of the road. A few seconds later the doctor asked Washington, "Did you notice that guy back there?" He had. "What's wrong with him?"

What's wrong with him? Just like that, from a passing observation? John admitted he had no idea. The doctor described the man's posture and the way he was walking, then said, "He has Parkinson's."

Danny Ricciardi, Frank Arbucci, and Da Boys went to St. Vincent together. They were excited about transforming their classroom education into reality, an opportunity to see how much they had learned. This is the rite of passage that every doctor goes through—and remembers. And while they were admittedly nervous about actually treating patients, they also were confident. As Frankie recalled, "We were in the hospital clinic and the very first patient of my career walked in. Danny and several of my colleagues were there. I shook my first patient's hand. My colleagues also shook his hand. As we had been taught, I began asking the basic questions. I fixed a big, comforting smile on my face and asked, 'So what's wrong today?'

"'I have a bad rash on my hand,' he said.

"My smile disappeared. I looked at his hand. Holy shit! I instantly diagnosed his problem: He was suffering from secondary syphilis. We had learned all about it. He had syphilis and it had spread in his system and was now literally coming out of his hand. As a group, we excused ourselves and ran to the men's room. We started washing our hands. And then washed our hands again. And then got penicillin shots."

Those first classes on St. Vincent laid the groundwork for what was to become an extremely successful program.

CHAPTER 18

"Long Live the Revo!"

NO CLASSES TODAY. REVOLUTION.

—Sign outside St. George's University classroom, March 13, 1979

Two years after welcoming our first students, we had four entering classes on Grenada, we had a growing and enthusiastic faculty, we had an established and popular visiting instructor structure, we had broken ground on a new library and lab buildings, we had established our presence and had one class on St. Vincent, we were successfully fending off competitors and beginning to negotiate contracts with mainland hospitals for clinical positions, and we had proved on the national tests that our students were competitive with their domestically educated peers.

We had overcome countless difficulties, settled with Prime Minister Eric Gairy, and, it appeared, were ready to prosper. Everything was running smoothly. What could happen?

On March 13, 1979, roughly two months after our fourth class had begun, I suddenly found myself in the middle of a coup d'etat.

As we had been warned, we stayed out of Grenadian politics. In fact, on a LIAT flight to the island, a student was seated next to opposition leader Maurice Bishop, who began discussing the political situation. The student stopped him, explaining, "We're guests of the Grenadian government. We're grateful that they have us here as medical students." Then he refused to engage in a political discussion.

But we certainly were aware of the growing tension on the island. Gairy and Bishop had been rivals long before we settled there. Gairy had gained power by uniting city and rural workers into a trade union. He organized the Grenada People's Party in 1951, preaching against the economic domination of British planters and traders. He had been a leader of the independence movement, and after Grenada was granted Commonwealth status, he became its first prime minister. He was a national hero.

But after he began consolidating his power by limiting civil liberties, granting additional powers to the police and army, and arresting members of the opposition, he had lost much of his popular support.

Maurice Bishop, who had studied law in London, emerged as the leader of the opposition in 1970 after successfully defending twenty-two nurses arrested for participating in an antigovernment demonstration. His Communist-leaning New Jewel Movement had been formed in 1973, intending to pressure Gairy to resign. When that failed the NJM organized an island-wide strike. During that strike Bishop's father, Rupert Bishop, was shot and killed by police for resisting arrest while blocking entrance to union headquarters, and Maurice had been imprisoned and beaten.

By the time we landed there, Gairy and Bishop had forged an uneasy coexistence. Our faculty and students got to know both men—in very nonpolitical ways. Vish, for example, regularly shot pool with Bishop. They played through the weekend nights at a private club. Both Gairy and Bishop controlled some real estate, and some of the students rented apartments from Gairy at the bottom of a hill, while others rented cottages from Bishop's family at the top of the hill. Being at the bottom, Gairy controlled the flow of water up the hill, so at times people higher on the hill had their water shut off—supposedly due to shortages.

On occasion Maurice Bishop would personally collect the rent. Steve Lakomy remembers having a conversation with him as political tensions were rising. "Aren't you afraid that the government is going to murder you?" he asked.

"No," replied the charismatic Bishop. "They would not murder me because I am too popular. They wouldn't dare do that."

On March 12, Gairy was in New York to attend a United Nations conference on unidentified flying objects and other cosmic phenomena. He was always trying to make Grenada the center of UFO research. He used to talk about its beautiful clear skies. He wanted the UN to build listening posts on the island to search for signals from outer space.

I was scheduled to meet with him in his suite in the Waldorf Astoria Towers at 10:00 a.m. the following morning, the thirteenth, to discuss school business. Six hours earlier, at 4:15 a.m., forty-six New Jewel Movement soldiers, armed with eighteen rifles and handguns as well as a few Molotov cocktails, had attacked the army barracks located right next to our True Blue campus. This was the type of coup that might have been scripted by a low-budget movie producer. The plan of attack was simple: Get to the barracks before the soldiers wake up.

The NJM troops occupied the barracks while the Grenadian troops were still asleep, then turned on the lights. The two hundred or so men in the barracks surrendered, one person was reportedly killed, and one person was injured. The soldiers were escorted out of the barracks, which were set on fire.

Several armed revolutionaries were waiting at Pearls Airport when the air traffic controller and customs agent arrived to go to work at sunrise. "The airport is not opening today," they were told. "The country is having a revolution."

The most important objective was Radio Grenada, the island's only radio station. Just as the rebels had done at the airport, several soldiers got there before the station manager, engineer, and announcer arrived to open up and seized control. Throughout the rest of the day, they regularly interrupted programming and commercials to inform listeners, "There has been a revolution in Grenada. All people are to remain in their homes." And then they would return to scheduled commercials. "...so don't forget to brush your teeth every morning."

There were fourteen small police stations on the island, almost all of them manned by only two or three officers. The rebels had only enough men to take control of three of them. But they announced on Radio Grenada that most of the stations had been captured and warned police officers in those remaining few stations to immediately hoist a white flag or they would be treated as the enemy. White flags, or where flags were not on hand white T-shirts, went up as the officers waited patiently for someone to whom they could surrender to arrive.

Later that morning the "Prime Minister of the Revolutionary Government," Maurice Bishop, made a radio broadcast declaring, "Freedom will be restored. Foreign residents will be quite safe.... Supporters of the former Gairy government will not be harmed. We want no violence.... The revolution is for work, food, decent housing, and for a bright future for our children...."

All phone lines had been cut, making it impossible to contact anyone either inside the country or internationally. Pearls Airport was closed. The docks were closed. The new government declared the day a public holiday—but later instituted an 8:00 p.m. to 5:30 a.m. curfew.

I was getting ready to go to my meeting with Gairy when my father called to tell me a revolution had taken place. "What are you talking about, Pop?" I said, sort of dismissing him. "I have a meeting with the prime minister in a few hours. There can't be a revolution."

All I knew about revolutions in small countries was what I had learned in Woody Allen's comedy *Bananas*. We thought we had planned for every foreseeable possibility. But a revolution? I couldn't imagine what was going on in my father's mind. He had been an extremely successful developer on Long Island until his son convinced him to make a substantial investment on an island in the Caribbean that a Communist government was in the midst of taking over. One thing he knew for certain: There were no Communist revolutions in the Long Island real estate business.

I met with my father, Pat Adams, and Ed McGowan in our Bay Shore office. We had no idea what to do. A report from Grenada quoted a spokesperson for the revolutionary government warning that the country would prevent "foreign imperialism." While no one knew exactly what that meant, we were aware that when Fidel Castro had overthrown the

Battista government in Cuba he "nationalized" all private holdings. Communist governments in other countries had also seized Western property. If the Grenadian rebels did the same thing, not only would the medical school be out of business, the founders would lose their investments.

We didn't know how to proceed. I told them I had to go into the city to meet with the prime minister. Or perhaps he was the former prime minister. It was confusing. "You can't go," they told me. "There's a revolution. Call him."

Call him? To do what? Reschedule till the revolution was over? "What am I going to say?"

"Tell him you heard on WCBS there's a revolution. Ask him what's going on."

I got Eric Gairy on the phone. There is no proper etiquette for this situation. If the revolution failed, we were going to have to continue dealing with him. I had to be careful to be suitably supportive. "Mr. Prime Minister," I began, "I understand there are reports on the radio of some crazy thing happening. I assume you're aware of that."

"Of course I'm aware of that," he said curtly. "These boys, they'll pay for what they've done."

"Well," I continued, trying to adopt the proper tone, "I know we had a meeting scheduled for today, but I'm sure you're going to be busy." Admittedly, I wanted to stay as far away from him as possible. "Oh no," he responded, "I must see you."

"Really?" I replied with as much enthusiasm as I could generate.

"Yes. In fact, come now."

Meanwhile, we had managed to make contact by telex with Geoffrey Bourne, who was in Grenada. It was a very confusing situation, he reported, and everyone was supposed to stay off the streets. But it appeared that the Gairy government had been overthrown by Maurice Bishop. The school told students to stay wherever they were but had no way of reaching everyone living off campus. Thus far, though, as far as could be determined our students were not in danger.

I couldn't understand why Gairy needed to see me. We met in his hotel room. His reason quickly became clear. "We have many urgent things to do," he said. "But I think you have a good connection in the White House." He was talking about Geoffrey Bourne's son Peter, who was a special advisor to President Jimmy Carter. "We must speak to the president right away about these boys. These boys are Communists. The United States must intervene quickly."

All I had wanted to do was open a medical school, a place where qualified students could get the opportunity they had been denied. Now I was being asked to help prevent the Communist takeover of a Caribbean nation. I didn't have a lot of hope I could accomplish anything. The concept that the United States military would actually send troops to prevent a Communist government from taking over Grenada seemed pretty implausible to me. More than implausible—impossibly absurd. Who would believe that was possible? But I couldn't tell that to Gairy. I owed him more than that. The school owed him more than that.

I used our two-dictionary code to send a telex message to Geoffrey: The prime minister really needs somebody in the White House to tell the president that the rebels are Communists.

He responded in code that he couldn't risk making that call from Grenada. His reason was convincing: We should assume that Bishop's supporters were listening to all our communications. If they learned that a school official had asked the American government for help defeating the revolution, we would be done on the island.

That made sense. I asked him to contact his son suggesting he call me in New York. I spent the rest of the day with Gairy as news filtered in bit by bit. In the afternoon, mercenaries based in Atlanta contacted him and offered their services to take back the country by force. It was very possible a well-armed and trained private militia could have overwhelmed Bishop's small number of poorly equipped rebels and restore Gairy to power. "There are some people from the outside who want to help," he told me. "But if we do that, we will spill the blood of my people."

To Gairy's credit he turned down the offers. He was convinced the revolution would not stand, that loyalists would resist and the Grenadian people soon "will be begging me to come back." He wouldn't risk that by mounting an armed invasion.

It was early evening before I finally spoke with Peter Bourne. He was properly and officially evasive. But generally, he told me without telling me that the United States government was not going to get involved in the internal affairs of a small Caribbean island. As he seemed to be saying, even the thought of something like that seemed absurd.

The *New York Times* reported the revolution in a single column on page 9, describing Sir Eric Gairy as "a union leader and nightclub owner who has tried to persuade the United Nations to investigate unidentified flying objects." The coup barely caused a ripple in the States, easily dismissed as just another revolution in a banana republic, but potentially it was devastating to us.

Our faculty and students learned about the revolution on the radio. Later in the morning Geoffrey Bourne contacted Maurice Bishop to offer congratulations. Like many of our students, Raz Giliberti walked out of his dorm room and into the revolution. The first thing he saw that morning was "a Rastafarian holding the largest gun I'd ever seen. It actually turned out to be a tear gas gun. 'Go back, mon,' he told me. Why, I asked him, what's happening? 'Revolution. Go back to sleep.' That probably summed up the level of excitement on the campus."

Radio Grenada told people to wear a white T-shirt with a red circle to indicate solidarity with the new government. Our students didn't know how to react. Fran McGill decided she wouldn't go to class that morning—until Timmy, the van driver who drove her to the campus each morning, showed up. "You are going to school and you will be safe because I am in the People's Revolutionary Army." It was a dangerous situation—the same people driving students to school or selling trinkets on the beach suddenly were parading around with deadly weapons. Fran got in the van and went to school.

Larry Adams was living in a cottage a few miles from the school. He remembers, "We were in disbelief at first. We are little Grenada, nobody would overthrow this little country. Why take over the Spice Island? Does somebody need more nutmeg? Was there a world shortage of spices? We didn't take it too seriously. We got dressed to go to class like any other day. Our minivan showed up, but the driver said, 'Today's a revolution. Can't take you to class.' We ignored him; we were going to school. That was our attitude: This is our last chance. We're getting an education here no matter what it takes.

"We jumped in the van and insisted he drive us to class. Normally there was some traffic and people walking along the side of the road. But instead, it was eerily quiet.

"Somebody finally said that maybe we shouldn't go to class. We discussed it and decided since we were more than halfway it probably made sense to keep going. We drove past the army barracks, which was still smoldering, and eventually got to the campus. Our driver dropped us off and hightailed it out of there. When we got to the classroom door, a handwritten sign taped to it read: NO CLASSES TODAY. REVOLUTION.

"We walked the two or three miles back to our cottage. Eventually, we got a message from the school: Keep quiet, don't talk to anyone, don't say anything political. Keep your mouth shut and we'll see what happens. I don't know that I ever saw any real soldiers; mostly it was a bunch of Rastafarians in beat-up Toyotas pretending to be soldiers, driving up and down the roads pointing rifles out the windows. We did hear about people who had shot themselves in the ass or the foot coming into the hospital emergency room for treatment."

In fact, the only reported encounter with the rebels took place when Morrie Alpert decided to surrender. The radio station was located next to an area known as Cinnamon Hill, where several faculty members and students lived. As Dr. Alpert returned to his house early in the morning, completely unaware of the takeover, he ran into the rebels who had taken over the station. Morrie put up his hands and surrendered.

The Grenadians rejected his surrender.

The only anxious moment took place early in the afternoon. Our business manager, Gary Solin, was in his house when a jeep screeched to a halt directly in front. Two rifle-carrying rebels jumped out and banged on the door. When Gary opened it he recognized the men but had no idea what they wanted. By this point anything was possible. "Oh Gary," the soldier said politely, "we are sorry to disturb you, but we wondered if you could lend us your video machine. We would like to show some movies to our troops."

One of Bishop's lieutenants showed up at True Blue in late morning. There has been a revolution, he announced, and Mr. Maurice Bishop and the People's Revolutionary Government are in control. He assured them that they were completely safe and urged them to continue their studies. "This is a political issue," he said. "We are not here to harm you but instead to help you achieve your goal." But what many students noted was that this spokesperson was wearing jeans! They unpacked their own jeans and began wearing them. It was not intended to be a political statement.

The first indication that there had been casualties came that evening when the newly named Radio Free Grenada broadcast an appeal for a doctor to come to the station, where the new government had set up its headquarters. Dr. Alpert and a visiting former colleague from Albany Medical College responded—and treated one man for a dislocated shoulder.

Meanwhile, on Long Island our students' parents were panicking. They had not been able to contact their kids. We had nothing to tell them. We weren't getting any real information other than everything on the island seemed calm. In addition to the telex, several students with ham radios were communicating with ham operators in the States, but most of our students were essentially trapped in their rooms and had no more information than we did.

Bishop's New Jewel Movement established its control over the island. I consider myself a loyal person, and I will be forever grateful to Eric Gairy for welcoming the school to Grenada, but whatever my own feelings were at the time, my job was to protect the university. While the new government's initial assurances were welcome, we really had no idea what Bishop intended to do about the school. I finally told Gairy I had to meet with Bishop. He understood that this was my obligation as chancellor of St. George's University, not my personal decision.

Among the few American-owned businesses on the island before we arrived was Key Punch Universal, which employed Grenadians to transform telephone records into pre-computer punch cards. The owner of that company was Walter Nelson, who lived in Connecticut. As two of the island's largest employers, we decided to meet with Bishop together. That gave each of us a little more clout. The meeting was held in Gairy's former office in St. George's. I'd been there many times before, but it definitely felt different.

Bishop was welcoming and reassuring, telling us, "I want to give you assurances you will operate your business better than ever. There will be no interference and there will be no corruption."

It was a long meeting, lasting more than three hours, and throughout it a large woman wearing a bright yellow T-shirt proclaiming "Long Live the Revo!"—the slogan of the revolution—walked in and out. Sometimes she offered us soda or water; at other times she sat down and joined us for several minutes. Finally, I asked Bishop who she was. "Oh, I should have introduced you," he responded. "That is Phyllis Coard. She is the wife of our minister of finance."

The minister of finance, trade, industry and planning was Bernard Coard, a graduate of Boston's Brandeis University with a degree in economics and with Bishop the co-chairman of the New Jewel Movement. I've always believed that Maurice Bishop became prime minister because he had the better backstory: His father had been killed fighting for unionists, and he had been imprisoned by Gairy. He also exuded personality, while Coard had lived out of the country and lacked Bishop's easy charisma.

I got to know both Bishop and Coard reasonably well. Most of the time they stayed out of school business. Most of the time. Our charter agreement with the government required us to provide scholarships for deserving young Grenadians as well as provide $100,000 worth of medical equipment for the General Hospital. The first time that annual payment came due under the new government, Bernard Coard informed us that part of those funds had to be used to buy two brand-new fully-equipped ambulances. It seemed like a reasonable request. I knew absolutely nothing about emergency medicine, and less about ambulances, so I contacted a high school classmate who had become a hospital administrator for advice. He told me that the type of ambulance Coard wanted was far better equipped than the General Hospital itself. I explained that to Coard, then suggested the money might be better spent improving the hospital, not providing essentially luxury ambulances. "A patient would be better off staying on the ambulance than going into the hospital," I said. "Is that really what you want?"

Coard was very offended. "You are not to tell us how we run our health-care system here on the island," he warned me. "We demand this. We have asked for ambulances and by law you must honor this request." I remember thinking at that time, *Boy, this is a tough guy, and I don't think he likes Americans very much.* That concerned me. But I didn't have any choice: We purchased those ambulances for them.

In the days following the revolution, I began receiving praise for my insistence on opening up a second campus on St. Vincent, which provided both leverage and a refuge if we needed one. Many people believed it was more than luck, that somehow I must have known a coup was brewing. "Trust me," I told them, "I did not. I'd love to take credit for it, but I had no idea this was going to happen." In response they would wink or smile or nod. Sure you didn't, Charlie.

About two weeks after the Bishop government took control, Cuban workers began arriving. In many small ways life on the island was about to change.

It would be several years before I would speak with Eric Gairy again. After the American military "intervention" in October of 1983 deposed the remnants of the revolutionary government, he returned to the island to live. He had lived in exile in the United States, surviving, he said, by "love envelopes" from the Grenadian people. The Bishop government had tried to destroy his reputation, at one point claiming he practiced witchcraft while serving in office, but he still retained some political popularity and harbored dreams of returning to power. But his time had passed.

In 1987 we invited Eric Gairy to be honored at a celebration of our tenth anniversary. Before issuing that invitation, we consulted the prime minister at that time, Herbert Blaize, who agreed it was appropriate. I was really pleased—we owed our existence to Gairy, and this was a chance to say thank you. Also I hadn't seen him in a long time. During those earlier years he'd always arrived on campus in a white Cadillac limousine, small flags on its bumpers, trailed by motorcycles. This time, though, as we waited for his arrival, standing in a line, I heard in the distance what sounded like gunshots. It wasn't; as the sound got closer I realized it was a car backfiring. Suddenly the car came into view. It was an older white sedan, and it continued backfiring—*bomp*, *bomp*, *bomp*—as it climbed the steep hill to the campus. The first thing I noticed was it was missing a hubcap. It was so sad. Gairy was trying so hard to re-create his glorious past, holding tightly to his dignity.

We welcomed him with the same respect as we had in those earlier heady times and gave him an award. We didn't have much of an opportunity to talk at that event, so he invited me to his home. Vish Rao went with me. He was living in a small but well-kept apartment above the Evening Palace. By that time he was frail; like that backfiring car, this once statuesque, vibrant man, this booming force, was bent forward and had lost much of his eyesight. He was much too proud to carry a cane, so instead he waved a three-foot-long pencil from side to side to locate objects in front of him. "Mr. Modecai," he greeted me, he had always liked to call me that, "Mr. Modecai, do you still have your suits?"

He was referring to the three-piece suits I always wore when we'd met. We had joked about who was wearing the better suit. "Yes, Mr. Prime Minister," I replied, "I do."

"You haven't seen my suit collection. Let me show you my suits." His assistant opened a closet door to reveal several old and soiled suits hanging there.

"Nice," Vish said softly. "Very nice."

That was the last time either of us saw him.

We had managed to survive another crisis. Cuban workers arrived on the island in increasingly large numbers. There was a regular Thursday night curfew and blackout during which cargo was unloaded from Cuban and sometimes Russian ships, then trucked to various locations. There were rumors that these shipments included weapons, but we were careful to mind our own business.

Within a few months we had managed to return to normal. While Bishop ranted publicly against American imperialism, he was always supportive of the school. "It brings direct material benefits," he told *Time* magazine. "There is also the spinoff effect on the economy. The many students living here are renting homes, buying food, going out for entertainment…"

The situation had settled down. Lectures and labs were being held as scheduled on both Grenada and St. Vincent. People were moving safely around the island. I remember sitting in my Bay Shore office one day several months later with several people, including Andy Belford and Peggy Lambert, as we laughed about everything that had happened thus far and asked jokingly, What else could go wrong?

That's when the volcano erupted.

CHAPTER 19

The Elephant in the Room: US Clinical Placements

"We knew we could work as hard as we possibly could work, and we could get good grades and learn anatomy and physiology and the other subjects. But if we were not able to come back to the States and apply that knowledge, then this whole exercise would have been for nothing."

—St. George's University charter class member Paul Vallone

When I conceived of St. George's, I had drawn up a one-page business plan under duress. I had continuously revised it as we encountered new obstacles. I tried to anticipate and plan for as many contingencies as possible, but admittedly I had never planned for a revolution or a volcanic eruption.

La Soufrière on St. Vincent had previously erupted three times in recorded history: in 1718, 1812, and 1902. The 1902 eruption killed 1,680 people. The simultaneous explosion of Mount Pelée on nearby Martinique had killed 29,000 people. No one considered the possibility that La Soufrière might erupt again. Students often swam there as if it were a hot spring. Americans are far more familiar with extinct volcanoes like Diamond Head in Hawaii.

I was in the Bay Shore office on Good Friday, April 13, when someone told me, "You're not gonna believe this, but there's a volcanic eruption on St. Vincent."

"A what?" They were right, I didn't believe it. Maybe the earthquake a day earlier should have served as a warning. The timing certainly was fortuitous, although in this instance no one accused me of having inside information. We had decided to end classes a few days early to allow students time to get home for the coming Easter and Passover holidays, so more than half the class had left the island the day before the thunderous explosions announced the eruption.

Fortunately, La Soufrière is on the north end of the island, far away from our campus in Kingstown. Joan Mack remembers walking out of her rented home to see an ominous black cloud hanging over the volcano. She turned around. "Fill up everything," she told her fiancé. They filled their bathtub and every container they could find with water, then went to the hospital to see if they could help. At the same time a group led by Morrie Alpert flew in from Grenada to offer medical assistance. Their plane was the first flight in after the eruption, and as they landed people were using brooms to sweep volcanic ash two feet deep off the runway.

While there were no deaths, thousands of people had to be evacuated to the south side of the island. Many of them had been forced to leave their homes without necessary medications. Joan and several other students spent the next weeks collecting medicines from the hospital and getting them to the people who needed them. Dr. Alpert and John Madden went to the hospital's emergency room prepared to treat casualties. They found the blood bank was depleted. They needed blood donors and they needed them immediately. The St. Vincent government solved that problem: They took an ambulance to the prison, where thirty-three prisoners volunteered to replenish the blood bank.

When the American government offered assistance, Alpert asked for several hundred sets of IV fluids and tubing. They were delivered a day later—but without alcohol wipes, bandages, or even the catheters needed to use them. When Alpert asked where that equipment was, he learned another lesson: When dealing with the US government you'd better be specific. That additional equipment arrived a day later.

Once again, we had been very lucky. The number of casualties was limited, and although lava was still flowing into the ocean a week later, the medical situation on the island was almost normal. Kingstown Medical College, our campus on St. Vincent, survived the unexpected ordeal, eventually becoming an important resource for the school by enabling us to prepare our students for their clinical experience. But it did not solve our larger problem: How were we going to secure sufficient clinical slots in American hospitals to train our students?

Then I had another idea. Being able to secure relevant clinical training was key to our continued survival, never mind success. The transformation from medical student to doctor takes place in a clinical setting. Students spend their third and fourth years working alongside physicians and clinical lecturers in hospitals. It's hands-on medicine.

During these two years, students rotate through various specialties, getting exposure to everything from pediatrics to psychiatry. It also is the vitally important audition for a residency, the postgraduate medical training necessary to practice as a physician in the US and all developed countries.

Our problem was that most of those positions in teaching hospitals were controlled by the American medical schools. These schools had affiliations with nearby hospitals that guaranteed placement for their students.

The way the system worked was that hospitals paid medical schools for these student-interns, and the schools provided inexpensive, enthusiastic young people willing to work long hours doing basic tasks for essentially no pay. The more prestigious the school, the more the hospital paid for the affiliation. For the students, this "audition" provided hospitals the opportunity to actually see young doctors at work, and often led to administrators offering the best of them a coveted residency after graduation.

It was a structure that benefited both the medical schools and the hospitals. Following that residency, doctors often maintained a relationship with the hospital. They became attending physicians, meaning they would send their patients there. In many cases the financial survival of a hospital became dependent on patient admissions from former residents in private practice.

Medicine is a business. And that's the way the system operated.

Foreign medical schools had no direct path to clinical positions in American hospitals. Those students from foreign medical schools who wanted to work in American hospitals generally found their own multi-week rotations. They often had help finding those spots from a relative, friend, or contact. But when they did, most of the time they ended up working in a rural area or an urban hospital serving a mostly minority population that did not have an affiliation with a medical school.

The University of Guadalajara, for example, would hand its third-year students a curriculum to complete and evaluation forms to be filled out by doctors, telling them they would receive their diploma after they had enough of those forms signed. Essentially, they were on their own.

That was one reason I encouraged our students to transfer to domestic medical schools if they had the opportunity. It would guarantee them a clinical position, something we could not do.

Yet.

The whole system was a mess. The already existing shortage of doctors had been exacerbated by the Vietnam War. The army had drafted numerous young men who otherwise might have gone into medicine and also recruited medical students and doctors for its own needs. As a result, the serious shortage of doctors in America was being filled by foreign-trained students, which is why so many primary-care physicians in hospitals at the time came from Europe and Asia—especially China and India. Dr. Fred Jacobs, a noted pulmonologist and the father of one of our students, who later become the commissioner of health of New Jersey and eventually chairman of our Department of Medicine, remembers, "When I first came to St. Barnabas Medical Center [in Livingston, New Jersey], we had many residents who didn't speak any English. We literally had doctors who could not speak to their patients without an interpreter."

That wasn't limited to understanding English words; it included the entire language of medicine. Deepak Chopra, for example, had graduated from the best medical school in India, then was placed in a New Jersey hospital by a foundation that supplied foreign-trained doctors to community hospitals. They even paid for his airfare. During one of his first nights at this hospital, he was called to confirm that a patient had died of gunshot wounds—in the language of medicine, he had to "pronounce" the patient dead. The patient had no pulse. Dr. Chopra wanted to shine a light in the patient's eyes, a lack of response to that is a critical sign, but he had forgotten to bring his flashlight. "Does anyone have a torch?" he asked, using the British term for a flashlight. "I forgot to bring one."

A nurse responded softly, "Dr. Chopra, we want you to pronounce him, not cremate him."

Pronounce him? There was no equivalent terminology in British medicine, and Dr. Chopra had no idea what that meant. "Okay," he said, holding his palms over the patient, "I pronounce you dead!"

When we founded the school, we had not yet developed a strategy for securing clinical positions. We didn't panic, though—we never panicked. Well, I never panicked. Well, maybe I was actively concerned.

But I had remarkable faith that we would be able to find an answer. I accepted the reality that our solution might not be perfect, but I never doubted our ability to figure it out. Never. There was a solution, and we were going to find it. That confidence made all the difference. That, and not being bound by archaic traditions.

What I could not have known is that to do that, we would have to challenge, then revolutionize, the entire American medical system.

We began by hiring William McCord, the retiring president of the Medical College of South Carolina, to develop a clinical program. Bill McCord was a respected medical educator who had transformed a small South Carolina medical school into a university, and I figured he had contacts at hospitals throughout the country. We also asked students if they had any family or other contacts in hospitals that might accept our students.

We ended up handing those contacts to Jane Sutter, in admissions at St. George's, although we didn't quite know what to do with them. We were just trying to figure out how to proceed. Clinical placements were, as charter class member Paul Vallone remembers, "the elephant in the room. We knew we could work as hard as we possibly could work, and we could get good grades and learn anatomy and physiology and the other subjects. But if we were not able to come back to the States and apply that knowledge, then this whole exercise would have been for nothing."

I was very careful to not let my optimism or enthusiasm distort the situation to our students. I never made a promise I didn't know I could keep. That was important. The two questions I was most often asked were: When are we going to get cadavers, and will we get clinical placements?

There was no path to follow. We were pioneers. I just did what made sense.

I've never been shy about selling a quality product. I had learned that from my father—he built quality houses and sold them at a fair, affordable price. Everybody benefited. I set out to find hospitals in the United States that would take our students for their fourth year. At the same time, as back-up, I contacted hospitals on every island in the Caribbean, scrambling to find clinical spots for those students in their third year.

Initially I intended, hoped actually, to spread our students across the Caribbean for their third year. Every island nation had its own hospitals, and in many places there was a shortage of trained staff. *They'll be happy to have our people*, I thought. Naively. I encountered more resistance than I had anticipated. One nation turned down an offer of $250,000. Another country wanted us to set up a complete medical school. I was struggling.

When the AAMC learned about my plan, they opposed it. At a conference of the Caribbean ministers of health on Barbados, the president of the AAMC asked those island nations to deny us access to their clinical facilities. If that happened, we simply could not graduate doctors because we had no clinical facilities of our own. That forced us to find another solution. And the AMA actually unintentionally gave me the key to the lock for $3.

Its *Directory of Residents* was published annually. The *Green Book*, they called it. I bought two copies, $6 cash, plus the cost of a box of yellow markers. In this book the AMA, perhaps intending to make a point about the quality of these hospitals, listed both the number of residents on their staff trained domestically and the number of those trained outside the country.

I will be forever grateful for that decision.

The better hospitals essentially had their pick of residents, but rural hospitals and community hospitals had to take whoever they could get. Many of them were as desperate for help as I was to offer that help.

I skipped those hospitals closely affiliated with medical schools. I knew, for example, that Mount Sinai in New York, a prestigious hospital that gets residents from its own school, was not going to be interested. Instead, I searched for hospitals that had a large number of residents who had graduated from foreign institutions on their staff. That meant they probably didn't train or attract many graduates of domestic schools. I also looked for the busiest hospitals because I wanted our students to have real-life experience, and a lot of it. Those almost always were urban hospitals, which treated a diverse population with a broad spectrum of medical issues arising out of the density of city living.

The hospitals were listed alphabetically. The majority of our students were from the Northeast, specifically the New York/New Jersey metropolitan area, so I started with New York City hospitals. I was hoping to find hospitals that had 40 percent or fewer US graduates on its staff. Right near the top was Coney Island Hospital. This statistic leaped off the page at me…

Percentage of American medical school graduates: 0 percent. Percentage of foreign graduates: 100 percent.

0 percent? 100 percent? I was astonished. When I saw 0 percent of US school grads at Coney Island, I took my yellow marker and highlighted it. Then I found a second hospital with a similar distribution, a third, a fourth—all urban hospitals whose presence impacted their

communities. These were places that saved lives on a daily basis. There was no better place to get a crash course in hands-on medicine.

The *Green Book* included the names and phone numbers of the hospital administrators. I began cold-calling. The first two people I contacted were Leon Smith at St. Michael's Hospital in Newark, New Jersey, and Stanley Freeman at Coney Island Hospital in Brooklyn. I didn't have Google Maps back then, but I knew that we had many students who lived close to both hospitals. Danny Ricciardi and more than a dozen of his classmates lived within a long walk to Coney Island Hospital.

"My name is Charles Modica," I began my pitch, hoping they wouldn't hang up, "and I'm the chancellor of a new medical school in Grenada. St. George's. Maybe you've heard of it?"

Both men sort of knew something about some new medical school they had heard something about somewhere in the Caribbean.

I told them that we had several students who were American citizens whose families lived within proximity of their institutions and who had graduated from American colleges. "They're in Grenada now and they're getting ready to take their boards. I think a lot of them are going to do well on them. Would you be interested in allowing them to have fourth-year electives in your hospital? I know it's a little in advance, but…"

I remember Dr. Smith interrupting me to ask, "Well, would they want to stay here for their residency?"

Are you kidding me? I thought. "That would be tremendous. They live in the area, and you have a fine hospital."

The future of our university began to solidify with those first two phone calls. Bill McCord and I met with Smith and Freeman. We traipsed into their offices and showed them the students from their area who could do their fourth-year electives at their hospitals. I didn't think it was possible they would take a chance with third-year students—the year where medical students do their core training in medicine, surgery, OB-GYN, pediatrics, and psychiatry. But to their credit both of them asked us the same question: Why do we need to wait? We could get them their third-year rotations too. Is there a reason you don't want to send them?

I felt like a miner who had just discovered a vein of gold. An astronomer who had found a new planet. An art historian who had uncovered an unknown da Vinci. "No reason," I replied casually. "I just assumed you wouldn't take them." I asked Freeman, whose hospital was affiliated with Downstate Medical Center, "Don't you have Downstate students?"

He was candid with me. Shaking his head, he admitted, "We don't get any residents from Downstate—and one of the reasons for that is they don't send us any medical students."

This was decades ago, and the entire system is different now than it was then. But when he said that, I swear I heard the music of a celestial orchestra. "I didn't know that," I said.

"They're affiliated with us out of convenience," he continued. "They're almost required to do that because we're a city hospital, but they don't send us any students. They don't use us; they use Kings Hospital. We would welcome your students here for a third year."

Both men asked for a little time to meet with their clinicians to see how they would respond to the concept. It turned out that every core specialty, in both hospitals, agreed to the arrangement. Then we did something else very unusual: We changed the entire structure of the traditional relationship between medical schools and hospitals. Rather than hospitals paying the schools, we offered to share tuition for every student they took.

We offered to pay them to provide an opportunity for our qualified students.

It was a revolutionary concept, and it threatened the status quo. But it made great sense to me. Nonteaching hospitals were going to have to incentivize their faculty members to teach these students, and that was something we could help them with. I also was aware that many hospitals, especially inner-city hospitals, were barely breaking even, or even losing money, and these payments in some cases could help them keep their doors open.

We offered, I believe, $100 a week per student, which we would pay directly out of tuition with the proviso it had to be used to facilitate education. Although, admittedly, "facilitate education" is a very loose definition.

These were the first clinical positions in American hospitals we were able to secure. And it changed everything.

Once those two institutions were secured, we began approaching other hospitals. We hadn't even considered the possibility of finding slots for our third-year students. The concept was so revolutionary that it was a hard sell. Bill McCord, Jane Sutter, and sometimes Geoffrey Bourne traveled throughout America and the United Kingdom trying to secure slots for people. "I had no experience at any of this," Jane remembers. "But Bill McCord did, and I learned from him. He understood the process and laid it out carefully to hospital administrators how this would benefit those institutions. It was entirely logical and absolutely truthful.

"Why Charlie believed I would be able to do this, I have no idea. But that was typical Charlie, putting people in a position to succeed.

"With Bill's supervision, I sat down at my desk and organized all the contacts. I color-coded everything, red for this, blue for that. Then I started calling people. As we began expanding, I would get in my little Volkswagen with Bill and we would drive around the country. When we got ready to go into a meeting he would say, 'Wind me up!' and go to work selling our students. We were supposed to get written contracts with hospitals, but a lot of administrators who agreed to try the program were reluctant to sign a contract. There was a lot of legalese involved, but Charlie told me, 'Jane, I don't care if they write it on a paper napkin, we just need something in writing.'"

At first it was a difficult sell, and Jane and Bill and even Geoffrey had limited success. American hospitals generally believed our students were substandard, mediocre, maybe even unqualified because they had not been accepted by an American school, rather than accepting the fact that there were too few places for too many qualified people. It was a biased, elitist point of view, but that was the reality we were facing. While we were at least partially responsible for the open system that exists today, at that time several states, including Florida, had regulations restricting or even barring American students studying in foreign schools from taking clinical spots. Illinois even wanted to prevent students who had done their clinical work in small community hospitals from being licensed to practice in that state. Hospitals in other states stated flatly they had no interest in foreign-trained students. One of Connecticut's biggest hospitals wrote, "We accept only American medical graduates in internal medicine."

While we were laying this groundwork, I was very careful about what I told our students. "You're supposed to stay in Grenada for your third year," I said, "but there may be some opportunities for some of you in the States. Maybe even more than some of you. But I can't promise anything until we're certain." Until we had enough napkins. "Trust me, some of you will go, maybe even all of you. But I can't guarantee it."

That left them hanging. I didn't like doing that, but I didn't have a choice. We had managed to keep the first agreements private, contained within our small group. We believed that if we sent out any kind of official letter about this program, the AAMC or AMA would try to stop it. I was confident that once our students were on-site, the hospitals weren't going to kick them out. These were great young people, smart and dedicated. But I also knew if I were the medical establishment, I would try to stop it before it took hold.

American medical schools had a great deal going. Their students were getting a significant portion of their education at little to no cost to the schools, and we were upsetting that tradition. What we described as an inducement to encourage hospitals to take our qualified students they could recharacterize as a payoff. The *New York Times* would later report, after other Caribbean medical schools followed our lead, "U.S. medical education faces a threat from for-profit Caribbean medical schools which purchase clinical rotation slots for their students at U.S. hospitals. These offshore schools are monetizing a system that was previously characterized as a duty—the duty of the current generation of physicians to educate their successors."

The funds used to "purchase clinical rotations," the story continued, were "largely derived from federally subsidized student loans." When I read that sentence, I knew exactly what was coming.

Until the moment we offered to share tuition with hospitals, we had been nothing more than a minor irritant, but this turned us—and those schools who came after us—into a significant danger to their business model. I didn't know exactly what they could do to stop us, but I was certain they would oppose our disruption of the status quo. So we waited until the last possible moment before notifying our students of their clinical assignments.

Fred Jacobs, who had joined our faculty as a visiting professor and later became New Jersey's commissioner of health, was always troubled by "the optics" of referring to this as paying for slots. He described it far more eloquently, and accurately, as "affiliating with clinical training sites and sharing our clinical tuition with those sites actually providing the training."

It took time for us to get this program established. And while we were doing it, many of our students used their own contacts to find a place to get the necessary training. But what they also were doing was proving they were the equal—and sometimes better—than American students.

Slowly, as our students proved their value our network expanded. No other foreign school had ever attempted an organized effort to secure these positions. Of course, the advantage we had was the unshakeable determination of our students. They already had laid the foundation for the school in Grenada—now they were using their drive, ingenuity, and connections and plowing ahead in the United States. For example, Rudy Antoncic's brother's father-in-law was in a union associated with a hospital in McKeesport, Pennsylvania, which helped him secure a spot there. Philip Lahrman's uncle helped him get a rotation in a small hospital—even though that hospital had no residents. John Washington's grandfather had graduated from Meharry Medical College in Nashville, Tennessee, and then trained at the affiliated Nashville General—they offered him a position. Fran McGill's mentor while she was working as a critical-care nurse at NYU before attending St. George's had become chairman of medicine at Harvard and helped her get a position in a Harvard-run program at a Veterans Administration community hospital.

Whatever it took, our students figured it out. "We knew what we wanted, we didn't take anything for granted, and we worked our asses off," Larry Adams said. We were able to place Adams and several other students at the Sisters of Charity Hospital in Buffalo, way upstate New York. As he remembers, "We wanted to do a couple of rotations at the university-affiliated Millard Fillmore Hospital, which then offered a much wider program, but they turned us down. We persisted. We kept pushing and nudging and calling, just refusing to give up. We wore them down. I got to do a rotation in radiology, the only non-US medical student there."

Our students took clinical positions wherever they could find them. Many hospitals had never had a student from a foreign institution as a resident on their staff. It was haphazard at best. David Baras talked his way into the rotations he needed at different hospitals. He began at Methodist Hospital in New York, then spent a month at the VA hospital in Tampa, Florida, then six weeks at Charity Hospital in New Orleans, then finally six weeks in Burlington, Iowa. David and his wife, Mary Jo, were visiting her hometown of Burlington when he visited a local rehabilitation center. "It was a very progressive facility, within walking distance of Mary Jo's house. It was one of the first rehab centers in the Midwest to have a pool therapy program. By chance the person who ran the program, Dr. Stone, lived nearby. I knocked on his door, told him who I was, and asked if I could do a rotation with him, and he said, 'Sure, I'd love it.'"

Geoffrey Bourne was able to find several sites for us in the UK. Lou Guida was one of our first students to go there. As he says, "While I was in school I was sure Dr. Morrie Alpert didn't like me. One day he told me, 'Guida, you are going to England to do your externship.'

"'Dr. Alpert,' I told him, 'I don't want to go to England. I'm from New Jersey and I want to finish up there.'

"'Nope,' he said flatly, 'you're going to England.'

"I was told to report to Dudley, England, in the black country, to do my clinicals. The whole thing made no sense to me. I kept thinking, I did all this work and they're sending me to this place? But then I discovered 'black country' meant it was a coal mining region. Dr. Alpert knew I wanted to specialize in working with the lungs, and he sent me to a place where I would gain invaluable experience.

"The rotation was for six weeks. After that, I figured, I'll come home. It did not start out well. When I landed in London, I went to the travelers information desk in the airport and asked the woman sitting there how to get to Dudley. She looked at me and started chuckling. That was definitely a bad sign. Then she asked, 'Why would you ever want to go there? It's the coldest, dampest, darkest place you'd ever want to go.' When I told her I was a medical student assigned there, she frowned and said, 'Oh. I guess the guy didn't like you very much.'

"I took a train and a cab and found myself standing in front of the house where I was supposed to stay. I knocked on the door, I rang the bell—no one answered. It was getting dark, it was very cold, and then it started snowing. I was freezing, I was lost, and I was in despair.

"I stood on the corner and started to cry. I've struggled through two years of stuff in Grenada, I thought. There were days with no water, the electricity went out during tests; I got stopped by a guy with a machine gun during a revolution. It was supposed to get better after all that. Standing on a corner in a snowstorm in the dark in a strange place in the UK with no place to go definitely was not better.

"I figured the hospital had to be somewhere around there. I left my trunk on the street and started walking. I didn't see another person. I had never felt further away from my goal of becoming a doctor. All of a sudden, I saw what looked like a haunted house, but all the lights were on. I found a small sign that identified it as Buttonwood Hospital. I knocked on the door. An elderly woman was sitting at an old-fashioned telephone switchboard, pushing probes into slots. She opened the door and asked, 'Are you Lou Guida?'

"I got hysterical. I hugged her. They had dropped me at the wrong place, she explained. She gave me a cup of hot tea and the keys to the house. That house was a dreary, creaking old mansion. My two roommates were from Nigeria, and they promised me, 'You're going to have the time of your life here.'

"I wasn't sure if that meant it was going to be very good or very bad. I reported to surgery at six a.m. Monday morning. I was the only American. One of the British students warned me our instructor was supposedly a really tough guy and 'he doesn't really like Americans.'

"All right, I thought, how tough could he be? My experience had prepared me for…well, for anything. When that surgeon finally arrived, he asked each of us in turn where we were from. 'I'm from America,' I told him, maybe a little defensively. 'Okay,' he said.

"Then he punched me in the stomach. I was not prepared for that. Morrie Alpert may have been an arrogant little man, but he had never punched me in the stomach. At that moment everything I had been through the last two-plus years swelled up inside, and I responded in the only acceptable way—I punched him right back. I had known this man, a man who was going to have my future in his hands, for about thirty seconds and we were having a fistfight. After he got his breath back, he stuck his finger in my face and said, 'No one has ever done that before. I like you. You're going to operate with me!'

"Minutes later I was in the operating room with him, a nurse, and an anesthesiologist. The patient's belly was open and this doctor had done what needed to be done. Suddenly, he looked at me and said, 'Okay, finish up,' and walked out. I watched him leave. I looked at the patient and wondered what I was supposed to do. Then I saw him watching me. 'Get your ass back in here,' I screamed.

"He came back, smiling. 'Okay, you passed your first test. You didn't freak out.' Oh, he definitely was wrong about that. But I handled it. From that day forward that's what my stay in England was like. They watched me, they taught me, they trusted me. I called my parents and told them, 'I don't want to stay here six weeks. I want to stay for two years.' During that time, I learned medicine. You name it, I did it. I went on house calls, I did EKGs. I probably delivered thirty babies. By the time I got home I was so far ahead of US medical students I had my pick of residencies and did a three-year pulmonary fellowship in Philadelphia. It turned out Dr. Alpert wasn't as crazy as I thought he was."

It is during clinical training that a fledgling doctor is given responsibility for a patient for the first time. It's an awesome responsibility. John Washington remembers that feeling very well. He was about to leave the hospital one night when a nurse told him about a struggling patient. He told her to give the patient a certain drug and then went home. Then he stayed awake all night worrying about it. "That's all I thought about until I got to the hospital the next day. I was thinking all kinds of crazy stuff: Maybe it was the wrong drug. Maybe I prescribed too much. There was no one to tell me, yeah, that's the right thing to do. As soon as I got there I asked as casually as possible how the patient was doing, terrified they were going to tell me something had gone wrong. The hardest thing I had to do was not show my relief when they told me he was fine."

We successfully placed ninety-four of our charter class students in clinical positions. Eventually we were able to find spots for every member of the first two classes. They continued laying the groundwork for the students who followed them. As always, there were people who doubted they were adequately prepared to compete with domestically trained students, and they had to prove themselves. "What I saw during my clinical training," says Ed Hall, "was that the students in our charter class were the same caliber as the students who came from any first-class medical school."

"We blended in," Danny Ricciardi remembers. "Part of the time I worked with Downstate Medical School students, and we kept up with them. If you were good, you were good. My philosophy was simple: Screw you, you're not smarter than me."

"Everyone's expectations were, oh, you're a foreign student, you must not be very smart," Larry Adams said. "Here was the difference, in my experience. One day during my radiology rotation, the radiologist gave us X-rays to study. That night I went into the film room and did my homework. I was the only one there. The next morning the radiologist put up a film and asked, 'All right, guys, what is this?' The US medical school students were silent. He called on a couple of them, and they didn't know the answer. Then he called on me. I knew what it was because I had seen it the night before. I always felt I just wanted it more than most of those people."

Adams eventually did his residency at Long Island Jewish Medical Center. "We regularly did rounds with the chief of staff. He liked to ask hard questions, mostly to embarrass us. One day he started picking on me. I knew every single answer—because I had done what I always did: I had worked my ass off. I studied, I read the textbooks. He looked at me like he was flabbergasted; he wasn't used to that. When he left, a US-trained resident tapped me on the back and said, 'No way, Larry, nobody answers all his questions.' I didn't think it was a big deal, but apparently it was. We had to prove ourselves—we had to show we were the equal of US students.

"We knew it, and we did it."

The new arrangement was working very well. Our students got placements and performed well, the hospitals got paid and, in many cases, later got residents. Instead of people from other countries, for whom English was their second language, they got students who spoke New Yorkese. The feedback we got from hospitals was almost universally positive. After six months the head of the clinical program at Coney Island Hospital reported, "We have been very pleased with these students. They have been extremely diligent…and seem comparable to many students in American medical schools." The head of the program at Lutheran Medical Center described students as "a highly motivated group of high-quality students…who were well prepared for their clinical rotations." Eugene Braunwald, one of the nation's leading cardiologists, said Francis McGill's "performance has been outstanding in every respect. She now ranks with the best of the Harvard students.… Her attitude, professional behavior and potential performance as an intern are clearly outstanding." Jack Cush was one of our first students at Coney Island Hospital. He, like all the students in these inner-city hospitals, got amazing hands-on training at the front line of medicine from doctors who were at the forefront of primary and emergency care.

We received many more letters praising the program. Our students had proved they could hold their own in the classroom and the clinical setting. I keep repeating that none of this surprised me, because it didn't. I knew how I felt when I was in studying in Spain; above all other emotions I was motivated to prove that the people who had rejected me were wrong. What was most rewarding was that once our students demonstrated their capabilities and enthusiasm, hospitals began embracing the tuition-sharing concept. Bill Ventura did rotations at St. Michael's alongside students from domestic schools. "The residents would tell me, 'You guys are motivated, you guys want to learn. Those other people leave at three o'clock; we almost have to throw you out at night.'"

CHAPTER 20

Backlash: The Medical Establishment Reacts

"The resistance stemmed from a concern about the caliber of education at St. George's."

—Vice Dean of Medical Education, New York University

"So, it's kind of like when they say jump, I have to ask, 'How high?'"

—Me

As I anticipated, organized medicine began reacting. They criticized us in the media, in the state legislatures, in the courts, and in the hospitals. When they accepted the reality that we wouldn't go away, they created obstacles. We had to do a lot of juggling in those early days as sites succumbed to real or perceived pressure. Weeks after a program in Miami had begun, for example, it was suddenly shut down. Every day presented a different challenge. Raz Giliberti, who was living in New Jersey, had been assigned to a hospital in Bensonhurst, Brooklyn. When he got there at 6:30 a.m. his first morning, he was instead sent to South Amboy Hospital in Jersey. Someone then tipped off New Jersey's PBS station that this tuition-sharing program existed, and they decided to investigate. Raz and I were both interviewed for the story. "They asked me about my experiences," he recalls. "I gave them a glowing report. There was nothing negative you could pull out of it. The story that was broadcast two months later was a complete splicing of what I had told them. They pasted together segments of our interviews to produce a negative story."

Technically this story was accurate: We had not yet completed all the required paperwork. The program at South Amboy was closed, and our students transferred to Leon Smith's St. Michael's Hospital.

The system hoped we would disappear. Every state had its own licensing requirements, which, according to the *New England Journal of Medicine*, created a situation that "can be generally described as chaotic, lacking in any guiding philosophy, dubious in its equity and dangerously uneven in professional standards." Fighting for these slots was one long, endless cycle. We had to fight state by state. The more our students succeeded, the more new students were attracted to the university, meaning we had to secure an increasing number of clinical positions. On a few occasions we had to go to court to defend our program.

The most significant challenge came from New York State. In response to our placing more and more of our students in New York hospitals—along with our competitors coming in our wake—the deans of several New York medical schools convinced the state regents to enact a law essentially closing the state to our students. A commission appointed by then governor Mario Cuomo recommended that the state cut its residency programs by a third—and stop using graduates of foreign medical schools to fill its teaching hospital programs. In 1985, undoubtedly under pressure from the medical establishment, the State Education Department barred students from Caribbean medical schools from taking clinical positions in New York hospitals. For us, this was a legal volcanic eruption. It was potentially devastating.

It got worse. The state health commissioner added that he was considering denying graduates of these schools a license to practice in New York. At that time, 38 percent of all the residents in city hospitals were graduates of foreign medical schools. These were the hospitals serving poor and minority neighborhoods. Without foreign medical school graduates, these facilities would have struggled with drastic shortages.

Once again, we fought back. We were the first Caribbean school to officially request approval for our students to enroll in clinical programs. At that time there was no formal approval process. No one really knew what to do about our request. We asked them to provide some parameters, to establish a process. In response they sent us a long list of conditions we had to satisfy. One of the questions, I remember, asked about the status of our Faculty Senate.

Faculty Senate? Not only didn't we have one, we didn't even know what that was. Andy and Peggy did the research—then we created a Faculty Senate, along with its membership and operating procedures. New York State eventually set up an approval process, which was to include a site visit. These people were associate deans of the schools that did not want to see us approved. To guide us through this process we hired the recently retired executive director of the state licensing board, Ray Solomon. When you're engaged in a political fight, you need experienced political experts on your side.

The site team went to Grenada for inspection. While they were sufficiently impressed with the teaching facilities, the quality of the students, and especially the enthusiasm and caring of the faculty, they were unimpressed with the Admissions/Registrar offices in Grenada.

Following that inspection they gave us a list of thirteen deficiencies that had to be corrected or satisfied and six months to do it. It was a fair and professional way of proceeding. But it meant we had only six months to fulfill every deficiency. Six months to survival.

We were fortunate to have several strong supporters among our students' parents. They knew what their kids were going through, and why, and were helpful in many ways. One of them, Bernie Ferguson, did some research. "I just checked into this for you, Charlie," he told me. "One of the major problems is that you don't have an immunology lab."

"Rats," I agreed, "we don't." We had an immunology lecture. I didn't think we needed a complete lab. Most of the schools I'd used as models to set up the curriculum didn't have one either. "You sure we need it?"

He checked it out for me. Of the thirteen medical schools in New York State, only six of them had an immunology lab. Six. Not even a majority. Having an immunology lab was not a requirement. I met with Tom Moynihan, who had followed Solomon as the executive director of the state licensing board. He was the person we needed to satisfy; he reported compliance to the regents.

Moynihan was open and honest. It was obvious he was willing to give us a fair hearing. "We've got a great program," I told him. "The hospitals love us. I understand many of these conditions, they make sense, but a few of them are not reasonable. You're telling us we have to have an immunology lab, for example, but there are only six New York schools that have one."

He smiled and nodded in agreement. *He gets it*, I thought. "I know that," he said. "We've discussed that. You have to understand my job is to tell you that this is the report, and these are the problems you have to solve. I know you're disheartened about it, and I know you've got some terrific students." He tapped the report. "But you need to fix these things or they're going to stand in your way."

The subtext, I believed, was that he sympathized with us but couldn't acknowledge it. "There are different options we have right now," I said, and I'm sure he knew I was referring to legal action, "but I feel good talking to you about this because you see where I'm coming from. I've got my students down there who want to come to American hospitals. And you know the hospitals need these people. They've got to continue taking students from abroad. I'd like to know what I need to do to make this happen."

He tried to tell me what to do without telling me what to do. We had the right to another site visit, he reminded me, but in preparation for that he suggested, "Don't look at what other schools are doing. You know that one point you raised, Charlie?"

I got it. That "point" was the fact that less than half of the existing schools had the immunology lab we were being penalized for not providing. He was warning me not to make that argument. He simply wanted us to figure out how to thread a needle with an anchor. "So, it's kind of like when they say jump, I have to ask, 'How high?'"

"That's exactly what it is."

I paused. "Okay, Tom, go ahead and say it."

"Jump."

"How high?"

"You got it."

I told our board of directors we weren't going to argue, we weren't going to make this a long and expensive legal battle. Whatever they wanted corrected we were going to correct.

Putting in an immunology lab would cost $80,000. That was a huge sum for us, but what we were really buying was acceptance by New York State, and that was invaluable to us. The board asked me if I was sure if we fulfilled these conditions we would be approved.

"Absolutely," I said, hoping I was right.

We built our $80,000 immunology lab, fixed the other things on the New York State deficiency list, and requested another site visit. We welcomed them with confident smiles. I wasn't interested in making a point; I wanted our students to have access to those clinical positions.

Weeks later we became the first school in the Caribbean to be approved by New York State. Several months later we also became the first school approved by New Jersey. Our students could work in metropolitan-area hospitals. It was the first absolute milestone we had hit as an institution. It was game-changing. Champagne was flowing around the Bay Shore office—and, I am sure, wherever our students were!

After we were approved by the New York regents, Bob Ross and others immediately filed for approval for their students—and were immediately rejected. Ross couldn't figure out why we had been approved while he was rejected and asked to meet with me. We met in his office, the one with all the photographs of him with various presidents. "C'mon," he pleaded, "what'd you do to get that approval?"

"I don't know why I'm doing this," I replied, "but I'm going to tell you the truth. The truth is contained in three words: When they say 'Jump,' you say, 'How high?' Do that and you'll get your approval."

This was not Bob Ross's style—for many reasons. He refused to do that. He went the pugnacious route. But he was turned down several times and sued the state. For the next decade we were the only Caribbean school approved for clinical placements.

That victory did not stop the establishment from continuing to question this precedent of paying hospitals. To damage our reputation, to create a bad impression of our students, we were lumped in with the other Caribbean medical school start-ups, several of which admittedly were substandard, rather than acknowledging our accomplishments. Their argument, reported the *Times*, was that "those schools turn out poorly trained students who undercut the quality of their New York peers learning alongside them at the same hospitals."

Those organizations were created to protect patients. They did that by establishing standards. It was a valid argument...but it didn't apply to our school. We continued to do everything possible to meet and even surpass those standards.

Undercut the quality? That infuriated me. We had a substantial amount of evidence showing that we were producing young doctors every bit as good as those graduating from American schools. But it was more than that. The fact—*fact*—was that we were supplying clinical students and residents to rural and inner-city hospitals that otherwise had a difficult time attracting staff, especially primary-care physicians. We were fulfilling a desperate need.

The majority of graduates from the American schools gravitated into the higher-paying specialties, creating a shortage of primary-care doctors that was being filled by foreign-trained men and women. Those facilities welcomed our students. "There is a great advantage to us," the doctor who ran the clinical program at Brooklyn's Methodist Hospital told *New York* magazine. "We cannot attract for residency slots in our hospital students who have gone to U.S. medical schools. They just don't want to come to Brooklyn. But when we take the offshore students for their clinical studies, they often decide to stay on with us and do their residencies."

In 1995 one of the original class members, Danny Ricciardi, who had become a successful rheumatologist in Brooklyn, joined our faculty as a clinical dean. That meant he helped secure clinical slots in metropolitan-area hospitals, then monitored their progress. If a student had an issue, Danny was the guy who tried to solve it.

Danny always is Danny—smart, gregarious, ingenious—and always finding connections where they are needed. And he was very successful in finding spots for our students. In 2000, because of his work in the city, Danny was appointed to the sixteen-member board of New York's Health and Hospitals Corporation. HHC ran the city's eleven public hospitals, in addition to other medical facilities, and had about 3,500 clinical spots to fill. Generally, they accepted a mix of students from both domestic and foreign schools, including ours. The city was aware of Danny's association with St. George's when he was put on the board.

By that time the landscape had changed drastically. More medical schools were competing for clinical spots at fewer hospitals. The soothing concept of the family doctor with his black bag visiting patients in their homes was as long gone as the pay telephone. Many unprofitable community hospitals had closed. With these changes, the traditional model of doctors teaching the next generation as a duty to medicine was rapidly disappearing.

As our enrollment continued to increase, this threatened to become an extremely serious problem. We were enrolling eight hundred students a class cycle, at least three times as many as most American schools, so we were far more affected by this growing shortage of available clinical positions than they were. By the early 2000s we had about two thousand students in clinical rotations in ninety-eight American cities. In addition to protecting those slots, we had to continue securing more of them.

Danny was aware that HHC, rather than being reimbursed for training students, was actually paying its member hospitals tens of millions of dollars for that training. It made no sense. As Danny pointed out, even he was smart enough to figure out that being paid is much better than paying for the same service. Also, as New York's budget problems grew, its public hospitals were increasingly desperate for new sources of revenue. So he began speaking to the executive directors of the member hospitals, offering to share tuition of the students they accepted. These hospitals had long welcomed our students—Danny and his classmates had established that beachhead at Coney Island Hospital decades earlier.

It took two years before he was able to convince Lincoln Hospital in the Bronx to sign an affiliation agreement. Then, one by one the other hospitals in the system bought into the concept until we had exclusive agreements with six of them. HHC had become a very valuable resource for us.

Then I had an idea. Again.

Rather than negotiating separately with each hospital, what we really should do was make an overall deal to include all eleven institutions. Danny presented the concept to Mayor Mike Bloomberg's administration. It got bounced around, but no matter how they looked at it, it came down to one simple truth: Instead of paying, these hospitals would be paid. The city eventually issued an RFP, a request for proposal. In addition to payments, we sweetened the offer, the most important one being one medical school and one nursing school scholarship at St. George's for each hospital. Provided they accepted at least twenty-four of our students, each of those eleven hospitals could offer scholarships to young people living in their area.

Six weeks after the charter class had started classes in 1977, we celebrated that the door locks we'd ordered had arrived. Each small step was a minor victory. Now we were tossing around tens of millions of dollars. Even Danny was dubious. I had to convince him this made sense. Eventually we closed the deal at $10 million a year, plus the scholarships. (The final agreement included 110 scholarships.)

In return we were given exclusive rights from among all international medical schools to about half the available clinical slots. The other slots were reserved for domestically educated students.

It seemed like an enormous payment—okay, it was an enormous payment—but until this agreement HHC had been paying medical schools for their affiliation. It was a huge win for the city, and for us. But when the agreement was announced there was a tremendous uproar from other hospitals in the city, especially the private institutions.

Within months, again following the path we had forged, Ross University and others had negotiated smaller contracts with teaching hospitals in different parts of the state. For some of these struggling institutions, these payments literally made the difference between staying open and continuing to serve the local community or having to close their doors.

While we had expected some opposition, the actual response might more accurately be described as restrained apoplexy. The *Times* reported, "Critics worry that the hospital corporation, whose mission is to serve the city's poor, is conferring prestige on a foreign school whose curriculum, they say, is more vocational than research-based and often caters to affluent students who could not get into schools in the United States... the contract turns a meritocracy into a bounty system in which struggling city hospitals collect more for every St. George's student they take, and could squeeze out local students."

Research based? Our curriculum essentially mirrored domestic institutions. Local students? Our students in many cases were from the metropolitan area, about as local as it is possible to be. It appears these people preferred "struggling city hospitals" to continue struggling.

The vice dean of medical education at NYU, whose students now have their entire medical school tuition covered by a wealthy donor, explained, "The resistance stemmed from a concern about the caliber of education at St. George's." The dean did not mention that, according to the State Education Department, about a third of all physicians licensed to practice in New York had attended foreign medical schools.

Perhaps the weakest argument came from the executive director of the Associated Medical Schools of New York, who according to the newspaper complained to the state licensing board that "as American medical schools tried to increase enrollment to address a shortage of doctors the contract would threaten access for local institutions and put pressure on them to pay hospitals more." In other words, he admitted, we were threatening their good deal. There was only limited evidence American medical schools were significantly increasing enrollment to deal with the serious shortage, and he completely ignored the reality that we already were fulfilling it with qualified young physicians. It made me furious;

NYU medical school is free for their students, yet they still were trying to prevent our students from completing their education.

In response to these attacks one of our students, Jennifer Gola, a Princeton graduate who had been rejected by US schools and completed her clinicals in HHC hospitals, told a reporter, "The Einstein [medical school] students did the exact same thing we did. We were standing next to each other on ward rounds, presenting patients together at clinic and presenting cases to each other. We had the same supervisors." And had to pass the same licensing examinations.

While the domestic medical schools inferred that our graduates were somehow inferior to theirs, there has never been a shred of evidence presented by any organization to support that contention.

I always urge people to compare the percentage of foreign-trained residents at inner-city hospitals or rural hospitals with graduates of American schools. By 2020, St. George's had become the largest provider of doctors in the American health-care system. Let me repeat that: By 2020, St. George's had become the largest provider of doctors in the American health-care system. Perhaps even more important, in a system estimated to be short as many as one hundred thousand primary-care physicians within a decade, three-quarters of our graduates enter primary-care specialties.

When I founded Fire Island's first water taxi service, my goal was simply to move people from one place to another. When I founded St. George's University, my goal was to provide a place for qualified students to attend an English-speaking medical school and eventually become licensed physicians in the United States. Neither goal ever changed.

Maybe those angry bureaucrats and administrators should put at least part of the blame where it belongs: with geopolitics.

CHAPTER 21

Coup d'état and Confusion

"I saw one of the armored cars coming up to the fort. That's when the shooting started."

—St. George's University administrative secretary Anthia Parke

When we founded St. George's University I knew there would be problems I couldn't possibly anticipate. We were pioneers, and there was no way of knowing what lay over the horizon. That didn't really concern me—I have always been pretty good at dealing with the unexpected without panicking. I am a dreamer and a realist, a creative problem-solver. I take pride in the fact that I am adaptable, flexible, resilient, and determined.

I also had my father's gift of being able to recognize those problems that couldn't immediately be solved, and rather than getting bogged down trying to solve them, I would find ways around them.

Somehow, we found ways of dealing with all the problems that had arisen. There certainly had been a lot of them, but I don't recall ever complaining. I don't recall ever wondering, *What else could go wrong?*

But even I was dumbfounded at first when the United States Marine Corps invaded Grenada to rescue our students.

Like so many newly independent nations, Grenadians were trying to determine which form of government would enable the country to develop. Grenada had historically been a peaceful place, and an orderly society was in place upon becoming independent. That democracy was still building its institutions when we were chartered, but growing pains included being courted by a foreign socialistic influence—Cuba. That influence ran amok, eventually leading to the United States stepping in to help the democratic system of government to prevail and thrive in the forty years since then.

Following the one-day, mostly peaceful revolution, Maurice Bishop had essentially fulfilled his promise to leave the school alone. The new government appeared to be reasonably accepted by the Grenadians. Among the first projects Bishop had begun was the construction of a new international airport at Point Saline, which was close enough to the True Blue campus for dirt and rock from explosions to pepper our rooftops.

Grenada needed the airport. Getting on and off the island was always a hassle. Pearls' runway was too short for large, modern jetliners. A new, larger international airport would open the island to increased tourism and trade. Building a new airport was complicated and expensive, and the Bishop government had asked Cuban premier Fidel Castro to help out.

Cubans had begun arriving on the island only days after Bishop took charge. Among them were diplomats, laborers, some medical personnel, and a few soldiers. Most of them lived in the rebuilt military barracks, near True Blue. The first few weeks after the revolution had been difficult; from time to time students could hear distant, sporadic gunfire. But eventually the situation had settled down into a new kind of normalcy.

Most of the encounters with the Cubans were positive. Cuban healthcare professionals began working at the hospital; one orthopedic doctor even joined our clinical staff and began teaching students. Occasionally, Cubans in trucks driving to work would pick up hitchhiking students and give them a lift. Vish Rao became friends with several Cuban doctors; Bob Jordan became friends with a truck driver who had once worked as Castro's personal chef. I attended several social events at the Cuban embassy. Cuban workers participated in students' baseball, basketball, and soccer games. We got used to them being there. When Danny and

Da Boys returned to the island for their final semester, for example, they set up a small business selling cheap digital watches to the workers. They would buy watches for $3 in Brooklyn and sell them for $25 on the island. And after just about every Cuban had bought a watch, Da Boys began selling them batteries.

The only obvious reminders of the Cubans' presence were the Fidel and Che Guevara posters that were pasted on walls and the daily ranting against American imperialism on Radio Free Grenada. That and the incessant blasting for the new airport.

The school became an even more important economic engine for the island. The presence of Cuban and Grenadian troops drove away what little tourism already existed. Grenada had been known as a safe haven for yachts, a good place to anchor in the Caribbean and enjoy the beautiful beaches. But when soldiers began conducting surprise inspections of these boats, supposedly looking for pornography, vacationers stopped coming and the economy suffered.

Nothing like this had ever happened in Grenadian history—nor would it again—but for a brief time we had to figure out how to deal with this government. The good news was because of our economic value those soldiers actually protected the school.

It took a little time, but gradually we got used to the presence of soldiers in our midst. There were few encounters. Lou Guida remembers being awakened by voices outside his rented house late one night a few weeks after the revolution. He peeked out and saw several armed soldiers of the People's Revolutionary Army climbing out of a truck. He got down on the floor and crawled around the house, waking his roommates, warning them. "We didn't know what to do," he said. "We had no idea what was going on."

Suddenly there was an insistent banging on the front door. They had no choice, they decided; they had to open it. The soldiers were standing there. They apologized for waking them up, explaining they were on maneuvers and were desperate for water. Lou and his roommates invited the patrol in. They came inside for a glass of water.

That was the reality of life on Grenada at that time: Welcome to the Revolution, with the Cuban influence transforming the peaceful nation into a more militant one.

We reminded our students to stay out of any political discussions. Basically, we advised them, keep a low profile, mind your own business, focus on studying, and don't go to any parties where guns were present. We were maintaining a delicate balance. There was no getting around the fact that we were trying to operate a for-profit medical school in a quasi-Communist country in the middle of the Cold War. Most Americans believed Castro was a danger to the United States, so it made sense trying to limit his influence in the Caribbean. The presence of Cuban workers on the island obviously would concern our State Department. But the Grenada Revolution was popular among Grenadians, and in reality Bishop was more of a socialist than a Communist. People trusted him.

Relations with the United States were essentially nonexistent. The Reagan administration had refused to even recognize the new government. After being rebuffed by America, Bishop began strengthening ties with Soviet Bloc countries, as well as China. He was trying to build a more diverse economy, among other initiatives opening a food-processing plant and a chocolate factory. He proposed building two new three-hundred-room hotels to make the island more attractive to tourists. But it was the international airport that was going to open up Grenada to the rest of the world. The planned facility would have a nine-thousand-foot-long runway, sufficient for jumbo DC-9s and 747s from Europe and the United States to land—and it would have lighting that enabled it to remain open at night.

Grenada desperately needed a modern airport. Pearls was...charming, but inefficient. By 1980 the school had its own plane, a six-seat Beechcraft, and a pilot. We used it primarily to ferry visiting instructors to and from Barbados and St. Vincent. One morning Geoffrey Bourne and several other faculty members were scheduled to fly to the tiny island of Carriacou, but at the airport they discovered our plane was blocked in by several other small planes and a DC-3. So they took the situation in hand, literally. This is the kind of airport Pearls was at that time: They began pushing our Beechcraft through the parked planes, moving small planes to the side so they could squeeze through. They finally created the opening they needed by moving a plane to the side of the DC-3. They then got in and taxied to the top of the runway. They sat there waiting for permission to take off—but instead they were ordered by the traffic controller, "Put that plane back where you got it from."

They dutifully shut off the engine and as directed pushed and shoved the other planes back into place where they had been. They then got permission to depart. That was Pearls. Not quite a do-it-yourself airport but certainly insufficient to service tourism. If Grenada was going to prosper it had to be replaced by a modern facility.

The government decided to build the new airport at Port Salines. We were told we had to move several of our prefab buildings, including our open-air lecture hall, about five hundred yards to make room for an airport service yard. Constructing new roads and a modern runway required a considerable amount of blasting. We worked out a system: We put a siren on the roof of our new library building. The building was concrete, making it the strongest one on campus. Each time they were ready to dynamite rocks they gave us a warning. When the siren went off the students in the lecture hall moved into the library. When the siren signaled all clear they returned to the lecture hall, made sure its roof was still intact, and the lecture resumed.

Like Eric Gairy, on occasion Bishop would visit the campus. He was always accompanied by security, but they kept their weapons in the cars. In fact, in 1981 we invited him to speak at our first graduation ceremony held on the island. This was a choice, not a command. It reflected our desire to maintain a positive relationship with his government.

Bishop was in a complex situation. He wanted to establish better relations with the United States, but the co-leader of his New Jewel Movement, Bernard Coard, was a Marxist who was pulling the revolution much further to the left. Bishop tried to reach out to the Reagan administration, but there had been no response. The State Department apparently believed Cuba was helping to build the runway for military purposes, ignoring the reality that Cuba was actually much closer to the United States than Grenada—and Barbados already had a runway long enough for military transports to land.

I did not want to get involved in the political situation, but eventually I had no choice. During the summer of 1983, Bishop was in New York for meetings at the United Nations and we met several times. He wanted to establish a better relationship with the United States, he told me. He wanted to moderate the revolution. I was elated. "Is there anything I can do to help?" I asked.

"Yes," he told me, "there is." He wanted me to find someone in the Reagan administration to open a dialogue. Unfortunately, I knew only a few low-level people. I reached out to the State Department and relayed Bishop's request. A couple of days later I got my answer: "You need to tell the prime minister that he has to apologize for his harsh rhetoric before anyone in the government will meet with him."

Well, they did have a point. The Bishop government had been pretty outspoken in its criticism of America. I conveyed that response to him in the nicest possible way. "I think they're saying that if you just toned it down a little, they might be willing to talk to you." I was hopeful this would mark the beginning of a new and better relationship between the two countries.

It did just the opposite. Coard and other New Jewel Movement leaders had learned that Bishop was trying to establish a line of communications with the United States. I will never know if that came from my meetings with him or from his meetings with other people, or if it was because the Reagan administration refused to meet him, which left him stranded. That's always been a mystery. Wherever they got that information, it led to a serious rift in the People's Revolutionary Party. On October 13, Maurice Bishop was placed under arrest in his home at Mount Wheldale, and Coard assumed power. I was doing my best to keep track of what was going on down there, but it was a very murky, very volatile situation. We told our students to stay on or near the campus.

Grenadians loyal to Bishop were outraged. Large demonstrations took place almost daily. On the nineteenth, a group of his supporters broke down the front gate of his house and rescued him. Bishop had been tortured, they discovered—his captors had burned him with cigarettes and deprived him of water. After being stabilized, he was taken to military headquarters at Fort Rupert, where it was believed he could be protected.

The situation escalated very quickly. Anthia Parke, then our administrative secretary, was in her office on the campus when a friend called to tell her a massive protest rally was taking place downtown at eleven o'clock in support of Maurice Bishop. At lunchtime Anthia took a bus into the capital. "Everybody was just headed up to the fort," she recalled. "People were happy Bishop had been freed, and they were going up there to protect him. I followed the crowd. There was a truck at the entrance to the fort with a lot of schoolchildren on it. One of those kids told me Mr. Bishop was going to be talking to the people very soon. I looked at my watch. It was twenty minutes before one o'clock. 'I would love to hear what he is saying,' I responded, 'but I have to get back to work.'"

Meanwhile, Coard and his associates, including Lieutenant Colonel Ewart "Headache" Layne, fearing Bishop would be able to regain control of the government, ordered four armored personnel carriers to go up to the fort and break up the rally, rearrest Bishop, and imprison him.

As Anthia began leaving the demonstration, she says, "I saw one of the armored cars coming up to the fort. That's when the shooting started. The truck with the children on it was covered with smoke. Everyone started scampering. I crawled through a window to get away. I ended up in the back, in a courtyard surrounded by woods. The army people were surrounding the perimeter of the fort. They had machine guns and they were shooting wildly. I heard one of the soldiers telling the others, 'Slow down, slow down.'

"The shooting slowed down. Next thing I remember was being on the hood of a car, climbing onto the top of a wall, then jumping over it. I got tangled in the brush. I ran all the way down the hill until I could get a ride to my home. I was on the porch of my house telling my family what was going on downtown when I heard more gunfire. Later that day

I found out that was when they had lined up the prime minister and all his ministers against a wall and shot them."

Eight people, seven men and one woman, Jackie Creft, the minister of education and the mother of one of Bishop's children, had been put against a wall in the inner courtyard and murdered. A number of protestors were also killed. Although that number has never been accurately determined, the best estimate was "many people."

I was stunned. Absolutely stunned. I couldn't believe it. Just couldn't believe it. In Grenada? It was hard for me to believe these killings had been ordered by Coard, because he was not a dumb man. These killings made no sense: Maurice Bishop was a popular leader; the Grenadian people would never support people who murdered him. My theory at the time was that some young kids in the fort had done this on their own. Maybe they panicked. We would never know for certain, and there have always been different versions of what happened at the fort that day.

Vish Rao and Bob Jordan had been proctoring the anatomy midterm in the lecture hall when the shooting erupted. While it was literally many miles away and none of our students were ever in danger, the sound of gunshots was unnerving. They had no idea what was taking place, so they made an effort to keep everyone calm. "Focus," Vish told the students. "This is your midterm. You'd better concentrate on that. Afterward we'll find out what's happening."

A few hours later the Coard government announced a curfew. I was in New York, getting information from Anthia. She told me General Hudson Austin had made a radio address to the nation announcing Bishop's death. General Austin? That surprised me. Hudson Austin was a former prison guard I had met several times. He was not nearly as bright as Bishop or Coard. As soon as I heard that, I was pretty certain that Coard had not ordered the killing.

It was really difficult for me to understand the situation. I knew all these people. I had been with Bishop in New York only a few weeks earlier. This was so far from anything I had ever experienced it made little sense to me. Why suddenly had the government been ripped apart? Many years later Hudson Austin claimed that in addition to the political division, Coard feared that Bishop was moving closer to the United States. He also was very jealous of Bishop's popularity. Whatever the reasons, the result was the same. The Grenadian government was in chaos. We had already dealt with so many unusual and unexpected problems just to keep the school running. But assassination? The murder of civilians?

As it turned out this was only the beginning. It made me nostalgic for the problems of the good old days that did not involve geopolitical concerns

The island was shut down. Everyone was ordered to stay in their homes. Stores were permitted to be open only during a few designated hours. The school was closed. Students and faculty who lived off campus gathered in a few centrally located designated houses.

A few hours after making his radio address, General Austin went to Geoffrey Bourne's home to assure him our students were safe. There has been some bloodshed, he told Dr. Bourne. "We're going to try to control the country," he said. "Don't worry, your students are safe."

"But there's a curfew," Geoffrey pointed out, "and we have classes."

"No, no, no," Austin told him. "The students can still go to class. We'll give escorts for them. You have permission." He gave Bourne his home phone number in case we had to get in touch with him. It's always reassuring to have the commanding general's home phone number "in case." In case of what? After that Geoffrey met with Austin or his representative every day to make sure we knew what was going on.

I reached out to my low-level contact at the State Department, a man named Richard Brown, and told him everything I knew. He listened and responded, "You can't trust him."

It was a completely helpless feeling. "I don't know who I can trust," I said. "But Austin's the guy who made the speech. I know his background."

Brown very patiently explained that the US government had intelligence that was very different from what I was being told.

Well, I hoped that was true, but nothing I had seen or been told made me very confident. "Look," I responded, "this guy is the head of the army. With all due respect, I'm not going to tell the CIA anything, but this guy was a prison guard. They made him the general because they didn't want to have to worry about anybody's political ambitions." Basically, I was telling him not to overestimate Austin. He wasn't a threat to anyone.

He did not want to hear that. The first hint I got that our government might have other plans came a few days later, when we were asked by the State Department and the National Security Council to sign a declaration officially requesting a US intervention to protect our students.

Protect them from *what*? I asked, Why in the world would I want to do that? I told Brown that our students were not in danger. They were going to classes. We were right in the middle of midterms. Our students were not in danger. The new government had been adamant about that. Believe me, if our students were in any jeopardy, we would have gotten them out of there immediately, whatever we had to do, even if we had to row boats ourself. I was not yet ready to sign anything.

My concern, my fear, was that our government was going to use this as an excuse to rid the Caribbean of another Communist outpost. I made it clear to the State Department that while I didn't support what was taking place in Grenada, I was confident that in a little while it was going to settle down. In fact, Gary Solin, our bursar, issued a teletyped statement mostly for parents that stated, "The situation here is very calm. Everyone is safe. The government has met with us and assures us of no problems and complete safety."

That was absolutely accurate. We could see that ourselves.

Richard Brown pushed back. Gradually it began to dawn on me: The government of the United States wanted me, wanted the school, to provide an excuse to take military action against Grenada. A representative of the Coard government went to the school and met with students, telling them, "You are safe. We are protecting you." When asked from whom they were protecting the students, he responded, "External forces." Which meant, I supposed, that the Grenadians were protecting American students from the American government.

Several students decided to leave the island on their own. One of them was living with his wife and two roommates in an apartment above a golf course. He and his wife were on a bus to the airport with a retired US Army Ranger and an air force captain when they were stopped by Cuban forces. As he relates that moment, "The Ranger and the captain turned pale when they saw the Cubans. They looked at me and said, 'Don't do anything. Don't move.' Basically, make like a dumb American. After a few minutes they left us alone. As we drove past Mount Saint Catherine, these guys pointed out to me what they described as a SAM missile site and listening post in the crater. It was one of the highest points on the island and perfect for an antenna."

Who knows if there actually was a missile site or listening post there. It was possible. But those were the kinds of rumors that were spreading throughout the island. It was impossible to get any reliable information other than what I was being told by telex code.

Brown and I spoke almost daily. I reiterated my strong position: "We don't want to ask anybody to do anything." No justification was apparent for any American involvement and the risks that may bring. I knew the island; I knew the leaders. I didn't believe our students were in any danger.

"We can't tell you what to do," he said, trying to tell me what to do, "but if you have any concerns about your students, you should sign it."

It was much too official for me. But I had to take some action. It was pretty obvious that in addition to the safety of our students and faculty, the future of the school on Grenada was in jeopardy. Taking on the AAMC was one thing, but this? There were no simple answers, nothing that led to a predictable outcome. Whatever steps I took could save the school or destroy it.

The only thing I knew for certain was that I didn't want our government to make any moves that might endanger our students. But if they were going to take military action, I wanted them to do it in a way that made sense and that kept our students and faculty out of what might become harm's way. I went to Washington with maps and photographs pointing out the school. Here's where the helicopters can land. Here's trees and wires. I told them our people would even spray-paint Xs on the ground to indict safe landing spots.

Communications were limited and poor. We were hearing conflicting stories. We were hearing stories from students that they were being warned by Grenadians to leave as quickly as possible, while other students were being told stay there, stay calm. Parents were justifiably worried. The lack of information raised the already high level of concern. With the perception of potential danger increasing, the time seemed right for me to start proactively addressing it. "Look," I told Brown, "I'd like to find a way of letting those students who want to leave get on commercial flights once the airport is open. What do you need me to show you that Hudson Austin is working with us?"

He responded, "If you are unwilling to ask us to do anything"—meaning provide an excuse to take military action—"one thing you could do is get Austin to demonstrate good faith. If you really believe this guy, get him to allow the State Department to land some people at the airport to meet with students and make sure they're safe. Do that—get Austin to open the airport for us."

That night I called General Austin at his home. This whole thing was bizarre. I was calling one of the leaders of a violent government takeover at his home. I assumed my call was being monitored, maybe even by both nations. His wife answered. It was so normal it was crazy. "Is the general home?" I asked. When he got on the phone I told him, "The State Department is very concerned about the students. Truthfully, I'm worried about what they might do. I was hoping you can open the airport for us and I'll send a small plane from Barbados with some State Department people on it, just so they can see for themselves that everything is okay."

He readily agreed. "Just tell us when they will be arriving. But no military people, just civilians." The fact that he so quickly agreed thrilled me. I thought it might be possible for us to get through this without anyone else getting hurt.

I spent the entire next day going back and forth on the phone making arrangements. But the more I spoke with Richard Brown, the more skeptical I became. He told me repeatedly, "You can't trust Austin. You can't take his word," as if trying to convince me. When the arrangements were finally set, he said, strangely I thought, "Charles, this should be kept between us because we don't want anyone else to know what's going to happen. Can I have your assurance this is going to be kept completely confidential?"

I agreed, but I had an eerie feeling about the whole situation. Why wouldn't they want parents to know the airport had been opened for State Department personnel to visit their kids? This was a very positive step, I thought. I decided to take action. Maybe I'd seen too many James Bond movies, but it seemed to me too often characters kept information secret that put them in danger, when spreading that information would make them safe. Maybe I was a little paranoid, but it seemed clear to me that Brown had his own agenda. He had put me in a situation where I had to choose between reassuring parents or pretending our students were in jeopardy. To me the choice was clear: I owed a greater duty to the parents and students than to Brown.

Assuming his name really was Brown.

I got in my car and drove until I found a pay phone, which I knew would not be tapped, and called WCBS news radio. Because we had many students from the metropolitan area in Grenada, the coup and the killings had been widely reported. "My name is Charles Modica," I said, "and I'm the chancellor of St. George's University in Grenada. The police there have just announced that people from our State Department have been given permission to land there tomorrow morning to meet with our students." They asked me a few more questions, which I used to make the point that everything there was calm and our students were safe.

Within minutes WCBS was broadcasting my interview. I was feeling pretty good about having made that call. Now the State Department couldn't pull any surprises. But before I got back to the office my beeper went off. It was a 202 number. Richard Brown. I stopped at the next pay phone and returned his call. Truthfully, though, by this point I didn't care what he thought. I wanted to get my message out, and I'd done it.

"Chaaaarrrles," he said, drawing out my name. "I thought you agreed it would be better not to publicize tomorrow's visit. We just heard you on the radio telling everybody there was going to be a State Department visit tomorrow. What was that all about?"

Rather than debate with him why I'd prioritized my best judgment about how to safely transport the students over his agenda, I feigned ignorance. "Oh shit, Richard," I responded as honestly as I could make it sound. "That was on the air? Already? Wow. That was supposed to be broadcast after the visit. I am so sorry." That was the best bullshit story I could come up with, but what I really was telling him was *screw you.* I made up a story that was barely plausible rather than admit I didn't trust him. That pissed him off. He made it pretty obvious he did not like losing control of the situation.

My job, my concern, my only objective was to protect our students and staff. It seemed clear to me Brown had other primary concerns, other dominant objectives.

The next morning, a Saturday, two members of the British foreign service accompanied a State Department employee stationed on Barbados to the island. After landing at Pearls they were driven to True Blue. Our students were permitted to leave their homes for this meeting. Each student was handed a card to be filled out if they wanted to be evacuated because they were concerned about their welfare. The details of an evacuation plan were not stated, but they were told they would have to reimburse the United States government for any cost incurred in their transportation.

Only a few students took the cards; the vast majority of them said they did not feel threatened. While this meeting was taking place, I was receiving telex messages using the old two-dictionary code. Basically, I was informed, the State Department employee was trying to convince the students to fill out the cards. "Right now, we can get you off the island," they were warned, "but what happens if there's trouble?" As it turned out, fewer than 10 percent of our students wanted to leave. One of them who stayed, Joe Racanelli, explained to a reporter why that number was so low: "Older students have more to lose. They had given up jobs; they had families. This is their last shot to become doctors."

Geoffrey Bourne told me that the State Department representative was so upset by that dismal response that she started crying. The three visitors then started pushing harder, urging students to reconsider their response, telling them repeatedly that no one knew what might happen and if something did happen they would be stuck there. Bourne said it seemed like they were hinting they had important information they were not permitted to reveal. After the meeting they flew back to Barbados and admitted that very few American medical students wanted to leave. As one newspaper reported, "They were too intent on their studies to be interrupted by the little local difficulties on the island."

I had arranged to meet with interested parents on Sunday morning at a gate at the American Airlines terminal at JFK airport. It was a large open space, and we were expecting a big crowd. As I drove to the airport early that morning, I heard the terrible news that terrorists had attacked the US Marines barracks in Beirut, Lebanon. They had detonated a truck bomb, and an unknown number of Americans had been killed and wounded. They were reporting that we had suffered a massive number of casualties. It was awful, horrible. But it seemed impossible to me that this would affect the school.

I met with more than two hundred anxious parents. I told them everything I knew, reassuring them that their children were safe and informing them we were chartering flights to leave from Barbados. But I understood the fears, so we took steps to respond to those concerns. If their son or daughter wanted to come home, that was being arranged. During this meeting I was asked if there was anything parents could do to help. "I'm concerned that our government might want to evacuate our students," I responded. "And I think that any type of military activity might create a danger that doesn't exist right now. If you agree with me, I recommend that you send a telegram to the White House asking the president not to act precipitously."

The response was almost unanimous. That night the head of the Parents Coalition sent a telegram to President Reagan asking him to show restraint. But what none of us knew was that by the time it got there it already was too late.

CHAPTER 22

Operation Urgent Fury

"I went back into my house and got down on the floor. Within minutes I heard machine-gun fire."

—St. George's University student Henry Collins

President Ronald Reagan had already made the decision to invade Grenada. Ships from the US Navy's Second Fleet, led by the aircraft carrier *Independence,* which had been sailing to Lebanon to support that mission, were diverted to the Caribbean. Of course, we still didn't know that.

We spent Monday making preparations for the charter flights that would evacuate students. Pat Adams flew to Barbados to try to get to the island, but all flights were canceled and he couldn't rent a boat to take him there. Instead, he was stopped by two American soldiers who overheard him asking questions. After confirming his identity and his purpose, he was brought to an office and asked to point out the location of the school's buildings on a large map. John Madden, who was doing his residency at Brooklyn's Coney Island Hospital, also was stuck on Barbados. He had been scheduled to work at the school as a visiting instructor, but he was told his flight to Grenada had been canceled "because there are tanks on the runway." Tanks on the runway? *That can't be right,* he thought, *there are no tanks on Grenada.*

On Monday, Americans began learning the full extent of the casualties of the terrorist attack in Beirut. It was truly awful, devastating. Islamic Jihad had detonated two truck bombs, killing 241 Americans, including 220 Marines who had been asleep in their barracks, and 58 French paratroopers stationed there on a peacekeeping mission. It was a stunning attack. The problem for the administration was that the situation in the Middle East was so confused, so chaotic, that there was no obvious way to retaliate. There was no enemy force to go after—we were fighting shadows.

The success of these attacks made America look weak and vulnerable. President Reagan was being strongly criticized for sending our troops there without providing sufficient security. He needed to find a way to regain the confidence of the American public and he needed it right away. It was my belief that President Reagan was influenced to order this incursion by the colossal failure in Beirut. He needed a sure thing. And conveniently there was this so-called Communist coup in Grenada.

Our charter flights never got there. Before dawn Tuesday morning, Henry Collins, a student living near the airport, heard a large propeller-driven airplane circling above the runway—flying without lights. "I knew it was circling because it was blocking out light in a circular pattern," he remembers. "We'd heard all the rumors about an invasion, but I couldn't figure out what this plane was doing. It couldn't land because the Cubans had put all kinds of heavy equipment on the runway.

"At about 5:25 I went to the bathroom. All of sudden I heard the plane making an approach. It was just getting light. I ran outside with my pants around my ankles. A C-130 was streaking from west to east, just off the ground, and people were jumping out of it. My brain didn't process this until I saw arms and legs and then parachutes open.

"I went back into my house and got down on the floor. Within minutes I heard machine-gun fire. An antiaircraft gun across the street started shooting at the planes. In response, a helicopter gunship opened up on that gun. That was the beginning of the invasion. The firing went on for about three hours. It was deafening. There would be a little lull, then it started again. During one of those breaks I went out onto my deck: two Marine Corps gunships were hovering over the beach at just about my eye level. I could see the faces of the pilots."

Operation Urgent Fury, the invasion of Grenada, had begun.

Fred Jacobs, whose daughter was a student, had been communicating with her by ham radio. He was in Short Hills, New Jersey. Early that morning he'd received a call from another ham radio operator informing him, "They're invading, but nobody knows who the invaders are." Initially, many students believed it was the Cubans. They didn't know that American forces had landed until 82nd Airborne troops burst into the dormitory at True Blue and ordered everyone to get down on the floor.

"It was surreal," US Air Force veteran Bob Jordan recalled. "We were standing on the roof watching A-6s and A-7s dropping bombs around us. We knew the war was real when we saw one of our Cobra helicopters get hit and crash onto the beach. Then…an American destroyer about a mile offshore pumped several rounds into the fort right above the hospital."

I had gotten a message from the school when the planes started circling. I called Richard Brown at four o'clock in the morning. "They're telling me that planes are circling. Is that Americans or Cubans? Can you give me a heads-up?"

"I'm not giving you any information at all," he said coldly.

I was furious. "Okay," I said, "but you're up at 4:00 a.m., so I'll make my own assumptions."

"You can do whatever you want, but I'm not making any comment to you."

Students stayed down on the floors of their rooms, propping up mattresses against the windows and glass doors. Within hours several students set up a makeshift infirmary in the cafeteria, using tables as beds. They tore up clean sheets and pillowcases to use for bandages and over the next days treated wounded Grenadians and Cubans, among them three civilian women who had been wounded in a crossfire. They did emergency medicine, wrapping wounds, applying splints, and monitoring patients. Several Cubans had been seriously wounded, and at least one of them died on a cafeteria table. Other students assisted military medics treating wounded Americans in a makeshift clinic set up in the library. "It looked like something out of *M*A*S*H*," said student David Breslin. As it got dark and the generator ran out of fuel, they began treating patients by lantern and flashlight.

Henry Collins lay on the floor of his rented house "waiting for some guy to come in and shoot me. I could see shadows and boots moving by under my door. I just held my breath and kept thinking, *Holy shit! I'd never been in a situation even close to this before.*"

We were sitting in New York, mostly feeling helpless. Throughout much of the invasion, our only source of information from the campus was a student named Mark Baretella, who stayed on his ham radio with Fred Jacobs for two straight days. Mark had been using his shortwave set to speak with his parents, but after Coard had taken over he'd hidden it in a body bag in the anatomy lab. When the shooting started, he'd retrieved it and established contact with Jacobs. Communications to the island initially were so bad that Fred's wife had to relay information from Grenada to the State Department to let them know what was going on.

At one point the State Department began asking for intelligence: How many Grenadians soldiers were on the beach, for example, and what weapons were they carrying? Fred refused to even ask Mark those questions. He wasn't going to ask an innocent spectator for information that would have made him a legitimate military target. Baretella did ask Jacobs to tell the State Department that Grenadians were shooting at American helicopters flying directly over the dorms, and students were afraid one of the choppers could get hit and crash into their dorm. Within minutes the helicopters moved away. Later we learned that a military officer was listening to this conversation on his own ham radio and had relayed the request.

The media knew as little as we did. When the networks found out Fred had established communications with someone on the island, they camped out on his front lawn. Dan Rather in particular was furious when Fred refused to put him directly in touch with his contact. Ham radio operators around the country heard some guy in New Jersey was the main source of communication with the island and began monitoring his conversations. Mark, a second-year student, was reporting mostly from under a table in his dorm room, doing a wonderful job reassuring anxious parents that their children were safe: "We're still holding here," he said, then asked for "a shipment of about four thousand White Castle hamburgers."

Vish Rao managed to make contact with his father-in-law living in Carteret, New Jersey. He was pretty sure Grenadians were listening to these calls, so Vish and his father-in-law spoke in their mother tongue, Telugu. He asked his father to call me in Long Island and convey his messages.

As information trickled in from a variety of sources, it was becoming clear the invasion had been planned with an emphasis on speed but not thoroughness. The military, it turned out, had very little intelligence about the island of Grenada or the school. The information I'd handed to Richard Brown had never reached the military planners. In fact, when a battalion commander informed his officers they were heading to Grenada, he was asked, "Why are we invading Spain?"

Our troops had not been given maps; they had no way to find their way around the island. Instead, soldiers had to rely on the colorful tourist maps from the Holiday Inn showing the locations of the main attractions. Most of the "intelligence" provided to the troops came from a recent article about the island in *The Economist*.

It was a mess, and we were in the middle of it.

An estimated 1,900 Marines and US Army paratroopers, plus a token number of soldiers from six Caribbean nations—including St. Vincent and Barbados—had begun landing that morning. Navy SEALs had been assigned to secretly land and position beacons for the 82nd Airborne. But unexpectedly high winds had blown their parachutes off course, and four men tragically drowned. Others landed in the ocean and boarded an inflatable Zodiac craft—when its engine failed the men had to be rescued. It also meant that the 82nd was essentially landing blind. They had absolutely no idea where they were or where they needed to go, but even if they knew their mission, they lacked the information they needed to get there.

There was little coordination between the services. One commander admitted he was surprised when the 82nd Airborne showed up because he had not been informed that they were part of the incursion. In fact, even though I had supplied the information, the military was not even aware that the school had two locations until they were on the island. It was only after saving the students at True Blue that they learned there was a second campus on the beach, as well as numerous students living off campus.

It was obvious that this incursion, as the US government was describing it, had been a last-minute decision with little time to plan and coordinate.

Communications were a serious problem. The hastily assembled forces did not have compatible radio equipment. Planning was so poor that when US Navy SEALs got pinned down rescuing Governor-General Paul Scoon and his family, an enterprising SEAL found a pay telephone and used his calling card to call Fort Bragg. He was connected to air control, and from that phone booth he was able to direct helicopter fire on approaching enemy forces.

To provide real-time information, Jane Sutter, in Florida, was patched into invading troops by ham radio. "They told me they didn't have any maps," she recalled. "I didn't know who I was talking to, but they needed directions. They would tell me where they needed to go, and I directed them by referring to landmarks. 'Up this hill there are two medical facilities in houses. See that restaurant on your right? Keep going past it, then walk up the hill and make a turn. You'll find a…' It went on like that throughout the entire day."

The bravery of the troops was extraordinary. Delays had forced the paratroop landings to take place in daylight, exposing them to enemy fire. To cut down that risk, soldiers jumped from five hundred feet, reducing their time in the air to twelve seconds or even less. The first wave landed and had engaged enemy forces when the second wave was dropped. When the Cubans and Grenadians began firing on the vulnerable paratroopers, the *Military Times* reported, "The Rangers rose from the ground as one organism, screaming their war cries and assaulted straight across the runway toward the enemy guns. Within 10 minutes those guns fell silent."

Fighting continued throughout the day and into the evening. American troops quickly secured True Blue but didn't get to Grand Anse for several hours. Nobody on the island knew what was going on or what they should be doing, other than not getting shot. During the initial attacks, navy planes had hit the wrong buildings; instead of military headquarters they had bombed a prison and mental hospital. Several people were killed, and both prisoners and patients walked out the front doors.

With students living all over the island, there was no way of accounting for everyone. We later learned that about thirty Grenadian soldiers had kicked in the front door of a house in which six students were living and briefly detained them. One of them, Bill Rifley, told reporters he'd hidden in a small cupboard when the troops broke in but after a couple of hours he had to come out because he was sweating so profusely he was afraid of dying from dehydration. Those Grenadian soldiers were led by a twenty-one-year-old, who apparently was more frightened than the students. They had broken into the house because it sat on the peak of a hill and provided a good view of the school and beach. The troops just watched out the windows and raided the refrigerator. The students weren't in danger from the soldiers—for a time they even were left alone with a machine gun. After several hours they were moved to a nearby house, and the following morning they snuck out to freedom.

President Reagan was using the incursion to rally support—which would, I believed, divert the attention of the nation away from the carnage in Beirut—and putting my students, people for whom I was responsible, in danger. At a press conference he said, "When I received reports that a large number of our citizens were seeking to escape the island, exposing themselves to great danger, and after receiving a formal request for help…from our neighboring states, I concluded that the United States had no choice but to act strongly and decisively." He had authorized the incursion, he continued, "First, and of overriding importance: to protect innocent lives, including up to one thousand Americans whose personal safety is, of course, my personal concern…" Later, just to make sure his message resonated, he reiterated, "American lives are at stake."

Yes, they were. I was beyond irate. Our students had never been in any danger—until he authorized the invasion. I was also terribly concerned the Cubans or Grenadians might shelter with some students or faculty members for their own protection. I was practically besieged by the media. I found myself holding press conferences. Me. Holding press conferences. On Tuesday afternoon I met with reporters in the lobby of our Bay Shore building, and I told them exactly how I felt: "The safety of our students could be threatened." I told them about the telegram that the Parents Coalition had sent to Reagan, imploring him not to invade. I told them everything I knew at the time.

I probably knew more about what was happening on the ground than the White House. The military had shut down the phones on the island, but I was receiving messages in our telex code on a regular basis. Richard Brown couldn't figure out how I was getting information.

I did numerous interviews, trying desperately to get our message out. I taped an interview for *The Today Show* in which I questioned the need for the intervention.

Minutes after it was broadcast my father called me. Then Pat Adams called. They were horrified. They didn't like that I was so critical of the president of the United States. Although they shared my concern about the students in the midst of a military action.

I shuttled from station to station. I spoke with radio and print reporters. I was interviewed on CNN. I was on live with Dan Rather on the *CBS Evening News*. I was on Ted Koppel's *Nightline*. By the end of the day I had toned down my message, but it was too late. My criticism was already out there.

At the insistence of my father, Adams, and Ed McGowan, I flew to Washington to speak directly to State Department representatives. I met with Richard Brown and several other people, none of whom could accurately be described as friendly. They wanted to know why I had been so obstinate. Really? I thought that was pretty obvious. "I'm worried about the students," I told them. "That's my only concern."

I spent most of the day at the State Department. I was told the president was very upset about my remarks. This sums up how bizarre this whole situation was: The president of the United States was mad at me. I need to repeat that: The president of the United States was mad at me. Oddly, because I had already struggled through and survived so many incredible situations, the fact that the president of the United States even knew who I was, much less cared what I thought, didn't seem unusual.

During those meetings, State Department personnel showed me a pile of unclassified documents that outlined a very different scenario than I had been led to believe. They had minutes of secret meetings during which New Jewel Movement leaders discussed holding students hostage—if the US military invaded. That was the "if" about which I had been so concerned. They had other papers showing that the Grenadians who had been giving me reassurances actually had very little power. They showed me notes from Bishop's diary that suggested the new runway could be used by Cuba and the Soviet Union for military purposes. They showed me evidence that a request to land a Pan Am passenger jet or dock a cruise ship to safely evacuate our students had been turned down by the Coard government. They told me they had considerably more classified information, but it all added up to the same thing: There really was no reason to be confident our students would have remained safe.

After seeing these documents, and given the reality of the situation, I began backing off my criticism—way off. Did I say the president of the United States was mad at me? Maybe he wasn't entirely wrong.

The State Department asked me to compose a letter to be given to students as they left the island. They wanted me to tell them, in my own words, that although their parents had been against military intervention, and I had made similarly strong statements, we had acted in good faith—and without having the information I had been shown by the State Department. I agreed—but stipulated the letter could be released only after every student had been safely evacuated.

As I was getting ready to leave, I was asked if I would speak to the media regarding my change of attitude. I would, I agreed; I told them I would be willing to issue a press release saying I had made a mistake.

While I believed that, at least to some degree, I also was well aware that the government could make a bad situation a lot worse for the school.

But my bottom line at this point was that I was willing to agree to almost anything that would help get our students out of a combat zone. I needed to backtrack. Loudly. Publicly. This was important to the administration. I was the only one who had attacked the president on this incursion. In addition to Republicans, I also had been contacted by several Democratic politicians, among them the powerful New York senator Daniel Moynihan. They asked a lot of questions. That's why it was so important to the administration that I recanted publicly.

Rather than a press release, it was suggested, "We think the press knows you're here, so when you walk outside you may have the opportunity to get that message out right away."

I smiled, knowing I had been set up. "Let me get this straight. There's press waiting outside?"

"Just walk out. They'll recognize you."

I was getting a crash education in how the world really works. I walked outside and stood there. As many as fifty reporters and cameramen were there. I was ready for them. Not a single one of them paid the slightest attention to me. I didn't know what to do. Go back inside and come out again? Suddenly NBC's chief diplomatic correspondent, Marvin Kalb, rushed up, stuck a microphone in front of me, and asked, "Chancellor, do you have a statement to make?"

Oh jeez, I thought, *this is so rigged*. The State Department had staged my mea culpa. So I mea culpa'ed. I said what I needed to say: The evidence shown to me by the State Department had "convinced me that the president was justified in making his decision." I stood there swallowing crow until every network had gotten its sound bite and every newspaper reporter had a quote.

The actual evacuation began that day. There were about 200 students at Grand Anse, 180 students at True Blue, and another 200 people in safe houses around the island. About thirty of them were squashed into Vish Rao's house, which was less than a mile from the beach, and an additional twenty people were in apartments next door. The plan was for helicopters to airlift everyone off the beach. The problem was that we couldn't get that information to everybody.

In midafternoon Vish decided to drive his little Chevy Chevette to Grand Anse to find out what was going on. He tied a white T-shirt to his antenna, and he and Bob Jordan drove there without incident. At Grand Anse they were told the helicopters were going to begin the evacuation in about a half hour. Their problem was how to get the students from Vish's house to the beach. "There was an old 1940s Bedford truck parked by the beach," Vish said, recalling that day. "It was being used to taxi students between the two campuses. I asked Bob to drive my Chevette back because it was new and I was nervous it was going to get bombed, and I would follow him in this truck. Then I realized it was a double-clutch truck and I didn't know how to drive it.

"One of our Grenadian employees was staying at Grand Anse for safety, fearing he might be arrested by someone. The situation was very confused and there was no information, so no one knew what the Americans, the Cubans, or the Grenadians were doing. He taught me how to drive that truck in five minutes. When I got back to my home, I told the students I was rescuing them and they piled on board. It took two round trips to get everyone safely to the beach."

Other students somehow had gotten the word to get to the beach and walked several miles to get there, some of them with a Marine escort. On the beach the Marines formed a human cordon from the door of the dorm to the water's edge using their own bodies to shield the students. The troops opened fire to suppress any enemy attempts to shoot at students, while the helicopters fired into the Grenadian military barracks. Later we did find bullet holes in the dorm exterior, but there was no way of knowing when those shots were fired. As the students ran for the choppers, they were told to keep their heads down and move as quickly as possible. Leave your belongings behind. Don't stop for anything. There was a lot of shouting, but no panic. The students waded knee deep into the ocean and were lifted into the helicopters. There were no injuries during the evacuation. Thank you, Marine Corps.

Bob Jordan had decided to stay there and watch the campus. His histology assistant, who wore a leg brace that made it difficult for her to move quickly, stayed with him. In addition, he was caring for a friend's pregnant German shepherd named Brandy and did not want to abandon her. Their problem was finding a safe place to stay hidden. "We moved from the first dorm building to the second dorm," he explained. "As soon as we got to that end of the building, we heard a huge explosion. One of the Cuban antiaircraft guns firing from an old hotel nearby had been blown up. There was a great amount of firing going on all around us; we were in the middle of a real battle. And we were alone on the campus.

"We moved again, this time into my office, and hid under my desk. Minutes after we got settled, two more explosions blew out all the windows. We were not safe there either. We eventually made it to the adjoining anatomy lab. There was a freezer in there to store our cadavers. It had a thick door with a small window in it. And the walls were reasonably solid. We crawled into it. There was no power so it was very dark in there. There were about thirty partially dissected cadavers laid out on heavy wooden shelves. My assistant and I each found an empty shelf and laid down on it. Brandy got under a shelf. Then we waited.

"And waited. Without electricity and without any circulation that freezer got very warm. After about a half hour the firing seemed to be moving away from us, and I crawled through the corridor into my office and looked through the broken window frames. Maybe five hundred yards across a field I saw several Grenadian soldiers running along the street. That wasn't good. They were retreating, and if they found us hiding there, who knew what they might do?

"When Maurice Bishop was killed on the nineteenth, we had just finished midterm head and neck exams and had closed the laboratory. We were six weeks into the course, and all the skin down to the thorax had been removed from the cadavers. That left a bony, muscular skull and thorax with the eyeballs still in place, staring out of the skulls. Several of the partially dissected cadavers had been left upright on gurneys, propped into a sitting position to enable students to identify the various parts. They looked a bit like props from a horror movie. If you weren't used to seeing this, it was gruesome, it was terrifying.

"Night was coming and I figured if anyone looking for a safe place to hide shined a flashlight into my office and saw that staring back at them, then we would be very safe.

"We stayed through the night. Nobody came near.

"In the morning I went back into my office and looked out again. There was no movement. I watched for a while. I didn't see anyone. Literally, not one person. We thought it was safe to come out. The evacuation was complete, and the troops had moved inland. It was an unbelievably strange sensation, like civilization had disappeared. We walked through the dorms and saw abandoned backpacks on the floor. Whoever had owned them had obviously left in a hurry. We went outside. The beach was deserted. There were backpacks, rucksacks, rifles, and bullets lying on the sand. Not too far away a downed helicopter was in the surf. Finally we saw two people way down the beach and walked towards them.

"Later we stopped briefly at two cottages at the Spice Inn, a resort hotel, but we decided that was not a safe place to be. Instead, we spent the night inside the hotel's walk-in freezer. That turned out to be a good decision, because sometime in the night the shooting started again. We could hear bullets hitting all around us. Several gas and propane cylinders had been shaken loose and were just lying there; it was pretty obvious that if a bullet hit one of them we would die in the explosion. The first thing we saw when we emerged the next morning was that one of the cottages in which we had taken refuge had been bombed. We had been lucky, very lucky."

The media coverage of the incursion was the first time most Americans had ever heard of St. George's medical school. And some of the reports were very positive. *Miami Herald* reporter Carl Hiaasen knew about the school because he'd written a long story about it several years earlier in *Tropic*, the paper's Sunday magazine. "While it has been harshly criticized by the American Association of Medical Colleges," he wrote, "...its students consistently score well on the national achievement tests."

As planes carrying 585 students and an additional number of faculty and family members began landing safely back in the States, we didn't even have time to take a relieved breath. As had been true many times in the past, once again we were trying to solve a problem no one had ever faced. We had a university to save.

CHAPTER 23

My Own Operation Urgent Fury

"We have a commitment to Grenada and its people, but we also recognize that students who feared for their lives before and during the invasion might not want to return there."

—Me

In less than a decade I had progressed from placing a small ad in the *New York Times* to being the given reason the United States of America had invaded a Caribbean country most people had never heard of. Yet somehow, the chain of events seemed logical.

That invasion turned out to be a far more hazardous mission than anyone anticipated. During the four days of fighting 19 American soldiers were killed and an estimated 150 were wounded, 45 Grenadians were killed and 358 wounded, 25 Cubans were killed and another 59 were wounded, and at least 24 civilians died—including those victims in the bombed mental hospital.

After the fighting ended troops discovered several warehouses filled with Soviet and Cuban military equipment. According to reports, it was enough to equip six infantry battalions, far more than ever could have been used on Grenada. It seemed obvious that Grenada was being used to store arms and perhaps as a staging area for future operations in the Caribbean.

We were incredibly fortunate; in almost four days of combat and a complex evacuation, not a single student was seriously injured, and they were all brought home safely. "Kissing the ground and embracing the officers who met them," *Newsday* reported, "the first group of Americans to be evacuated from Grenada arrived in the United States yesterday, glad to be home and full of tales about witnessing a military invasion firsthand."

Several weeks later the White House invited the evacuated students to a ceremony held on the South Lawn. The 490 students who made the trip waved small American flags and cheered the president. Meanwhile, all kinds of rumors were spreading about the coup and the incursion. The morning of that reception the State Department reported finding a mass grave near the airport containing 100 to 150 bodies, including that of Maurice Bishop. But by late that afternoon a spokesman completely retracted that claim, admitting, "I guess we blew it."

There was no mass grave, and they had not identified Bishop's body. In fact, his body had disappeared and has never been positively identified. There have been endless rumors about its disposal, from being burned to being buried, but his remains have never been found.

As soon as the last few students were back in the States, we turned to the next problem: What are we going to do? How do we save the school? I kept thinking of a phrase that had been used during the Vietnam War: In order to save the village, it was necessary to destroy it. That sounded a little like what we were facing. In order to save the medical school students, was it necessary to put that medical school out of business?

Reopening was going to be difficult. A headline in the *Baltimore Sun* warned, "Invasion May Mean End of Med School," and the *Milwaukee Journal* agreed the "U.S. Invasion May Be Last Straw for Medical College."

How do you move an entire medical school? Financially, it may have made sense to shut down the school, at least for that year until we could assess the situation and the possibilities. We could have walked away and cut our losses. "Could" being theoretical, but it wasn't reality. We never considered that, not for a second. I had sold these students a dream. We were going to enable them to become doctors. That's why I founded the school, and I believed it just as strongly at that moment as I had on the day we welcomed our first students by helping them haul mattresses off a truck. The charter class, the Super Eights, the classes that followed them had persevered through so much to prove it was possible. We had graduates practicing medicine in America. We had educated doctors. So there was no way we were walking away. No way.

But "How?" was the question. For a while, at least, we couldn't return to Grenada. As a reporter described the situation there, "Here was a lush tropical island of heart-stopping beauty, an island of mountains and waterfalls, hibiscus and frangipani and an island of disabled personnel carriers, of military checkpoints on every road, of POW camps ringed with concertina wire.… About a minute from the airport, in a clump of bushes, lay a dead Grenadian soldier. For days he had laid unburied until he became a virtual tourist site. A cab driver headed for the airport asked a tourist, 'Have you seen the dead soldier yet?'"

Services on the island had not yet been restored. There was limited electricity, water, or even food on the island. Just like our semi-good old days. We leased the dorms at Grand Anse to the military, and soldiers from the 82nd Airborne were housed there. In addition to prisoners and mental patients having been freed, all the animals in the local zoo, including the alligator and the anteater, were loose, except, ironically, a single black vulture. And supposedly there still were some enemy troops in hiding in the hills, although according to the administration there were so few that it was "no worse than a gang in the South Bronx."

Our students—and even more vociferously their parents—made it very clear they were not ready or willing to return. "I'm not going back," a student named Tom Colonna told *Newsday*. "If I have to go back, I'm just going to drop out." So we had to find places they could continue their education. Students on St. Vincent could stay there. The Barbados government previously had told me it would welcome the school if we wanted to move, so they allowed us to temporarily relocate some students—obviously hoping we would find the facilities and political stability so enticing we would stay there.

We leased a partially empty nunnery, the Villa Maria Convent. After everything that had happened, the reality of negotiating a real estate deal with nuns seemed quite ordinary. The place was pretty run down but had enough space and included nearby St. Joseph's Hospital to make it attractive. We would be sharing it with several nuns who continued to live there, led by the remarkable Sister Mary Nelson-Francis, who would eventually move to Grenada and lead an orphans and elderly fund.

We converted the upper floors into lecture halls and put the anatomy labs in the basement. We rented additional space in hotels for students and faculty members. Getting fifteen cadavers into Barbados was even more difficult than it had been in Grenada. Bajan newspapers warned, "You can never tell who is going to end up on one of their tables."

We worked around the clock, and less than three weeks after the incursion, 207 students began classes in Barbados—among them Tom Colonna. The Bajan people made us feel welcome. As Barbados' UN ambassador Harley Mosely said during the opening ceremony, "If it is [Barbados's] opportunity to assist the university and School of Medicine in these troublous times…they could no more refuse assistance in the field of education than they could transform themselves into the North Pole."

The supporting infrastructure was extremely good, in many ways better than Grenada. It was so comfortable there, in fact, that my dad, Pat, and Ed wondered if it made sense to stay. I was firmly against it, telling them, "You know what? If Grenada ever needed us, it's right now." Just in case a move became necessary, though, we did ask the government for permission to maintain a permanent presence. To my surprise there was strong local opposition to that. The University of the West Indies Medical School, which was already operating on the island, the opposition political party, and the island's Association of Medical Practitioners all made wild assertions about us. A spokesperson for the university predicted ominously that we would overwhelm the Bajan hospitals it was using for its own clinical positions.

Even after everything that had been said or written about us, these were whoppers. The students and our curriculum supposedly were "substandard and will undermine medical education in the Caribbean and lower the quality of health standards."

We responded to every attack. Fortunately, as a government minister calmly pointed out, "In the six months they've operated here they've bought in over $1 million to Barbados."

With so many students from the New York metropolitan area, it made sense to try to find a place for them to continue their studies at home. Fred Jacobs literally had skin in the game: His daughter was a first-year student. I asked him to help us find space for our people. Working with New Jersey governor Tom Kean and Abdul Islami, the medical director of St. Barnabas Hospital in Livingston, he arranged for about 150 students to continue their education there.

In New York, Republican Senator Al D'Amato, who was close with my father and Pat, arranged placement for two hundred first- and second-semester students on the Brooklyn campus of Long Island University. This was exactly the type of constituent service that had earned D'Amato his nickname "Senator Pothole." He got things done. In fact, the chiding announcement from his office noted, "Senator D'Amato's intervention in behalf of the Grenada students was achieved after [Democratic] Governor [Mario] Cuomo said he had explored the possibility of helping students but had found no way to do it. Apparently unknown to the Governor, L.I.U. and St. Barnabas officials had already reached agreement on the temporary plan."

Not every venue was welcoming. New Jersey permitted first-year students to resume studying at Rutgers Medical School, but the school made it difficult—our instructors weren't allowed to use their own slides, and the students could not even use their vending machines.

But somehow, within three weeks we had our students back in class. We regularly issued optimistic statements about returning to Grenada, but no one really knew when that would happen. "We have a commitment to Grenada and its people," I wrote, "but we also recognize that students who feared for their lives before and during the invasion might not want to return there."

At our Bay Shore office there was no such thing as normal. We worked around the clock just trying to stay in operation. We were communicating with students to get them to their assigned sites. We were moving instructors around. We had to get textbooks to students to replace those books that had been left behind. We had to adjust our whole record-keeping system to track academic progress. We worked with students to find additional clinical placements. We had to make decisions about finances and consult licensing boards.

If we had paused to look at this mammoth task we might have been overwhelmed. So we didn't. We practically lived in the office. The phones never stopped ringing; students and parents had endless questions—many of which we couldn't answer. We just didn't know, but as always, we would find answers. It was an impossible job but somehow, somehow, we got it done. We did everything possible to catch up and incredibly, our students lost little more than a week of school.

The new government in Grenada wanted us to return as quickly as possible. Americans had never been more popular there. The Grenadian people had welcomed the incursion and had started referring to it as "a rescue mission." Sir Paul Scoon, who previously held the mostly ceremonial position of governor-general, headed the government until elections could be held. He loved the school, he understood its value to Grenada, and he wanted us to reopen to demonstrate that the island was safe and stable. But as I wrote, I would not push students to return. For many of them it had been an extremely traumatic event, so they would come back on their own timetable.

When the election for a new government finally was held, Herbert Blaize became the new prime minister. I knew him; I knew the people he appointed to government positions. While I was never as close with Prime Minister Blaize as I had been with Gairy or even Bishop, he certainly appreciated the importance of the school to the island.

Our students had left almost all their belongings on the island. Eventually we gathered and shipped ten tons of books and personal items to a warehouse in Elizabeth, New Jersey. Students were invited to try to find their possessions, but a lot of them could not. There had been some looting and some valuables had disappeared. Steve Marcum was among the minority who found his backpack, although, he said, "I wasn't too happy to see the dirty socks. They weren't even mine."

Classes resumed on the island on January 10, less than three months after the evacuation, when we welcomed a new class. Students studying on Barbados were given the option of staying there to finish their classroom studies, and half of the second-semester class took that option. Those who did come back were welcomed by Grenadians. Mark Rubenetti remembers, "One person came up to me on campus and said, 'Thank you very much.' I said, 'I didn't do anything,' and he answered me, 'You came back.'"

After we reopened, the Parents Coalition decided to honor the nineteen servicemembers who had given their lives in the rescue operation. We designed a beautiful monument to stand in the center of the campus. I had an idea about doing something I had never seen before. Like all my ideas, I have no idea what sparked it, but I wanted to make this special, more than just a slab of bronze. So rather than just remembering those men by listing their names, we reached out to their families and got the signatures of each of them and had those inscribed on the front of it. The monument is made of bronze and is five feet tall. The three founders also had a miniature replica of it made that I could present to President Reagan.

I was invited to meet with the president to present this gift to him almost exactly a year to the day the incursion began. This was only a few weeks before the 1984 presential election. Several students who had been rescued also were invited to the ceremony. Not surprisingly, I was not welcomed in the White House by the State Department. Secretary of State George Shultz obviously had not forgotten the problems I'd caused. He barely acknowledged my presence.

I was standing right next to the president as he made his remarks. "Together we celebrate today, with joy, an anniversary of honor for America—your rescue and the liberation of our neighbor, Grenada, from the grip of oppression and tyranny.... At stake was the freedom of 110,000 Grenadians, the security of the democracies of the Eastern Caribbean, and, most important, the safety and well-being of you American medical students trapped by events that were totally beyond your control. So, we approved a military operation to rescue you, to help the people of Grenada, and to prevent the spread of chaos and totalitarianism throughout the Caribbean.…"

As I stood there listening to his remarks, I was kind of overwhelmed by the reality that I was standing a few inches away from the president of the United States in the East Room of the White House. It was one of those rare "if my friends and family could only see me now" moments. Fortunately, they could and they did.

"…Side by side, with forces from the neighboring Caribbean democracies…" he continued, "…the brave young soldiers, sailors, marines, and airmen accomplished their mission. They went to Grenada not to conquer, but to liberate, and they did. They saved the people, they captured tons of Soviet military equipment, and they averted a hostage crisis before it happened."

When the president was done, I continued my own apology tour. "Mr. President, as you know, I was probably the first person to voice reservations about your decision to go ahead with the rescue mission in Grenada last year," I began. I looked right at the president as I said it. If you've never eaten crow, it tastes like chicken. "I know I certainly was the most publicized. During my State Department briefing the following day, I realized there were factors unknown to me which required you to make a tough and immediate decision.… I have realized over the past year that you have taken the greatest risk of your political career when you made the decision to act, rather than ignore the plight of our students and the call for help from six Caribbean nations.

"You had little to gain in taking military action," I continued, carefully ignoring the disaster in Beirut. "Had the mission failed in any way, you would have shouldered the entire blame.… No wonder our renewed national pride has emerged from your ability to take action when necessary."

Honestly, it never occurred to me that we were involved in numerous battles with federal and state agencies over licensing and regulations and that undoubtedly there would be many more such battles in the future.

When I was done the president told one of his classic off-the-cuff anecdotes. "I just have to tell you a little story about Grenada. This young lieutenant marine, flying a Cobra helicopter…said that there was one thing in all the news stories about Grenada that was so consistent and so repeated that he decided it was a code, and he was going to break the code. That line was that Grenada produces more nutmeg than any other spot on earth…"

Code? Nutmeg? Wait a second. That sounded very familiar.

He continued, "Number one, that is true—they produce more nutmeg than any spot on earth. He said, number two, the Soviets and the Cubans are trying to take Grenada. And number three, you can't have good eggnog without nutmeg." Admittedly, I didn't have the slightest idea where President Reagan was going with this story, but he had the whole room laughing. "And number four, you can't have Christmas without eggnog. And number five, the Soviets and the Cubans were trying to steal Christmas. And number six, we stopped them."

Everybody started clapping. I'm sure that story made as little sense to everyone in that room as it did to me, but he still was the president of the United States. He looked at me and smiled. I can't tell you what went through my mind at that moment. I'm sure I was supposed to join in the applause. Instead, and truthfully, I don't have the slightest idea what I was thinking. I grabbed the president of the United States's hand and raised it in a celebratory gesture. Like a referee raising the winner's hand after a boxing match. Cameras captured the moment, and the photograph appeared on hundreds of front pages the following morning.

The president did not seem the slightest bit upset about my gesture. George Shultz, however, did not appreciate it. Not at all. Afterward, he asked me, "Boy…" Boy? "Did you plan to hold the president's hand?"

I shook my head. "No," I said, "it just felt like he wanted me to do it."

Shultz was so angry at my response that he turned and without another word walked away.

The following March more than twenty thousand cheering Grenadians greeted "Big Daddy" Reagan, as they referred to him, when he visited the island for the dedication of the monument. A large sign at the new Port Salines International Airport, with its beautifully long runway that American contractors had completed, read, WELCOME DR. REAGAN. NINETY-NINE PERCENT OF GRENADIANS THINK THAT YOU SAVED THEIR LIVES IN 1983—THEREFORE IT IS FITTING TO CALL YOU DOCTOR.

During those ceremonies one of our students, James Griffee, was presented with the Distinguished Civilian Service Award for "establishing a medical triage facility for wounded US Rangers" as well as "a vital communications link with the students at Grand Anse campus… contributing to the rescue of 233 American students."

Within a year we had graduated another class and were back in operation on the island.

CHAPTER 24

A Medical School Out of an Idea

"If my mother was here now she would say, 'My son, the doctor.'"

—David Baras, speaking at St. George's first graduation ceremony

Our problem was the recent past cast a shadow on our future. The good news was that more prospective students now knew about St. George's; the bad news was how they learned about it.

Some prospective students remained wary, but there was no reason for it. A stable government was in power, and there would never be another challenge to Grenadian democracy, but it was a fact we had to deal with. Peggy Lambert, our dean of enrollment, remembers how difficult it was to recruit new students: "It was very hard to explain to people that Grenada was actually a sleepy little island. The Americans had come in and gotten the Cubans out, transforming it back into this beautiful, safe, quiet, safe, friendly, safe country again.

"It was a hard sell. The first encounter most people had with Grenada was the invasion. That cut down significantly on the number of applications we received—although one of the soldiers who had landed on the island was so intrigued by the school he eventually applied and enrolled."

Peggy was right—it *was* a hard sell—and as a result the entering class was smaller than it had been in previous years. Any hope that the increased attention might rejuvenate the small tourist industry that had been destroyed by the Cuban presence didn't materialize. Prime Minister Blaize set out to change that, hiring a New York public relations agency to figure out how to create a new image for Grenada, a positive accurate portrait of the island that would attract tourists. And he asked me to help.

The fact is Grenada should be one of the top vacation destinations in the Caribbean. Anyone who has been there will confirm it is a safe, unusually beautiful, welcoming island. Have I mentioned it is an English-speaking island? But it was caught in a cycle: the lack of infrastructure kept tourists away, and the lack of tourists prevented the infrastructure from being built up. The prime minister told me that this big New York ad agency was "going to make a theme for Grenada and tell us how to market it." This was an important deal. He paid a lot of money out of the limited treasury for this project. But if it was successful, it would help transform the nation's economy.

I was invited to the presentation of the promotional campaign. It took place in a small auditorium in New York. The prime minister flew in for the event. The agency began by showing a series of slides, asking us to identify which Caribbean country the images brought to mind. That actually was easier than I thought: The beautiful waterfalls were in Jamaica, for example. The big hotels were on St. Barts. Then they showed slides of various beaches, and that was more difficult—the Caribbean is a region of beautiful beaches, making it almost impossible to determine the precise location from the slides. If they had shown a slide of the school, I would have recognized that too, but they didn't. Then they asked the key question: What is that thing that can be used to brand Grenada? What is it that made it unique? It has waterfalls, but everybody has waterfalls. It has beaches. What is it, they asked, that will set Grenada apart?

That was a great question. In the previous decade I had invested so much of my heart in Grenada, but this was the first time I had to pause and think about that. We had stumbled into Grenada because it was the only country that accepted us, but strong bonds had been formed. The agency presented its own concept: When you arrive in Grenada you know instantly it isn't like St. Barts or Barbados, where there are an abundance of tourist hotels and souvenir shops. The theme they suggested was: Grenada, the Caribbean the way it used to be!

I thought that was terrific. They were turning the lack of tourist facilities into a plus. They were promoting what we didn't have rather than trying to compete with the much more developed islands. And it was accurate: Grenada really offered a different, maybe more relaxing experience because it had remained quite natural. At a dinner afterward I told Prime Minister Blaize that I loved the concept, then asked how he intended to fund the advertising campaign. "As good as it is," I pointed out, "if you can't afford to show commercials on TV or radio it doesn't matter." It turned out the prime minister had a lot of plans but only a little money.

I had an idea. Where have we seen those words before? Anyway, I remembered how much our first students had appreciated the Gairy government welcoming them to the island with a steel band and rum punch. In minutes they had reinforced the Caribbean atmosphere. Eric Gairy always had a great sense of showmanship. The fact that it had made a strong and memorable impression on everybody was important.

I told that to the prime minister, then suggested, "If we could take this theme and meet every flight, even with just a steel band and punch, people would feel welcome and remember it. While they are waiting to go through customs, there can be a drink cart and tables for people. . . ." My mind was churning. I got caught up in the concept. I thought it was my latest best idea ever. It made great sense; the number of people arriving at one time was never more than forty-eight. It was doable, easily doable, and I was convinced they were going to do it. I reminded them that New York restaurants survive by word of mouth. I could almost hear people saying, "I go to Barbados every year and I have to stand in line, but you wouldn't believe what happened when I went to Grenada. It's like the Caribbean used to be!"

Sigh. It never happened. I brought it up to several successive prime ministers; they just never were able to go with it. So I backed off. But my feeling of gratitude toward Grenada and its people has never waned.

Although I never put flags on the front of my car, there is no stronger ambassador for Grenada in the United States than me. So knowing I have established and maintained a strong positive relationship with the government, businesspeople through the years have approached me to broker deals. If I thought it might be helpful to the island's economy, I made an introduction, always making it clear that I did not have any financial interest in it. After the invasion the Reagan administration did offer assistance, holding seminars in the Old Executive Office Building in Washington for manufacturers who might be interested in locating on the island. My role was to convince them that there was a large, stable workforce, that the local government was extremely cooperative, and the university could provide training. One group wanted to create a local gambling industry, but the government wasn't interested. A major sporting goods company explored making baseballs there, but that never materialized.

Eventually whatever interest there had been in economic development disappeared as the incursion gradually faded into American history. By 1986 the only remaining evidence of the operation were pockmarks in the outer walls of some buildings. The students who had been studying on Barbados were back in the States doing their clinical work, so we eventually closed that extension.

In 1987 we celebrated our tenth anniversary. When I had first envisioned the school, my father and I agreed that if we could survive ten good years it would be worth it. We had more than survived. Several hundred of our graduates were practicing medicine in the United States. We had about five hundred students either studying in Grenada or immersed in their clinicals.

Not only were we established. Not only had we proved we could graduate doctors as good as any people educated in the States. We were growing. And growing. Beyond anything I had imagined. Within another decade we had become a significant factor in the Grenadian economy, employing more than 150 local workers and contributing both directly and indirectly an estimated $6 million a year. We had contributed more than $1 million to the Grenadian General Hospital for equipment, supplies, and modernization—and five local graduates of the school were practicing in that hospital. We had expanded, establishing a premedical program and a liberal arts college mostly for students from the West Indies and developing nations. The three-year premedical program was designed to feed regional students into the medical school. The liberal arts school, tuition-free for Grenadians, had 270 enrolled students.

We have never stopped growing.

My original business plan projected the school would be financially sound if we enrolled two hundred students and a hundred of them graduated. We held our first graduation on May 24, 1981. Ninety-nine students paraded through the lush gardens of the Holiday Inn to the National Convention Center, whistling the "Colonel Bogey March," the theme from the movie *The Bridge on the River Kwai*.

That first graduation, the only graduation we held on Grenada, had been covered by *People* magazine, which accurately described that class as "dogged survivors." Dogged survivors—that was accurate. All the challenges that class had survived had knotted them together. One of our student speakers that day was David Baras, who stood tall and told his classmates, "If my mother was here now she would say, 'My son, the doctor.'" But his mother was not there. There were many parents who couldn't make it. So afterward Nelly Bourne went up to David and told him, fittingly, "Today I'm your mother, and you are a doctor!"

I knew exactly what Nelly meant. It's impossible to fully express how I felt that day. That level of pride and admiration can't be conveyed by words on a printed page. Many of these students were my age or older, but I felt a parental pride. I knew every one of them, and together we had carved a medical school out of an idea. I knew they were grateful to me, but I was equally grateful to them. Almost every single student had given up something important, from a secure job as a nurse or physician's assistant to operating a Dairy Queen, to pursue a dream. And they had done it. I watched them marching together, whistling, and I wondered, literally I wondered, How many people would have been willing to take that risk to fulfill a dream?

And for just an instant I remembered the first few days, when some people arrived in the night, took a look at the facilities, and turned around, leaving their dream behind. The people I was watching had believed in themselves, and as Robert Frost once wrote, they had taken the road less traveled...and that made all the difference.

"The graduation was sort of anticlimactic," Danny Ricciardi remembers. "The day that we had all gotten residencies, our best students as well as our flunkies, that was the really amazing day. That was the day we accepted the fact that we had made it. We were doctors. Us."

Two months after that first graduation, on July 23, in the Delegates Dining Room at the United Nations, sixty-six members of our second class, the Super Eights, also graduated. They had asked to participate in the first graduation, but I felt each class deserved its own celebration. This was the first graduation ever held at the UN, and that would become our tradition. I knew each of these students too. They had put up with the same hardships as the charter class. Our commencement speaker was Bronx congressman Mario Biaggi, who had been instrumental in our fights against the medical establishment. In his speech, he said, again accurately, that St. George's had succeeded "in transforming students from the ranks of the disenfranchised to the rank of Doctors of Medicine."

The achievements of those first classes were remarkable. They built the foundation on which we would grow. In January 1985, the *Journal of the American Medical Association* reported that St. George's was the number one foreign medical school in the initial pass rate of the ECMFG exam with 84.6 percent. Of our initial classes, 99 percent of our students had entered accredited residency programs, and 92 percent were board certified to practice medicine. 92 percent! Not one of them would have become a doctor without St. George's.

Almost all of them had been rejected by American schools. There hadn't been room in those schools for any of them—yet there was plenty of need for them to practice medicine. As Democratic congressman Frank Guarini told our 124 graduates in May 1984—contrary to the claims of the medical establishment—"The health needs of large segments of our population are neglected. We have poor people, elderly, minorities, rural people in America who do not have access to vital medical care. We need doctors for these underserved populations."

And we still do.

Those numbers did not include the 706 St. George's students who had successfully transferred into American medical schools, many of whom had graduated and were in practice. We were firmly established, most semesters the size of our entering classes was increasing, our graduates were moving successfully into hospital residencies or private practice, we had contracts for a sufficient number of clinical slots, and our infrastructure continued to expand to meet our growing student population. By 1998, 93 percent of our students passed the licensing exams on the first try, far above the 58 percent pass rate for other offshore medical schools. Our students were doing residencies in 364 hospitals in 41 states—with 21 percent of them eventually becoming chief residents. "Our pass rate is better than some of the Philadelphia schools I couldn't get into," Bard College graduate Shira Gertz proudly told the *New York Times*. "Which I guess just goes to prove that grades and MCAT scores have nothing to do with your clinical abilities."

When Carl Hiaasen had written his *Tropic* story about the school in 1981, they were nice enough to include a photograph of me in my three-piece suit standing in front of our new library. What they also were nice enough not to do was mention that it was our only new building. I was so proud of that building.

But from our very first days we knew we needed to continue expanding. We always wanted more and bigger and better. We reinvested in our infrastructure. A decade after the incursion we broke ground for a new campus.

Working with a bevy of experienced architects and engineers, Andy Belford planned a fifteen-acre campus in True Blue that included a new large lecture hall, a pathology lab, a physical diagnosis lab, student dorms and faculty housing, even recreation areas. We started building and never stopped. By 1998 we were in the midst of a $25-million building program that included a forty-five-thousand-square-foot library, additional classrooms, living space, and study space for two thousand students, even space for our proposed Cricket Academy where young West Indians would be trained for international competitions.

We had successfully weathered almost every conceivable type of storm except, ironically, a storm.

CHAPTER 25

Hurricane Ivan

"Don't worry about it. Hurricanes always veer north."

—St. George's student to her parents, September 6, 2004

While the tropical climate did make mosquitoes and bugs a continuing but solvable problem, it also added to the allure of a Caribbean island education. We also had been very fortunate—in a region known for hurricanes, Grenada had not been hit by a major storm after Hurricane Janet in 1955. Its location south of the "hurricane belt" kept it safe from the devastating storms that had struck other islands. So, when Hurricane Ivan approached in early September 2004, we were cautiously concerned but not overly anxious. Two weeks earlier, when there had been another "serious storm warning," we had partially evacuated the lower-lying areas of the campus, and the fact that it proved to be nothing more than a stiff breeze probably made us overconfident.

As Ivan approached on Sunday, windows across the island were boarded up. On Monday, for the first time in many years, we canceled classes for Tuesday and suggested students store water in their bathtubs and stay indoors. Some students were tracking the storm on the internet, but most of them were far more concerned with completing their homework. When these students had initially arrived on campus, they saw the intervention/invasion monument and heard stories of the early days of the school, of the shortages and primitive facilities. But since then, we had built a world-class infrastructure, a gorgeous modern campus overlooking the Caribbean, and a prestigious faculty. The only deprivation our students experienced was the occasional loss of electricity. And maybe even I had settled into a comfort zone. It had been a long time since I'd asked that fateful question: What else could go wrong?

So none of us were prepared for a storm as strong as this one.

A close friend of Peggy Lambert had a daughter in our new veterinary school. On the night of September 6, 2004, her concerned parents called. "Don't worry about it," she told them. "Hurricanes always veer north." That was what we all thought, having been lulled into a false sense of safety.

Hurricane Ivan hit Grenada on September 7 as a Category 4 hurricane, although it eventually grew into a massive Category 5 storm. Initially, remembers second-term student Camille Flanders, "We weren't worried." Like many other students, she packed an overnight bag and moved with her books, notes, and computer to a friend's house on higher ground. They hunkered down for the night, continuing to study as the winds increased, paying little attention—until water began flowing under the doors and through the window frame. That's when they stuffed towels against the openings and moved into a rear bedroom, away from any glass.

I was in New York, listening to reports. Having been through this type of warning several times before, I was not yet overly concerned. Whatever it was, I figured, it might require some maintenance, but it would not have any major effect. Within a day or so whatever small damage there was would be cleaned up or repaired and Ivan would be a memory.

That belief began changing when I somehow managed to get a satellite phone connection with our business administrator, John Kopycinski, who described in graphic detail the intensity of the winds. I could barely hear him above the storm.

The National Hurricane Center in Miami reported Ivan hit the island with sustained winds of 120 miles per hour, which rose briefly to 145 mph. People there said they actually could see the wind. That was accompanied, then followed, by torrential rain.

Even many of those structures whose walls remained standing lost their roofs, including the House of Parliament and some churches. It was the beginning of a terrible struggle for Grenadians, but they adapted, telling people, "It just lets God see us better."

When Andy Belford designed our new buildings, several of them only recently completed, he had incorporated some of the advanced structural technology created to deal with this situation. Basically, he adapted Florida's hurricane construction standards. The buildings were concrete and steel with reinforced foundations. Given our location and its mostly weather-benign history, some people wondered if we were spending too much money and being overly cautious. I knew we were about to find out.

Prime Minister Keith Mitchell estimated many buildings were damaged or destroyed. The new sports stadium, police stations, firehouses, churches, schools, warehouses, buildings of every type were at least temporarily unusable. The stone-walled prison that had stood since the seventeenth century was ripped open by the storm, allowing its prisoners to escape—among them many of the seventeen people who had been jailed for life for their participation in the 1983 Marxist coup.

As many as eighteen thousand people were left homeless, electricity was out, roads were impassable, and the nutmeg industry was decimated as almost all the island's half-million nutmeg trees were uprooted or snapped. That was an economic disaster that would reverberate for a decade—it takes a nutmeg tree that long to deliver its first crop. Student Nicole Organ described the bizarre aftermath: "There were all kinds of colors coming down the mountainside—sheets of metal, pieces of shacks and roofs."

Andy Belford had been right. The school had weathered the storm. We lost roof tiles, there were many broken windows, and we suffered some water damage, but none of our students were injured. All around us, though, there was evidence of this disaster. Whole towns slid down mountains; houses were just wiped away. Even Prime Minister Mitchell's house had been destroyed. An unknown number of Grenadians were killed or injured.

Once again, we went into crisis mode. The infrastructure was much too damaged for our students to stay there. Somehow, we had to get almost two thousand people off the island and into classrooms as quickly as possible. There were solutions—all we had to do was find them.

Peggy Lambert and I flew down there as soon as the airport was open. As we made our way to the campus, neither one of us said very much. I had never seen anything like this. Huge swaths of the island had simply been flattened. Considering the extent of the physical damage, it was astonishing that only about forty people had been killed—and none of them from the school. But a lot of people had been injured, and the hospital and clinics were overwhelmed. As our students had done during the invasion two decades earlier, they set up aid stations to assist as much as possible. The biggest problem they faced was a lack of supplies. "There was nothing dry," one student lamented. "We had some antibiotic creams and bandages to treat cuts and bruises, but there was nothing left to help people out."

Food, shelter, and power was limited and sporadic. We had our own generators that provided emergency power and allowed us to have some light at night.

There was so much that needed to be done so quickly, we just went to work. It was another situation in which the worst thing we could do was stop to consider the mammoth job that had to be done. If we did that it would seem overwhelming. Instead, we focused. Focused. Solve one problem, then move right on to the next. One at a time.

The first thing we had to do was secure the campus and ensure our students were taken care of. I reached out to security companies and arranged to bring in men to protect our facilities.

It would be weeks, maybe months, before the island was ready for the school to reopen. We began searching for suitable sites in the States for our students to finish the semester. What made it even more difficult than the last time we'd had to do this was the fact that the school had expanded; in addition to more medical students, we had opened a veterinary school and had to find placements for those students too. We also had a large number of international students who needed visas to enter the US.

As soon as we returned to Bay Shore, we went to our office and basically lived there for the next two weeks. By this time we had been working together so long that we knew each other's strengths and weaknesses. We knew who knew what was where, so people didn't need instructions or permissions from me. Those people who had not been with us through earlier crises had heard all the stories and embraced this one as their opportunity to help save the university. Everybody had a role. Nobody panicked; unexpected problems popped up and were solved. Peggy once described the way we worked as "mental triage," which probably was accurate.

The way we went about it reminded me of my childhood, when my father hired me to lay a floor. He wasn't interested in hearing about the problems I encountered or why it was taking so long or how difficult it was. He wanted the floor laid down. That was what he cared about. And that was our mindset: Get it done. Several thousand young people had trusted us with their futures, and we never forgot that.

The complexities of this situation at times made me look back wistfully on having to rebuild the school following the invasion. In some vague ways that was a rehearsal for what we had to get done now. Having done it before we knew it was possible. What made all the difference was that we didn't panic. We didn't waste time thinking about how difficult it was going to be to pull it off or bemoan the fact it was happening to us. We just went to work figuring it out.

A significant difference between our previous crises and this situation was the existence of the internet and cell phones. Technology enabled us to communicate both with potential landing sites for our students and all our students as a group rather than having to contact each person separately, as we had done previously. This saved an enormous amount of time.

The problems sometimes seemed endless, especially late at night when we were still in the office. While 80 percent of our students were

American citizens, our international students came from about eighty different countries. The State Department and Homeland Security provided temporary visas for them, as well as for our foreign faculty members. In addition to simply locating available teaching space, we had to rent housing and arrange transportation to and from the student and faculty housing and the teaching space. Then we had to ship personal belongings and, for our vet students, their animals. Collecting and shipping textbooks was inefficient of both time and money, so we purchased new books.

Years ago, I had formed a strong relationship with Barry University, a wonderful Catholic college in Miami. In 1997 I was elected chairman of its board of trustees. That was the first place we turned for space. Fortunately for us, Barry had opened a new student union only months earlier, and the former student center was vacant. We moved right in. We found spots for our first-year students at Long Island University's Brooklyn campus and New York College of Osteopathic Medicine in Old Westbury. The dean of our veterinary school, Raymond Sis, contacted friends of his, several of whom had participated in our visiting professor program, and successfully placed 95 second-year students and 10 faculty members at Purdue, 133 first-year students at North Carolina State College of Veterinary Medicine, and 66 third-year students at Kansas State.

Within two weeks we had relocated 1,300 students in six different locations. They were back in the classroom. Within two weeks.

We decided to keep our expanding School of Arts and Sciences on the island because most of our students were Grenadian or West Indian. Although classes were curtailed, initially to only a few hours a week, it allowed the students a safe place to be while their homes were being repaired. We also kept the master of public health students on the island because it was a perfect place for public health students to be.

We opened our dorms to construction workers from other Caribbean nations who were in Grenada to help repair and rebuild.

Once again, the only reason we were able to do this was the resiliency of the students. We'd gotten much bigger, we were graduating several hundred students a year into the profession, we had built a world-class campus—but we still were attracting the second-chance applicants. I never wavered in what I told the kids: If you can get accepted by an American medical school, go there. If you can transfer to an American medical school, do it. I'd tell that to my own family if asked. But. Big but...the reason for that is not that you will get a better education—our students have always done as well as many American schools on all the tests—but rather because the system remains designed for domestic schools.

Twenty-five years after we'd opened the front gate, young people continued to come to St. George's with something to prove. Hurricane Ivan was just another obstacle for them, and so they adapted to the situation. As fourth-term student Olivier de Raet explained to a reporter, "If we don't finish by Christmas, it would mean we would not be able to take our medical boards next summer. By not finishing the semester, we'd have to postpone our clinical rotations in the United States and postpone our graduations a whole year."

Our medical students were back in classrooms across America literally two weeks after Hurricane Ivan had come perilously close to leveling much of the island other than our campus. And with just a little jiggling of schedules, we were able to get our students graduated and into clinical positions on time.

We had navigated through so many incredible challenges that on occasion I found myself wondering what possibly could be next. In my wildest moments I have to admit that I never considered poison snake eggs. Nor did I envision a worldwide pandemic, throughout which our graduates would serve on the front lines of medicine.

CHAPTER 26

COVID and Beyond

"All of our worst-case scenarios in training couldn't prepare us for how bad this was. And it just kept getting worse."

—St. George's University graduate Dr. Michael Keenaghan

"There was never an issue about where I had been trained— and nor did I ever feel any less competent than the people I was working with."

—St. George's University graduate Dr. Bill Ventura

"Maybe more than anything else, it was that calm before that I will never forget." That was Dr. Michael Keenaghan, a 2006 graduate of St. George's working as a pediatric critical-care physician at Kings County Hospital in Brooklyn. "Everyone at my hospital was preparing for COVID. We'd all heard how bad the situation was in Italy. In only two days the numbers there had skyrocketed from reasonably bad to incredibly awful. Italian hospitals were overwhelmed. We knew it was only a matter of days until it happened here because we were following the same timeline; we were just about a week and a half behind. We thought we were prepared.

"We waited. Surprisingly, though, admissions to the hospital dropped to almost none. Patients just stopped coming in. Just nothing. Maybe they were wary about being infected by the early cases. The hallways were far more quiet than usual. Everyone was very somber. It was eerie.

"And then the ER exploded."

In 2020 the medical world went to war with the COVID-19 virus. Sometimes, in the turmoil of survival, it was possible to lose sight of our mission. But decades before, when I'd sat in the back of a medical school classroom in Spain with a small group of Americans, trying with limited success to understand an instructor speaking Spanish and wondering what part of the anatomy is *los dos puntos*—I'd had an idea. That idea had turned into a great university. We had constructed beautiful buildings, recruited a world-class faculty, expanded into four schools, and had a US-accredited veterinary school and master of public health program. We excelled in fulfilling examination and licensing requirements worldwide—but one thing had not changed: the desire of young people to become doctors.

That dream, that commitment to serve, was as strong in 2020 as it had been when the charter class was fishing for door keys. Since that time twenty-thousand graduates of St. George's Medical School had entered the global health-care system. While our graduates went into every medical specialty, we had become the largest provider of primary-care physicians in America. Our graduates formed the front line of medicine. That means in a great number of cases, the first physician a patient will meet is one of our former students. That's especially true in community hospitals, those places serving a broad, varied population.

It also guaranteed that when COVID hit hard our graduates were among the very first responders. In early February 2020, we had invited numerous hospital administrators and physicians to Grenada to assess the programs and lay plans for the future. It was the School of Medicine's Annual Clinical Meetings in Grenada. We had scheduled it long before anyone had heard of a highly communicable virus spreading rapidly in China.

Among our guests was Tita Castor, a physician from Queens, New York's Elmhurst Hospital. Elmhurst is one of the eleven Health and Human Services hospitals with which we had contracted for clinical positions, and several of our graduates were residents there. While Dr. Castor was in Grenada, she was informed she had been selected to lead that hospital's COVID-19 preparation and response team. I asked her if the hospital was prepared; she told me that her assistant previously had led the effort to combat Ebola and that they were preparing similar protocols. "As long as we don't get overwhelmed," she said, "we'll be fine."

Elmhurst Hospital was overwhelmed. In fact, all of New York's HHS facilities were overwhelmed. New York City, as a densely populated international hub, was hit first and hardest in the States. Communicable viruses prosper in cities. Michael Keenaghan recalls that at Kings County Hospital, "Outside in the back we had two refrigerated tractor trailers that we were filling with bodies. It wasn't for lack of trying; we did the absolute best we could. All of our worst-case scenarios in training couldn't prepare us for how bad this was. And it just kept getting worse.

"Physicians and nurses generally don't see death that much. We save lives, that's why many of us went into medicine, and I think we all felt like we weren't saving enough people. It was hard; it was very hard. We tripled the number of beds in the hospital. Every day I would think, *Well, at least it can't get worse than this*. Then the next day it was worse. We worked around the clock. The paging system code for cardiac arrest is 99. For more than thirty-six hours we had a code 99 at least once every ten minutes. One time I was running up the stairs and I just sat down for two or three minutes and thought, *What am I doing? Will this ever end?*"

At no time in our history was the education our students received more valuable, or put to better use, than during the COVID-19 pandemic. As Keenaghan said, "I remember one patient who survived that I really knew I'd made a difference. We were short of everything—equipment and staff. Especially staff. When I was at his bedside, I was doing everything; I was setting up his fluids, pushing all the meds, putting in all the lines. I was doing it because there was nobody else who could help. It continued for several days.

"One of my colleagues asked me how I knew what to do, explaining he'd relied on other staff members to do that part of the work. I told him, 'I just learned it along the way.' It was at that moment, and I will never forget it, that I felt that I had accomplished what I had set out to do in my career. My goal was to make a difference, and at that moment I was making the difference in one person's life. I was putting into practice what I'd learned in my clinical experience. I very distinctly remember hearing Dr. Ricciardi and Dr. Madden telling me over and over and over to ask questions, to learn everybody's job, to demonstrate every day how interested you are, and maybe the most important ethic we got from the school, work harder than everybody else. They drilled that into me: You have a strike against you; if you don't try harder than everyone else, you're not going to make it. They pushed me, and eventually that became the way I work."

Maybe nobody has written a song entitled "A Chip On Your Shoulder May Be Quite Beneficial," but it has proved to be a strong motivational force. Rather than fighting it, beginning decades earlier our students have embraced it. While Dr. Keenaghan was doing his fellowship training at Columbia, for example, he says, "I ended up working twice as hard to show that I was just as good as everybody else. There were some people who lifted their eyebrows when they learned I had attended St. George's, but within a couple of months, they literally were calling me to help them out. I remember when I was getting ready to take my pediatrics boards and my director, who had watched me working, tried to encourage me. His exact words were, 'Don't worry about it, Mike, you'll pass with flying colors. It's only foreign medical students who fail.'

"I had to remind him that I was a graduate of SGU."

It is tremendously satisfying to look back on what we have accomplished in almost half a century. The astonishing thing is how little we knew about the challenges we would face when we planned the school—and still didn't let that slow us down. The statistics are staggering: We've trained students from 133 countries, and our graduates are practicing medicine in more than 100 nations. As estimated 13 percent of all the doctors in Botswana, for example, are SGU graduates. In Trinidad and Tobago it's 20 percent. We've got doctors in South Africa and Taiwan and Malaysia.

It isn't just how many doctors we graduate—it is the contribution they make. As our current president, Dr. G. Richard Olds, pointed out to a Miami, Florida, reporter, "Zip codes with disproportionate shares of racial and ethnic minorities also tend to lack adequate access to doctors. Black and Latino Americans are roughly twice as likely as their white peers to live in areas with few or no primary-care providers....

"Perhaps the most dangerous doctor shortage we face is in primary care. By 2034, the Association of American Medical Colleges projects that the United States will be short as many as forty-eight thousand primary-care doctors. More than one thousand counties already lack enough primary-care physicians to meet demand.... Seventy percent of our medical graduates from St. George's University in Grenada go on to pursue careers in primary care, many of them in underserved areas."

Bill Ventura, for example, trained in cardiac anesthesia at Baylor Hospital, working in operating rooms with legendary heart surgeons Denton Cooley and Michael DeBakey. "There were ten operating rooms," he said. "And about half of them were DeBakey's. In one of those operating rooms, there was a brass or bronze mold of his hands. His gloves were stamped in gold, 'For the exclusive use of Dr. Michael E. DeBakey.' He had no idea about my background. Nor did he care. He came into the operating room, didn't acknowledge anyone else, did the operation, and left.

"This was the best medicine money could buy. The hospital had a connection with the Saudi Arabian government. One day they sent me to a floor to start an IV on a fifteen-year-old boy with diabetes. The door opens and it was like walking into a palace. There were Louis XV chairs, crystal chandeliers, and Persian rugs. *Am I in a hospital?* I wondered. But there was never an issue about where I had been trained—and nor did I ever feel any less competent than the people I was working with."

Ventura wanted to be a surgeon. After completing five years of surgical training, he was offered a position at a New Jersey practice. "It didn't appeal to me because I would have been low man on that totem pole, so I registered with a medical headhunting agency. They found opportunities for me in Florida, Texas, and Georgia. I was hesitant, but they showed me a demographic that made it clear those states were growing rapidly and would need doctors. I ended up interviewing with a health-care system in rural Georgia. They offered me a package that was too good to turn down. They told me I would be the only surgeon in three counties, but I also would have to be a general practitioner because there were too few doctors in that hospital system. It was really a backward area then. It couldn't have been more different than Houston, but I decided to try it.

"It was different from anything I'd ever known. I remember somebody taking me down to the sheriff's office, showing me where they used to hang people. I don't know if they were testing me or not, wanting to see if I would pack up and go back to New Jersey. But having gone through what I'd gone through I was used to making sacrifices in my life so I decided, what the hell.

"It turned out to be everything I had dreamed of—why I wanted to be a doctor. I knew all the people in the town. I knew the pharmacist; I knew the funeral director; it was a wonderful small-town practice. Not everyone had insurance; not everyone had money. There were times I got paid in fish wrapped in newspaper. I was given a live duck by another patient. I ended up becoming one of the old-fashioned physicians who treated everyone for everything. That's why I had become a doctor."

Another graduate, David Frank, traveled in an entirely different direction. After serving as chief resident at a Long Island, New York, hospital he went north…way, way north, accepting a job in the North Slope Borough in Barrow, Alaska, primarily treating Eskimos living in isolated villages. Rather than a small black doctor's bag, he was required to carry a rifle when he made his rounds in case he encountered a polar bear.

In so many instances that was what we did. We took people who wanted to be doctors but had been denied that opportunity and we provided a viable path for them. But…but they had to want it. And that has always been the difference in so many of our students. They want it. That is why so many of them end up on the front lines treating patients. Although most of them probably do not get paid in fish.

What's ironic is that while St. George's still is criticized for being a for-profit university, in the past decade the entire American medical system has become a corporate profit center. As the friendly "doc" with his black bag was replaced years ago by the single practitioner in an office, that stand-alone practice is now disappearing too. Most doctors are now salaried employees working for large health-care organizations. Everything they do is analyzed for its economic impact. They are allotted a certain amount of time for each patient; they can be limited in the tests they prescribe. And as the world of medicine adapted to changing times, so did we.

It would be impossible for me to accurately describe the contributions so many people made to the creation and growth of the university. Somehow, when we needed the right person, they were there. If you believe in faith, or fate, this is where it made an impact. We started with a motley crew of dedicated people who learned day by day. Because they laid the groundwork, we were able to recruit experienced, equally dedicated people who not only shared our vision but made it their own and had the ability to transform it into reality. It was pretty amazing and there is no rational explanation for it, but somehow, when we needed a person with a skill set, they showed up.

Geoffrey Bourne was an extraordinary man. In addition to helping create and saving the medical school, he once appeared on Johnny Carson's *Tonight Show* to describe how he had taught chimpanzees to type on a computer. But among his last and greatest contributions to the school before dying of heart failure in 1988 was recruiting Dr. Keith Taylor. Dr. Taylor had spent three decades in academic medicine at Stanford University, publishing more than one hundred papers and abstracts and gaining recognition as one of the nation's leading gastroenterologists before joining our faculty as a visiting professor. In 1989 I asked him to follow—not replace—Dr. Bourne as our vice chancellor. When Keith joined the administration as the second vice chancellor in 1989, Peggy Lambert later observed, "Both he and the university were at respective crossroads." (Admittedly, I don't think we realized that at the time.) "He was ending a long and distinguished career as a clinician and scientist at Stanford; we were ending a wildly successful period as the first offshore medical school catering specifically to American students.

"His résumé in medical education was long, impressive, and respected; ours was...well, scrappy and gutsy and successful, but a little rough around the edges."

Keith also was a dreamer, but his dreams were different than mine. Whatever my intelligence, I have always had the ability to appreciate people who understand things that I don't. And when necessary, get out of their way. Keith and I came from different worlds. He spoke the King's English; I spoke the President's American. Like many of his generation he didn't like speaking on the telephone; I practically lived on my phone. But most importantly, he loved academia and research and had dedicated his career to fostering it. I was more direct—I was able to recognize a need and find ways to turn a potential solution into a reality. So I loved the school for what it was; he came to love it for what it could become. He believed St. George's could become an international university. Maybe I was a little dubious about that, but given my own history how could I not support him?

An aspect of Keith's genius was his ability to convince the founders that we actually could profit by creating what would initially be a money-losing School of Arts and Sciences for international students. I believe it is accurate to describe their level of support for this idea as "dragged along kicking and screaming." As Peggy also said, accurately, "There were many people who held the perfectly sane view that St. George's should simply continue doing what we did extremely well—training American students to return to the US and practice medicine."

That was especially true since many of the students the arts and science school was created to attract would come from low- or moderate-income families that could not afford to pay a significant tuition. And typically Grenadian children ended their education after finishing secondary school.

"Let me make sure I understand this," I said to Keith. "You want to add a whole new school for people who wouldn't be able to pay enough to support it?"

I had become my father.

"That's right," he said, but he said it in a clipped British accent that carried with it confidence and authority. "The core is the premedical program that we need in order to recruit international students from around the world." What I hadn't really known was that in most countries, students enter five-, six-, and seven-year medical programs right out of high school. The four-year medical school after a bachelor's degree model is mostly North American.

This was Keith's dream. And in that dream he saw possibilities even I hadn't envisioned, and I'm usually pretty good at going pretty far out. To his credit he pushed and pulled and cajoled and squeezed and somehow managed to sell enough people on this concept that the school welcomed its first class in 1996. As part of our annual agreement with the Grenadian government, we agreed to pay 90 percent of the tuition for qualified island residents. When that college opened, 96 percent of all our students from all programs came from the States, a percentage that began declining as we fulfilled Keith's vision and we became a truly international university.

Presently more than one-third of our 7,500 students come to Grenada from eighty different countries. And of the one thousand students enrolled in arts and sciences, which includes everything from business and accounting to premed and tourism-relation courses, nine hundred of them are Grenadians on 90 percent tuition scholarships.

The undergraduate school also reinforced our already strong bond with Grenada. Eric Gairy and the Grenadian people had embraced us before we existed, at a time when no other English-speaking country in the world wanted us. In return, we provided an educational engine that generates more than a third of the island's annual economy. But what we also have done is contributed to the creation of a growing middle class on the island that had simply not existed. The School of Arts and Sciences offers degrees, diplomas, and certificates in fourteen areas, including accounting, biology, IT, sociology, psychology, biology, and nursing. For example, our honors program in Marine, Wildlife, and Conservation Biology recently was accredited by the Royal Society of

Biology. It was the first program in the Western Hemisphere and only the eleventh worldwide outside the UK to obtain this distinction.

Because we are a for-profit institution, by law we are not permitted to accept grants. We taught medicine to medical students; we had not expanded into the rest of the academic world. (Unless you consider the Cricket Academy an educational facility.) Expanding our global footprint was part of Keith Taylor's vision, which is why he founded the Windward Islands Research and Education Foundation. WINDREF is a nonprofit research institute that essentially was founded by Keith, Peggy Lambert, and Dr. Calum Macpherson. The institute, which is funded primarily by grants from such organizations as the Gates Foundation, the United States CDC, the World Health Organization, and the World Bank, brings together researchers and scientists from around the world to discuss relevant subjects.

Let me be completely honest: This is Keith Taylor's doing. Well, Taylor and Peggy Lambert, plus Calum Macpherson and Geoffrey Bourne and Vish Rao, and all the many people who invested their lives in the university, who signed on along the way and propelled us forward. My dream was educating physicians; I absolutely did not expect that one day we would be sequencing genes for COVID research or conducting programs like the "Investigation of Disease in Pre-growout Fish in a Commercial Aquaculture Operation in Ecuador," or exploring the "Bioethics of Climate Change" as we did when we hosted the Global Virus Network's Virology Workshop for Journalists in 2014. That conference was designed to have medical researchers give Caribbean journalists a basic understanding of viruses, enabling them to ask the right questions and provide clear information to readers. Who knows, that might have made some small difference in 2020.

Following Keith Taylor, Peter Bourne, Geoffrey's son, became our third vice chancellor. Peter had been associated with the school almost from the very beginning and seemed a natural fit. Among his initial ideas was establishing our School of Veterinary Medicine. This actually was something we'd considered years earlier, when it had been recommended by consultants hired by the founders. It made great sense; vet and medical students take a lot of the same first- and second-year science and anatomy courses. And, just like medicine, there was a serious shortage of vet schools in America and a large reservoir of people who wanted to pursue that career and couldn't get into a program.

Sound familiar?

It seemed like a perfect fit. But when we began digging a bit deeper, we discovered we were not the only people aware of this shortage and that at least eighteen new vet schools supposedly would be opening in the United States in the following few years. We also found out, to my surprise, that creating a vet school was prohibitively expensive for us. We got hold of a feasibility study done by the University of Nebraska that estimated the cost of building a first-class veterinary hospital and hiring a faculty at about $25 million. Which was just about $25 million more than we could afford at that time.

But Bob Ross had successfully founded a vet school on St. Kitts in 1982. Truthfully, I'd always wondered if we should have done it, if we should have made that commitment earlier. When Peter Bourne suggested it, Professor Calum Macpherson, who had helped create WINDREF, was enthusiastic. "We looked to see what else could be established given our infrastructure and expertise," he later explained. It made great sense. For some courses, we realized, we could utilize some of the same faculty. We actually could have future veterinary practitioners in the same classroom setting as future medical practitioners.

We finally made a commitment to go ahead in 1998. It was like watching the cycle repeating itself. There was a sense of renewal, even though we were building something new. The first dean of SGU's School of Veterinary Medicine was David Hogg, a respected veterinarian who already was on our staff—teaching comparative anatomy to med students. He previously had started a vet school in Zambia, so he knew what had to be done.

We adapted the same formula that had proved so successful when we started the medical school. Our first-semester vet students took the same courses as our med students: histology, physiology, neurology, and immunology. But as they progressed into animal studies, we recruited faculty just as we had so many years earlier—hiring them when needed. We also depended heavily on our visiting professor program. We were able to bring in experts on specific subjects from America's best vet schools.

When I grew up on Long Island in the 1950s, there still were farms with cows and horses and goats. That had been a long time ago. I never expected to own cows. But in addition to our small animal clinic, we had to create and operate a farm, or, as it officially is known, our one-acre Large Animal Resource Facility. On that farm we maintain small bovine and equine herds: horses and cows.

But maybe what was most reminiscent of the beginning of the medical school was the type of vet students we attracted—dedicated, sometimes desperate men and women who just needing an opportunity. Lauren Rooley was typical, as she explained in 2017: "I tried to get into veterinary school in my hometown, and when I didn't get in, I applied elsewhere. I spent several years failing to get into vet schools. I was close to giving up completely. I had one last bit of fight in me and applied one more time. As the days ticked down I got one rejection after another until I received an email from St. George's. I remember that moment very clearly: 'Dear Mrs. Rooley, we are excited to inform you…'

"I didn't even read anymore. I started to cry. No, not cry, sob! I called my mom, still sobbing.… I know this experience is going to help me become the doctor I want to be. A kind, generous, compassionate, hard-working individual…"

The educational structure is only slightly different than the med school. After spending three years studying on Grenada, our vet students do hands-on clinical work at one of thirty-one affiliated vet schools in the United States, the United Kingdom, Canada, Ireland, and Australia. We also have a program in Africa. Our students can take a six-week course working with the wildlife in Uganda's Queen Elizabeth National Park, under the supervision of Makerere University. They also can elect to take an entire semester at that university. We are one of the few vet schools accredited in both the States and the UK, and since its founding in 1998, we have graduated more than two thousand veterinarians.

It's difficult, but it's fun, to compare the way our first classes created a university culture with the way students do things today. Of necessity those first classes created a transcription service requiring people to tape-record lectures, other people to transcribe them and then make copies, and still others to distribute them around the island. There were students who really needed the money they made, but most importantly the transcription service certainly helped bind those classes. They took great pride in it.

Now it is as archaic as rotary dial telephones. Compared to that, Calum Macpherson says, "In the vet school we use innovative teaching techniques. All lectures are recorded and students can play them back any time of the day or night. All the lectures are on PowerPoint, on ANGEL, on the internet, so they can see color pictures of everything they're dealing with."

But of all the similarities between establishing the medical school and the vet school, it was this one reported by a vet student that reminded me of an unforgettable situation. "Currently," she wrote to a friend, "we are eagerly awaiting donkey cadavers to use in my comparative anatomy lab. Apparently, they got lost in the mail, which begs the question: How exactly does one lose donkeys in the mail?"

Later in that same note she reminded me just far we have come. While once our students had to be concerned about food, running water, and electrical outages, she also wrote, "Kind of weird but as vet students it's practical to have short nails. Mine grow like crazy here, especially during the wet season!"

Of all the magic and mysteries of Grenada, until I read this I had never known that its climate causes fingernails to grow faster.

EPILOGUE

Looking Forward, Looking Back

St. George's University has continued expanding. We began offering a master's degree in public health that can lead to a variety of careers in the health industry, enabling us to make a true international footprint, as well as a School of Graduate Studies that offers more than thirty different programs. We became involved in marine biology, a natural fit for a school on an island, and did I mention we host a Cricket Academy?

In addition to supporting the modernization of the General Hospital, the university has continued to provide access to important health benefits for Grenadians. For example, after graduating in 1982 Raz Giliberti became our first student to specialize in ophthalmology. Raz, who eventually became a clinical dean, founded an eye clinic for island residents on the Grand Anse campus in 1986. It's impossible to estimate how many thousands of people have been treated by Raz and other ophthalmologists he recruited—among them his daughter Francesca Giliberti, SGU class of 2010. The clinic has also brought several Grenadian children to New Jersey for corneal transplants. The success of Raz's program led to the creation of similar clinics for Grenadians in a variety of specializations, from cardiology to OB-GYN.

To house all these initiatives, the university infrastructure has continued to expand. I remember being so proud of our first new building, our small library, which opened in 1978. That was symbolic as much as functional; we were building a foundation in Grenadian soil. After that we just kept growing. When Mike Keenaghan stepped onto the True Blue campus in 2002, he recalled, "There was still a lot of construction going on. But it was breathtaking. I remember just looking at it and thinking, *I get to study medicine here?*

"We had beautiful lecture halls and new dorms that, we were told, were right on the spot the original classes started the school. We heard all about those early days; when I was there we briefly lost electricity about once every three weeks, and at times the internet was spotty, especially during high demand, and we complained about that. I remember wondering about those first classes—how did they do that?"

Andy Belford had been the motivating force, the energy behind our expansion program. We had begun discussing building a new campus in the early 1990s. Well, some of us started talking about it. Construction was something I knew quite a bit about; it was in my DNA. I knew it from floor tiles to roof shingles. But I also knew that it was expensive, and being careful about spending money also was in my DNA. Andy was persistent, though. He believed firmly that it wasn't his money, and he wanted to spend it! As he said often, if the school was going to continue to grow, we needed a larger, modern infrastructure. The questions were where and what?

We already had a presence on St. Vincent, but we had previously agreed that we would not increase our facility there. Following the intervention, I decided to explore the possibility of opening a site on St. Kitts, which had been granted independence a year earlier and already had an airport large enough to service jumbo jets. The government was really interested in having us there. I wanted to learn more about it. So I asked ninth-semester student Raz Giliberti and four of his classmates to establish a beachhead there. We structured a ninth-semester program there for them, which included working in the island's hospital in the morning and attending lectures afternoons and evenings.

They spent the entire semester there and passed their final exams. While they were on the island they looked for space for classrooms and housing, and they met with government officials to explore the possibilities. Though it was tempting, eventually I decided against it. Several years later I considered opening an extension of the school in the States, as others had done. I went so far as to get blueprints for an existing building to determine how difficult it would be to transform offices into classrooms and lecture halls. Theoretically, it was possible, but the existing regulations would have been difficult to overcome.

Our future was tied to Grenada. We made the commitment to build a world-class campus on the island. Until that point we had put up whatever structures were needed when we needed them. "Just on time" buildings. We were literally staying one building ahead of the students.

The founders were getting older and were not necessarily in favor of spending several million dollars. Gradually, though, we were able to talk them into it. Well, maybe argue them into it would be a more accurate description. My father had always pushed me to stand up to him, and I like to think he enjoyed these discussions. I would fight with all of them, then Andy would step in to officiate. In his own magical way, Andy not only convinced them this was necessary—he somehow persuaded them it was good business to spend the money.

With expert assistance, he designed the buildings, then worked with a Grenadian contractor to get them done. In fact, just about the only building on the entire campus he did not help design and build is, ironically, the Andrew J. Belford Centre.

Andy had his own dreams, and he didn't let my opinions get in his way. For example, we "actively discussed" where the new dorms should be built. I thought they should be placed in various spots between the academic and service buildings to ensure a flow through the entire campus, while Andy strongly believed they should be in one section. We'd talk about it at length and finally agree where we were going to put each new building. As construction proceeded, I got regular reports in Bay Shore from Andy, telling me, "It's going great, we're putting that building right where we decided." Then I would get down there and it would be in an entirely different place. "Andy," I'd wonder, punctuating that by throwing my arms up in the air, "I thought we agreed we were putting that building over there?"

"Don't you remember, Charlie," he would correct me. "We talked about it and agreed..."

Andy was one of my oldest and most trusted friends. As kids we'd literally strung a tin can phone line between our houses. I decided that I would agree if Andy said I said it.... Besides, it was too late to move a building. Andy also had a way of working with our contractors that was uniquely Andy. He did whatever was necessary to get things done. It was hard for me to criticize this, as it was exactly the type of thing I might have done once or twice or a hundred times in my career. At times a contractor would ask him, "Has this been approved?"

Andy would nod his head firmly while saying softly, "Just about."

Andy's biggest frustration came when a member of the administration—from me on down—got too deeply involved in the building process. I remember when we were building faculty housing and an administration member's wife made her luxurious tastes known by ordering an extremely expensive dinner table and gold-crusted dinner plates. Andy had been there when every penny made a difference, so this type of extravagance just drove him crazy. The breaking point for him came when plans for one residence stipulated pine beams; the administrator's wife objected vehemently, demanding he use cedar beams. Cedar was almost four times as expensive as pine, and Andy fought her on it. Finally, in frustration, this woman looked at Andy and said huffily, "Andy, when Jordan's Queen Noor comes to visit and looks up at the ceiling and asks, 'What are those beams made out of?' you don't want me to have to say, 'Pine,' do you?"

It worked out well; Andy installed pine beams, and Queen Noor never complained.

Not surprisingly, and not unanticipated, as we expanded, we ran into unexpected problems. By this point most people would figure little could surprise me. This one surprised me. After purchasing the University Club, a beautiful place for our guests to stay, we decided to enlarge the narrow strip of beach in front of it. That put us in the fascinating position of having to import sand to the island.

We bought several tons of sand and had it loaded onto a barge. While the barge was en route I received a phone call informing me there was something wrong with the sand. Really? I was dumbfounded. I had always believed sand was sand. What could possibly be wrong with sand?

As difficult as it was to believe, I had bought bad sand. Apparently, someone found eggs in the sand from poisonous snakes not found on Grenada. If we had spread that sand and those eggs had hatched, we might have disrupted the ecology of the island. This put us in the even stranger situation of having to clean our sand.

I wondered, *How do you clean sand?* We found a deserted island and spread out our sand in the sun. That killed the eggs. Then we scooped it up and delivered it to Grenada.

I watched with mixed emotions as, building by building, our original campus disappeared. The structures at True Blue were knocked down and replaced by bigger, better, and beautiful modern buildings. At Grand Anse Beach the geodesic dome, which had been our lecture hall, then was used by government forces to store ammunition before the invasion, had been blown up by American forces. But we put a high chain-link fence around the rest of the campus and locked it. It's still there, most of it, a place of incredible memories. The low cement retaining wall separating the dorms from the beach—a wall on which Danny and Da Boys and then successive waves of students had sat in the early evenings to smoke a cigarette or have a beer, to sing songs and trade rumors—is still there. It was the front stoop of the school, now surrounded by silence.

In other places at the abandoned Grand Anse site, grass is pushing up through cracking concrete, the exterior paint has been bleached by sunlight, and a few long-forgotten messages remain tacked to the bulletin board. The Tuesday morning test has been canceled for eternity.

When a member of the charter class who had lived there visited several years ago, he opened the door of the room in which he had lived—and a bat flew out.

St. Vincent is gone too. As a result of our expansion program, we finally had sufficient classroom and dorm space to house all our students. We briefly considered just reducing our footprint there but eventually decided that made little sense. We closed the Kingstown Medical College in 2008.

Once we decided our future was entirely in Grenada, our expansion program took hold. There are presently about sixty buildings on the forty-two-acre True Blue campus, many of them named after those people who literally made them necessary: Lou and Marion Modica Hall, the Bourne Center, Patrick F. Adams Hall, Keith Taylor Hall, Morris Alpert Hall, Eric Gairy Hall, and, fittingly, the Andrew J. Belford Centre. In addition to classrooms, lecture halls, dorms, and service buildings, these include a state-of-the-art stimulation lab where students learn and practice basic medical procedures like intubation or starting an IV—using mannequins rather than cadavers. And while once physical workouts consisted of swatting mosquitoes or walking down the beach at night to the Holiday Inn for a shower or biking the mile-plus on the "campus treadmill" between True Blue and Grand Anse, we built a large state-of-the-art fitness center.

We needed all of it. St. George's University currently has 8,600 students, a little more than two-thirds of them Americans, and a faculty of about 2,100. Since 1981 we have graduated slightly more than twenty-four thousand people, including twenty thousand physicians. We now put more than one thousand future physicians into residencies every year and have been America's leading provider of first-year residents for the last decade.

Just think about that. Almost without exception every one of those men and women had been rejected by American medical schools. Years ago, the lack of opportunity would have forced them to find other professions. Instead, most of them have enjoyed successful medical careers. They run hospitals and departments. They have become specialists and run family clinics and have served on the front lines against diseases. There already is a significant shortage of doctors; now just imagine how much worse the system would be with twenty thousand fewer of them. It's not possible to even guess how many tens of thousands of lives have been saved or changed by these people the American medical establishment once decided weren't qualified to be doctors.

Here is the reality of the medical profession: Patients don't care where their doctor went to medical school. Most of the time they don't know. But they do rely on the fact that this doctor has been tested and vetted by the appropriate organizations. At the height of the pandemic, Mike Keenaghan remembers, "Physicians from across the country were volunteering and coming to New York to help. We needed them—we were desperate for assistance. One afternoon I ran into a female physician in the hallway trying to find her way around the hospital. She had come to us from, I believe, Wisconsin. She was a pediatrician who had been put on an adult inpatient floor where she was doing almost critical-care-level work. She had no idea what she was getting into when she volunteered, but she wanted to help. I had no idea what medical school she attended, nor did anyone else. Nobody asked; nobody cared. She did what we all have been trained to do—treat patients and try to save lives."

Although the establishment absolutely hates admitting it, we also have fundamentally changed the American medical education system. Many of the strategies we pioneered out of necessity have become common practice. This includes things like tuition-sharing with hospitals that provide clinical positions, which has been a great financial boon to a lot of institutions, and our visiting instructor program. We changed the traditional clinical training structure; rather than a student spending their entire clinical program in one place, we relied on the kind of cool sounding "distributive learning." Students generally used to go from their medical school down the block to an affiliated university hospital where they would be taught by university professors in a standard manner. Previously, some foreign schools simply had allowed students to arrange their own clinicals, and when they had somehow managed to get it done, the school gave them credit.

We adapted that. In most instances we got the clinical slots, but fulfilling their clinical requirements required moving them to different facilities. The upside of that, the unintended consequence, we discovered, was that the wider range of experiences resulted in better prepared doctors. They got a real medical smorgasbord, working at a wide range of facilities.

Today many medical schools are putting their students in clinics, in outpatient facilities, in different types of hospitals serving different patient populations, so they get a diversity of experiences. We did this out of necessity, and when the advantages became obvious, other educational institutions adopted it. According to Dr. Ninad Desai, chief of pediatrics at Kings County Hospital and chairman of our Pediatrics Department, "That diversity makes them much, much stronger than standard medical school students who are in this cut-and-dried location and get cut-and-dried exposure."

One thing that has never changed is the determination of our students. Way back in our third year a woman named Dianne Beresford sold her house and her car and her husband took a leave of absence from his job as a firefighter so she could pursue her dream of becoming a physician. More than two decades later she is still practicing internal medicine. That was decades-old history.

But only a few years ago another woman, Rachel Lewis, who had graduated from Amherst as a political science major and worked as a paralegal, decided she wanted to follow her father into medicine. After taking requisite postgraduate science courses at NYU, she applied to more than a dozen medical schools—and was rejected by all of them. Remember, she was an Amherst grad. She saw a small ad for St. George's—on a New York subway—applied, and was accepted. Perhaps speaking for Dianne Beresford and the nearly twenty thousand graduates through all our years, she told the *New York Post*, "You have to have a burning, unending desire to put yourself through something like this."

A burning desire. I like that. That remains an accurate description. As Danny Ricciardi said, "The one thing that my class still has in common with today's students is that they want it as much as we did. That's a very general statement to make, but in my work with the school I see how dedicated these students are. It's impossible to look at them and not remember us."

"We knew we had to be better," remembers Sherry Singh. "We had to show up earlier, present more, and work harder to achieve the same goal as an American-educated student. That perseverance shows through clearly in our performance."

"I had this feeling my whole life that I wanted to be a doctor," Mike Keenaghan explains. "And then to be told by medical schools I wasn't good enough was unbelievably difficult. That led me to a different level of trying harder. Because of that I used to tell myself, it's okay if I don't sleep tonight as long as I'm learning everything. During my clinical rotations I tried ten times, twenty times harder than anyone else because I knew I was going to have to get a residency, a letter of recommendation, or really, just to show people I was worthy of having my MD."

The creation of a large university, the reality that someday we would become the leading provider of doctors into the American medical system, was not even a small part of my thinking when I started writing, printing, and distributing my *Foreign Medical School Catalogue*, "Senior Editor Charles R. Modica." What I expected it to do was carry along on the already existing flow rather than change its course and carve an entire new direction. It has been a totally unexpected life; it has taken me to places with people I could never have imagined. It has been rewarding beyond my most substantial dreams. We have changed so many thousands of lives. Including my own.

The success of the school, the fact that a medical school located in the Caribbean could be financially profitable, eventually led to a lot of large corporations kicking our proverbial tires. We were not immune to the reality that medicine, which for centuries had been considered a calling, had suddenly become a corporate profit center. Most of the other legitimate Caribbean medical schools had been purchased by financial entities. We received a lot of offers and resisted them. We turned down numerous offers. For more than a decade Charles Adams met with at least one or two parties every year to see if there was a good fit. It took many years to find a partner who appreciated the real value of what we had—not simply monetary but the "it" that had governed our decisions since the fire department was pumping drinking water into the swimming pool.

We also weren't in a hurry to sell, even as we watched our competitors being purchased. It was difficult for me to sell those things I loved. The water taxi service I'd started on Fire Island had grown into a significant business, but when I no longer had the time to run it I just gave it to my brother. So I was not in the business of selling businesses. We didn't even know how much the school might be worth.

This school was never about dollars and cents for me, and that never changed. This was my baby. But over time I began thinking about the future of the school and what was possible. It slowly became apparent to me that it was time to start chapter two: transforming what was essentially a school in the Caribbean primarily for American students into a more international university, a place where we could train doctors and public-health workers and veterinarians and accountants and businesspersons who would then return to their countries—places in need of these young people like Botswana, South Sudan, and throughout Asia—to improve health care and add to a growing middle class. And we couldn't do that without investing considerably more than we had available.

To fully become what St. George's University was capable of being, we needed greater resources. Handing over control was somewhat disconcerting. While I remained chancellor and we would continue to make the day-to-day administrative decisions, it felt like I was sending my college off to college. I was proud but wary; I was happy but anxious. We had enjoyed a tremendous amount of success—we could take great pride in the fact that we'd taken on the medical establishment and won. We were *The Bad News Bears*, *The Mighty Ducks*, *The Replacements*, *The Dirty Dozen*, and *Rudy.* We were the rejects who had fought through obstacles to emerge victorious at the end, to the cheers of the audience.

So when I stand in the balmy Caribbean breezes looking at this extraordinarily beautiful university, watching thousands of young men and women hurrying to their futures, I can't help but think about the people who made it possible, the people who were there at the beginning like my dad and mom, Pat Adams and Charles Adams and Ed McGowan; friends like Andy Belford, Peggy Lambert, Jay Wilbur, and Bob Ryan; educators like Geoffrey Bourne, Keith Taylor, and Vish Rao;

and the students who planted the flag like Danny Ricciardi and Da Boys, John Madden and John Cush, Raz and Joan and all of them, as well as the people who came later but all of whom, working together, made so many dreams come true.

Especially mine.

About the Author

Charles R. Modica, JD, is the Chancellor and Chair of the Board of Directors of St. George's University, a University he co-founded in 1977 in Grenada, West Indies as an independent School of Medicine. In the years since, Dr. Modica guided its development into an international center of higher education with degrees in medicine, public health, veterinary medicine, business, and other disciplines. As Ambassador-at-Large for Grenada, Dr. Modica has worked to promote the country's infrastructure in health, industry, business, and tourism. Dr. Modica has a strong sense of civic responsibility and currently serves on many charitable boards in Grenada and in the United States.